SUPERVISORY TRAIN[ING]

UNIT 9
Productivity Improvement

Participant's Manual

Associated General Contractors of America
Fourth Edition

Copyright Notice

Productivity Improvement
Participant's Manual
Fourth Edition
© 2002 AGC of America

All rights reserved. No part of this book may be reproduced, stored or transmitted in any form or by any means, electronic or mechanical — including photocopying, scanning or recording — or by any information storage and retrieval system, including the Internet or any online system, without permission in writing from AGC.

This product and all other materials in the Supervisory Training Program are copyrighted by AGC. AGC has registered its copyrights with the U.S. Copyright Office to fully protect its rights under federal law.

Reproduction of any part of this product for any purpose including reproduction to avoid purchase of additional copies of this or any other product — is a violation of this copyright. It is likewise an infringement of this copyright to create other works by paraphrasing, modifying or otherwise appropriating parts of this product without the written permission of AGC.

Productivity Improvement **was written by:**

James J. Adrian, Ph.D.
Peoria, IL

The Supervisory Training Program is developed, published and distributed by:

Associated General Contractors of America
2300 Wilson Blvd., Suite 400
Arlington, VA 22201

Phone: 800-242-1767

Fax: 703-837-5405

www.agc.org/stp

Printed in the United States of America

Royalties from the sale of the STP course materials are primarily used to fund revision and development of the STP and related construction training materials.

Table of Contents

Session 1: Introduction to Productivity Improvement ... 1-1
    Benchmarking Construction Productivity 1-2
    Group Activity: Reasons for Low Construction
    Productivity Increases........................... 1-6
    The Ability to Improve Construction Productivity 1-7
    Themes for Productivity Improvement 1-12
    Using on the Job What You Learned Today 1-23

Session 2: Improving Productivity Through Pre-Planning 2-1
    A Review of Session 1 2-2
    Increasing Productivity Through Pre-Planning........... 2-3
    Interfacing the Supervisor with the Estimate 2-5
    Exercise: Review of Contract Documents for Identifying
    Vital Few Work Tasks and Useful Many Work Tasks 2-11
    Exercise: Review of Supplementary Conditions.......... 2-16
    Pre-Planning Production Budgets 2-18
    Exercise: Pre-Planning Production Rate Goals 2-22
    A Pre-Planning Checklist 2-24
    Exercise: Additional Pre-Planning Tasks 2-26
    Using on the Job What You Learned Today 2-27

Session 3: "MORE" — Four New Skills for The Effective Supervisor 3-1
    A Review of Session 2 3-2
    The Traditional Approach to Supervising Construction
    Versus MORE.................................. 3-3
    Exercise: Using Past Project Accounting Cycle Data for
    Productivity Improvement 3-6
    Implementing MORE 3-7
        Measurement or Benchmarking 3-7
    Group Exercise: Productivity Fade 3-11
        Opportunity for Improvement Through Challenging
        the Work Process 3-13
    Group Exercise: Critiquing a Proposed Project Layout
    for a Highway/Bridge Project 3-18
        Risk Analysis for Productivity Improvement 3-19

Exercise: Using the Job Cost Report to Measure and
Monitor Productivity Risk 3-23
    Estimating Costs to Improve Focus on Improvement ... 3-25
Using on the Job What You Learned Today 3-28

Session 4: Personnel Management: Making a Job Look Like a Firm 4-1

A Review of Session 3 4-2
The Importance of Onsite Workers to Project Productivity .. 4-3
Exercise: Difficulty of Motivating the Onsite
Construction Worker 4-4
The Four Needs of Every Worker..................... 4-5
Exercise: Motivating the Onsite Construction Worker 4-8
Exercise: Preparing Production Budgets
for Crew Members 4-15
Exercise: Designing a Weekly Report for Workers to
Improve Communication 4-18
Incentives as a Motivational Tool 4-20
Classical Personnel Management Theories 4-22
Group Behavior 4-25
Exercise: Supervising Various Types of Work Groups...... 4-27
Using on the Job What You Learned Today 4-28

Session 5: Equipment Management for Productivity Improvement 5-1

A Review of Session 4 5-2
Improving Equipment Productivity 5-3
Exercise: Knowing the Hourly Cost of Labor
and Equipment 5-8
Exercise: Production Capability of a Machine........... 5-13
Exercise: Calculating Non-Productive Cost............. 5-16
Exercise: Pricing Change Orders..................... 5-22
Exercise: Calculating the Lowest Cost Method 5-33
Using on the Job What You Learned Today 5-34

Session 6: Productivity Improvement and Planning and Scheduling 6-1

A Review of Session 5 6-2
The Benefits of Planning............................ 6-3
The Relationship Between Jobsite Productivity and
Planning and Scheduling 6-6
Exercise: Planned Non-Productive Time 6-9

Preparation and Use of the Overall Project Plan
and Schedule 6-10
Exercise: Supervisor Decisions Using a Project Plan
and Schedule 6-22
Exercise: Updating the Project Plan and Schedule 6-27
Using One- to Four-Week Look-Ahead Schedule 6-28
Short Interval Look-Ahead Schedule 6-30
The Benefits of Using Checklists for Planning 6-32
Exercise: Preparing a Reminder List 6-34
Using on the Job What You Learned Today 6-35

Session 7: Managing Subcontractors 7-1
A Review of Session 6 7-2
The Need to Manage Subcontractors 7-3
Exercise: Addressing Subcontractor Concerns 7-6
Selection of Subcontractors 7-7
Exercise: Evaluation of Subcontractor Performance 7-9
Being Authoritative and Leading by Example 7-10
Managing Subcontractors by Encouraging Them
to Manage Themselves 7-12
Exercise: Evaluating Subcontractor Plans and Schedules . . . 7-19
Accountability Identifies Responsibility That
Enhances Productivity 7-21
Communication and Meetings 7-23
Building a Team Approach to the Project 7-26
Exercise: Team Building by Focusing on Common Goals . . 7-27
Using on the Job What You Learned Today 7-30

Session 8: Quantifying Lost Labor Productivity 8-1
A Review of Session 7 8-2
Loss of Labor Productivity (Impact) Owing to
Changes and External Events 8-3
Loss of Productivity: (A) Worker Ability to Do Work 8-6
Exercise: Calculating the Loss of Productivity
Due to Overtime 8-10
Loss of Productivity: (B) Continuity of the Work Process . . . 8-11
Exercise: The Learning Curve and Pricing a Contract 8-15
Loss of Productivity: (C) Environmental Factors 8-16
Exercise: Temperature and Lost Labor Productivity 8-22
Loss of Productivity: (D) Disruption of Work Process 8-23
Loss of Productivity: (E) Added Support Activities 8-27

Table of Contents

Exercise: Logistic Changes and Productivity Loss 8-29
Loss of Productivity: (F) Human Element. 8-30
Methods of Quantifying Lost Labor Productivity 8-32
Using on the Job What You Learned Today 8-39

Session 9: Record Keeping, Control, Changes and Defect Analysis 9-1

A Review of Session 8 9-2
The Importance of Good Jobsite Record Keeping 9-3
Exercise: Common Jobsite Record Keeping Problems 9-4
Project Control and Record Keeping. 9-5
Exercise: Using the Job Control Report as a
Productivity Improvement Tool 9-12
Change Order Work Versus Base Bid Work. 9-13
Exercise: Change Order Do's and Don'ts 9-14
Exercise: Data Collection for Project Productivity Defects . 9-22
Using on the Job What You Learned Today 9-23

Session 10: Improving Productivity with New Technology/Review 10-1

A Review of Session 9 10-2
The Importance of Information to the Construction Firm. . . 10-3
Exercise: Using New Technology to Increase
Productivity; Not Just Faster, But Better 10-6
Implementing New Technology for Labor Hour
Reporting 10-7
Exercise: Cost Benefit Analysis for Automated Versus
Manual Time Recording 10-10
Controlling Materials, Tools and Supplies 10-11
Exercise: Tools and Material Management 10-14
New Technology and Equipment Productivity. 10-15
A Daily Report, Jobsite Record Keeping and
Project Billings 10-17
Exercise: Implementing New Technology 10-21
Using on the Job What You Learned Today 10-22

Supervisor Best Practices for Productivity Improvement 10-25
Application for STP Completion Certificate . . . . **End of Book**

Introduction to the Course

Welcome to *Productivity Improvement*.

Purpose of this Course

The purpose of this course, *Productivity Improvement,* is to contribute to your professional development. If you are currently working as a supervisor, aspiring to become a supervisor or work with construction supervisors, this course will help you be more successful in your job. Although it is aimed specifically at onsite construction supervisors, all people involved in construction projects can benefit from the ideas and skills presented in *Productivity Improvement.*

Why Should You Study Supervision?

Contractors often have a difficult time filling supervisory positions with properly trained people. Supervisors are made, not born, but many companies are too small to have an in-house training program. Job demands on supervisors are increasing because of rapid changes in workers' attitudes and technology. Project locations are scattered over large geographical areas. New laws and regulations covering construction have restricted and complicated production and increased the focus on compliance, quality and cost control. Fewer people are entering the construction work force.

However, many opportunities exist in construction. There is new work to be done, as well as rehab, rebuilding and renovation projects. Increased competition brings pressure to do things more efficiently. Companies that meet these challenges by developing and maintaining an effectively supervised work force of well-trained people survive and prosper.

Construction supervisors are a critical link in the production and profit-making process, and much is expected of them. Supervisors are expected to control costs and meet specifications. They are expected to complete projects within tight time schedules and optimistic budgets; they are expected to maintain high morale among their workers; they are expected to be the contractor's representative on a daily basis, dealing with the labor force, subcontractors, suppliers, owners, architects, engineers, the public and other various inspectors and governmental officials. This is a very difficult job description. To be successful, supervisors must learn new skills and also must sharpen other skills they have previously learned.

The word *supervisor* is the title of a position. *Supervision* is the activity that is performed by supervisors. This course is designed to train supervisors and potential supervisors how to improve their ability to supervise, resolve problems and create win-win situations for all parties involved in a construction project.

A Supervisor's Role Differs from a Craftworker's Role

There are basic differences between a craftworker's job and a supervisor's job. Craftwork is technical work. Using a transit or level, using equipment to place and finish concrete, operating a scraper safely and productively, hanging iron and bolting it up, and reading and understanding slope stakes are all technical skills that are consistent from one project to another. Craftwork is personal, "I-centered" or "me-centered," and it is the first set of skills a construction worker learns.

Supervision requires the use of human and conceptual skills and is likely to be applied differently to different supervisory problems on the same project. To complicate this process, there are frequently no pat answers to supervisory problems.

Often, difficult decisions must be made, and sometimes these decisions are not clearly right or wrong.

Design of this Course

This course is designed to be presented in different ways. You may be attending ten classes where a session of approximately 2½ hours is presented each meeting. You should read the text in your Participant's Manual before coming to each class session. This will help you become familiar with important concepts and skills and will help you prepare for discussions and other class activities: If you are unable to read a session before class, come to class anyway. You will still be able to learn much by listening to and participating in class activities.

You may be attending a course where all ten sessions are presented in a concentrated format over a few days. If so, you will not have as much time to read ahead. Time will be allowed for you to review the material presented in the Participant's Manual.

No matter which attendance format is used, as you read, think about actual jobsite situations you have seen or experienced that illustrate the points presented. It's important to talk about your experiences during class discussions so everyone can understand how the ideas, skills and solutions discussed in the course are actually applied in the field.

In this course, you will not be simply sitting and listening; this is not a lecture course or a seminar! You will become involved in the discussions and activities in an active exchange of ideas, questions and solutions that will be relevant to you and your work. Much of what you and others in the class learn from this course will come from each other, and your active participation is essential. Case studies will be used to help you understand various concepts and skills.

Notes About Your Manual

You will notice some blank pages in your Participant's Manual and some pages that are partially filled with text. This manual is yours to keep and use as a reference on future construction projects. It is recommended that you make notes on the blank pages and in the wide margins where appropriate, and use a highlighter to mark or underline key ideas.

We need your feedback to improve this course and the manuals used to present it. You are encouraged to note your comments about the Participant's Manual on the participant registration and evaluation form, which is in the back of your Participant's Manual. Your instructor will direct you to complete this form at the end of the last class session, or you may complete the appropriate questions after each session.

INTRODUCTION TO *PRODUCTIVITY IMPROVEMENT*

Unless told otherwise, you are to complete the registration section and have it signed by your instructor. This or a registration form completed by the class sponsor should then be sent to AGC. A registration form is the only way to add your name to the list of people who have completed this course. Although your instructor will normally collect the participant registration and evaluation forms, it is your responsibility to see that your signed completed form is sent to AGC.

The evaluation section asks questions about the subject matter of this course and its value to you. Your comments will help AGC know how to make *Productivity Improvement* more effective when it is revised.

How This Course Is Organized

In the ten sessions in this course, a variety of methods will be used to help you and other participants understand the subject of supervision. Case studies, oral presentations, group discussions, group problem solving and interviews with other participants all will be used to accomplish specific learning objectives for each session. Your instructor will introduce many activities with brief remarks and then start a discussion that reviews key points in the reading.

You may be asked to complete some assignments outside of the regular class sessions and bring actual job situations to the class for discussion.

The text and study material are designed specifically for the construction industry. The material is not specific to site or type of construction because the skills presented can be applied by any supervisor. Class participants may come from various companies, general contractors, subcontractors, utility or heavy and highway contractors that perform different types of work, but the basic principles of the text are designed to apply to supervisory problems common to all construction projects.

STP Courses

There are ten related courses in the Supervisory Training Program. These courses are designed for field superintendents, people who want to become field superintendents and others who want to learn about important ideas and skills that effective superintendents need to know. From time to time, there will be references to these related courses in the Supervisory Training Program.

The STP courses are:

- Unit 1: *Leadership and Motivation*
- Unit 2: *Oral and Written Communication*
- Unit 3: *Problem Solving and Decision Making*
- Unit 4: *Contract Documents and Construction Law*
- Unit 5: *Planning and Scheduling*
- Unit 6: *Understanding and Managing Project Costs*
- Unit 7: *Accident Prevention and Loss Control*
- Unit 8: *Managing the Project: The Supervisor's Role*
- Unit 9: *Productivity Improvement*
- Unit 10: *General and Specialty Contractor Dynamics*

You can receive a special certificate of recognition and wallet card from AGC when you have completed all ten of the STP courses. An application for this certificate is included at the end of your manual.

In addition, AGC has developed two 25-hour overview courses. *Construction Supervisor* is oriented to supervisors in building construction; *Heavy/Highway Construction Supervisor* is designed specifically for supervisors involved in heavy and highway construction.

A summary of the topics covered in the STP courses is shown on the following pages.

STP Course Summaries

Construction Supervisor and **Heavy/Highway Construction Supervisor** are each 25-hour **overview courses** that present ten key topics every successful supervisor must know. Each topic is covered in a 2½-hour session.

Construction Supervisor
- Leadership
- Motivation
- Communication
- Problem solving
- Decision making
- Cost awareness
- Planning and organizing
- Production control
- Accident prevention and loss control
- Contract documents

Heavy/Highway Construction Supervisor
- Leadership
- Motivation
- Communication
- Problem solving: problem identification
- Problem solving: the decision making process
- Cost awareness
- Planning and organizing
- Production control
- Accident prevention and loss control
- Project documents

Each of the ten courses in the main program is 20 to 25 hours of intensive training on a specific area of construction field supervision.

Unit 1: *Leadership and Motivation*
- Dollars and sense of people and construction
- Role of the construction supervisor
- Helping people perform better
- Leading others
- Positive feedback
- Team building
- Leadership skills in action

Unit 2: *Oral and Written Communication*
- Forms of communication
- Problems from poor communication
- Effective listening
- Components of conversation
- Communicating with your crew
- Good writing skills and habits
- Facilitating the meeting process
- The Internet and World Wide Web

Unit 3: *Problem Solving and Decision Making*
- Problem prevention and anticipation
- Identifying problems
- How to solve scheduling and technical problems
- Strategies for solving human performance problems
- Creative problem solving
- Barriers to developing creative solutions
- Establishing a problem-solving atmosphere
- Developing follow-up systems
- Changing your mind

Unit 4: *Contract Documents and Construction Law*
- Introduction to contract documents and construction law
- Creating a positive environment
- Contractual relationships
- Contract forms and documents
- Managing general conditions
- Good documentation practices
- Changes
- Differing site conditions
- Time impacts
- Negotiation of resolutions

Unit 5: *Planning and Scheduling*
- Preparing the project plan
- Developing using bar charts
- The critical path
- Computer scheduling
- Using the schedule on the jobsite
- Updating the construction schedule

- The schedule as documentation
- Analyzing a change

Unit 6: *Understanding and Managing Project Costs*
- The birth of a job
- Selection and award of contract
- Types of construction contracts
- The conceptual estimate
- The detailed estimate
- Financial risks
- Losses from criminal activity
- Cost control for change orders
- Subcontractor backcharges

Unit 7: *Accident Prevention and Loss Control*
- The high price of accidents
- Safety communication and motivation
- Documentation and inventories
- Using reference materials and advisory services
- Project security and traffic control
- Using the project schedule to prevent losses
- Selecting methods and equipment to prevent losses
- Assigning responsibility and equipment maintenance
- Common construction hazards
- Government regulations and inspections

Unit 8: *Managing the Project: The Supervisor's Role*
- Preconstruction planning
- Planning, organizing and staffing
- Developing the project plan
- Planning for production and support
- Cost and risk control
- Policies and procedures
- Purchasing and receiving
- Subcontractor management
- Project layout
- Project start-up and close-out

Unit 9: *Productivity Improvement*
- Introduction to Productivity Improvement
- Creating a positive environment
- Contractual relationships
- Contract forms and documents
- Managing general conditions
- Good documentation practices
- Changes
- Differing site conditions
- Time impacts
- Negotiation of resolutions

Unit 10: *General and Specialty Contractor Dynamics*
- Construction systems
- Contractual relationships
- Value and impact of specialty contractors
- Selecting a specialty contractor
- Importance of open communication
- Prints and specifications
- Time management
- Productivity and goals
- Project closeout

Notes

Notes

Introduction to Productivity Improvement

Learning Goals for Session 1

After this session, you will understand how productivity is measured. You will understand how the supervisor can play a major role in increasing jobsite productivity and how a small increase in productivity can have a significant impact on the time and cost of a project. You will also learn ten new themes for increasing productivity.

Learning Objectives

To accomplish the learning goals, during this session you will:

- Meet the course facilitator and other participants in the class.

- Become familiar with the course goals, objectives and outline of **Productivity Improvement** and learn how the course will be conducted.

- Discover how productivity is measured by all industries.

- Benchmark productivity and productivity improvements in the construction industry versus non-construction industries and investigate the reasons for the differences.

- Quantify the potential for productivity at the construction jobsite and identify reasons for non-productive time.

- Learn ten new themes or philosophies for improvement of supervision and construction productivity.

To Get Ready for Session 1

Reading: If you have your manual prior to Session 1, read the preliminary pages and then read the pages in Session 1. If you don't receive your manual until the first session of the course, try to read this material within a few days after the first class meeting.

Major Activities for Session 1
- Get acquainted
- Get an overview of the content and organization of the course
- Complete the pre-knowledge survey
- Learn the definition of productivity and how it is measured
- Identify causes of non-productive jobsite time
- Quantify the impact of productivity improvement on project time and cost
- Apply applications of ten new themes for improving productivity
- Review this session

Benchmarking Construction Productivity

The Challenge of Being a Supervisor of the Construction Process

Construction can be considered as a manufacturing industry. In one sense, it is similar to the automobile business. Whereas companies such as General Motors take raw steel and use labor and equipment to turn it into an automobile the construction industry uses labor and equipment to turn materials into buildings, roadways, bridges, wastewater treatment plants and houses.

While similar to other manufacturing industries converting raw materials into finished product, the construction industry has several unique characteristics. For one, construction is more dependent on labor productivity than most other manufacturers. In addition, the construction process is subjected to much more uncertainty and risk than other industries.

Consider what a car would cost or what its quality would be if the car was built under the following conditions:

- The car was built on a driveway and was subject to variable weather conditions.

- Every car built was different; i.e., you never built the same model twice.

- Several hundred materials came from different geographic locations and had to be ordered and delivered to the driveway at the appropriate time.

- As many as ten different labor crafts were employed to work on the automobile at the same time.

- Numerous subcontractors were jockeying for position to perform work.

Obviously these are not the conditions under which an automobile is constructed in a car plant. Instead, it is typically the conditions under which many building projects are constructed. The point is that the construction process is a very complex one.

It can be argued that the construction supervisor must be smarter than supervisors in other industries. He or she is confronted with many more uncertain events and unique challenges.

It follows that the typical construction supervisor does many things right. He or she likely makes more daily decisions than supervisors in other manufacturing industries. Independent of formal educational background, the construction supervisor possesses much knowledge; knowledge of materials, knowledge of construction work processes,

---

The construction supervisor must be very creative and knowledgeable to manage construction productivity. The construction process is very complex and subject to a significant amount of uncertain events. Weather, unique projects, multiple labor crafts, multiple contractors at the same site and dependence on external party decision-making are only a few of the many factors the supervisor must manage.

knowledge of how to manage people and knowledge related to monitoring costs and project information.

The supervisor makes a major impact on each of the following project considerations:

- Project time (the duration the project takes relative to the plan)
- Project cost (the final cost of project relative to the budget)
- Project quality (the adherence to the project specifications)
- Project safety (no accidents)

While each of these factors is important, it is crucial that the supervisor promote safety first. Safety is the primary project consideration; if an accident occurs, all other factors are negatively affected.

While many factors in part affect the four variables noted above, the actions or non-actions of the supervisor also significantly determine the project time, cost, quality and safety. It can be argued that weather doesn't run the project, designers don't run the project, labor unions don't run the project; it is the supervisor that runs the project. If this is not the case, why is it that if two different supervisors are assigned to the same project, the project time, cost, quality and safety are different?

Productivity Defined

As smart as the construction supervisor is, and as important as he or she is to the success of the project, there is evidence that there is still considerable potential for improvement. This potential for improvement can be best viewed by looking at the productivity of the construction process.

Productivity is defined by businesses and nations as follows:

$$\text{Productivity} = \frac{\text{Units of output from a work process}}{\text{Person hours of input}}$$

In the case of the automobile industry, productivity would be measured as the number of cars produced per person hour. In the service industry it would be the number of services performed (e.g., customers waited on) per person hour. In the case of the construction industry, common means of defining productivity are:

- Cubic yards of concrete placed per person hour
- Square feet of contact area of forming placed per person hour
- Linear feet of pipe placed per person hour
- Pounds or tons of ductwork placed per person hour
- Board feet of lumber placed per person hour

> Construction is a manufacturing industry in that the supervisor is asked to use labor and equipment to turn materials into buildings, roads and residential units. Productivity is measured as units of output produced per labor hour of input. However, productivity can be improved by the efficient use of equipment as well as by the efficient use of labor.

Benchmarking Productivity: Setting Out the Potential for Construction Productivity Improvement

The term "benchmarking" can be viewed as a process by which we measure and compare two processes or two firms to determine how good one is relative to the other. In this way, we can find reasons or causes for one doing better than the other. By studying this, we can duplicate what was done right.

Consider the benchmarking of construction productivity increases relative to those of other industries. Shown below is a plotting of construction industry increases versus increases in all other U.S. industries combined as a function of time.

Productivity increases in the construction industry have lagged behind productivity increases in other industries. It is important for the supervisor to understand the reasons for this in order to address problems and thereby increase productivity.

Fig. 1-1

Productivity Increases (US Combined Versus Construction Industry)

- US Productivity Increases
- Construction Industry Increases

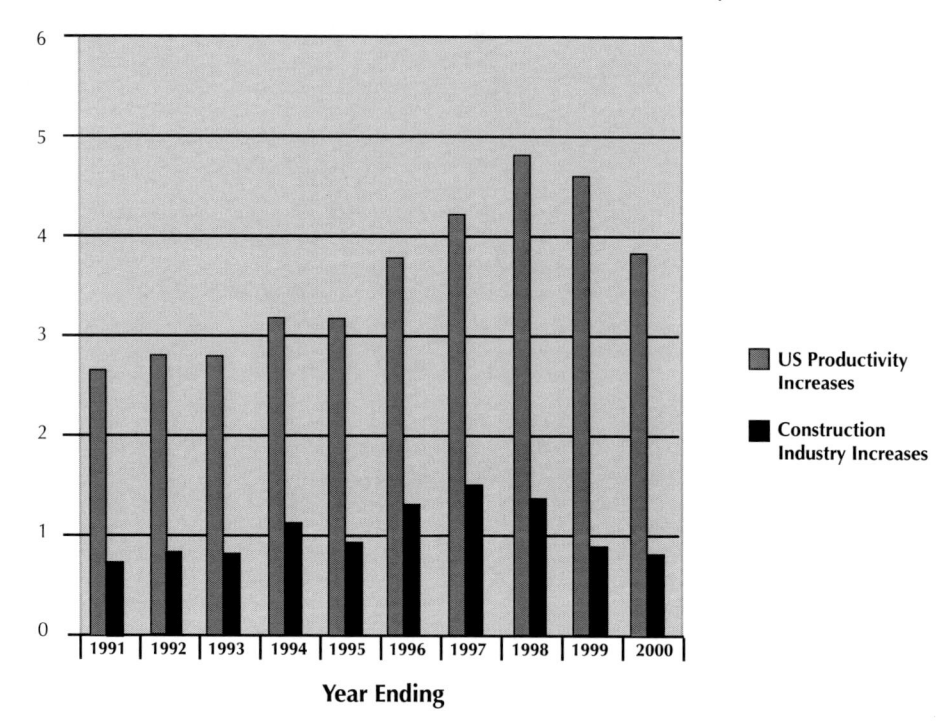

Year Ending

Figure 1-1 illustrates that while U.S. productivity increases have been on the order of 2% to 5% a year, the construction industry has witnessed productivity increases of about 1% a year; actually often dipping below 1%.

Introduction to Productivity Improvement

The data begs the question, why has the construction industry had smaller annual increases in productivity than other industries? One common argument or excuse is that some industries have been able to automate their work process by substituting machines for workers. Productivity is measured by dividing the units produced only by labor hours and not equipment hours. When an industry such as the automobile industry substitutes assembly line equipment for labor, it increases productivity simply because fewer labor hours are in the denominator of the equation for productivity.

SESSION 1

INTRODUCTION TO PRODUCTIVITY IMPROVEMENT

Group Activity

Reasons for Low Construction Productivity Increases

Government statistics indicate that the construction industry has had one of the lowest increases in productivity of all U.S. industries. One of the reasons obviously relates to the industry's inability to "automate" the construction process. Unlike the automobile industry, which has a relatively low ratio of labor to material going into the final product, the construction industry will always be dependent on a large percentage of onsite labor costs to construct the project. The supervisor cannot change this high dependence on labor (other than to occasionally attempt to fabricate materials off-site).

In an attempt to improve productivity by identifying what other industries (for example; automobile, pharmaceutical, retail) may be doing relative to the construction industry, identify three additional reasons why the construction industry has had slower increases in productivity than other industries. For each of the reasons your group identifies, write down some ideas on how to address the cause and thereby increase productivity.

- Cause for lower increase in construction productivity (relative to other industries)

    Possible ways to reduce or remedy the cause

- Cause for lower increase in construction productivity (relative to other industries)

    Possible ways to reduce or remedy the cause

- Cause for lower increase in construction productivity (relative to other industries)

    Possible ways to reduce or remedy the cause

The Ability to Improve Construction Productivity

Three Work States of a Worker or a Machine

When one views the construction process, one sees a complicated process. Many workers are doing different tasks; equipment is being used to move materials horizontally and vertically. Typically the construction firm and supervisor are managing several construction work processes at the same time. One crew of workers might be forming concrete, another performing excavation work, another crew fabricating pipe and another crew placing sheet metal work. Each of the worker crews may be using different equipment to perform their work tasks; a crane, a backhoe or a lift.

The supervisor has a challenge to keep various workers and pieces of equipment at a project busy. The supervisor might take the position that if everyone and everything is busy, the project is progressing on schedule and on budget. However, working hard does not necessarily mean working smart!

Construction is similar to other manufacturing businesses. Whereas the automobile industry uses labor and equipment to turn steel into cars, the construction supervisor uses labor and equipment to turn raw materials into buildings, roads and bridges and residential units. One might propose that the observer of the construction process is drawn to watching or monitoring "things" (a carpenter, a mason, a pipe fitter, a crane, a backhoe) turning material into finished buildings, roads and bridges, or residential units.

The supervisor should be more attentive to what these "things" are doing than what they are. During the workday, a worker or a machine at the jobsite is in one of the following three states at any point in time.

- A **productive state**; i.e., putting in finish material (doing "value added" services)

- A **non-productive state**; doing something that does not add value to the work process

- A **support state**; doing something that appears necessary but is not a task of putting in finish material

Examples of each of these three work states are as follows:

Productive work states:
— Two workers properly installing a concrete form
— A crew of workers placing conduit for electrical wiring
— An operator and a backhoe digging a trench

Note: It is important for the supervisor to observe what labor and/or equipment are doing; not just what they are. The construction supervisor should strive to increase the time that labor or equipment is in a productive state.

— A carpenter nailing up framing

— A crane bucket dropping concrete into a formed wall.

Non-Productive work states:

— Workers doing punch list work

— Workers waiting for material to arrive at the project

— Equipment standing idle because of no work to be performed by the equipment

— Workers looking for tools

— Equipment idle because it is broken or in state of repair

Support work state:

— Workers carrying material from one location to another

— Equipment moving from one work task to another

— Workers meeting with a supervisor to have work methods explained to them

— Equipment moving material that is in the way of workers

Ideally the work process would include only productive time. This will never happen, given the complexity of the construction process to include multiple crafts, numerous different types of material, unpredictable weather, etc. However, many construction projects are characterized by having too much non-productive time in the process. Shown in Figure 1-2 are the work states of labor at an example construction project.

Note: Support time should not be viewed as totally non-productive. However, like non-productive time, it can often be reduced with improved supervisor planning and creativity.

Note: Non-productive time and support time should be viewed by the supervisor as an "opportunity" to improve, not only as a problem. If there were no problems, there would be no opportunity to improve.

Fig. 1-2

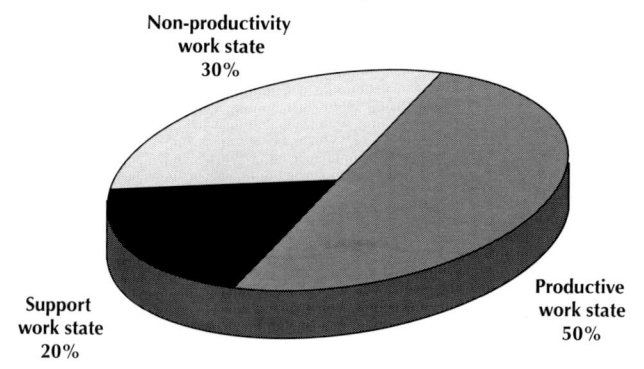

- Non-productivity work state 30%
- Support work state 20%
- Productive work state 50%

Clearly the workday shown in the above figure is not representative of every project in regard to non-productive or support time. Some projects are better, some are worse.

The figure above illustrates the work states for labor for an example project. The productive work states in this example are only around 50%. How about the work states of equipment? Like labor, equipment at a project site is in one of three states; productive, non-productive or support. Many types of equipment (e.g., earthmoving equipment) have meters on them to measure usage. It is not unusual to see equipment that has only 800 or 900 hours of usage on it in a given year. Given the fact that there are 52 weeks in a year and eight hours in a workday (2,080 work hours in a year), even if a firm does not work overtime, it follows that equipment is in a non-productive or support state more than 50% of the time.

All industries have non-productive and support time in the work process. For example, even a highly industrialized industry such as the automobile industry has assembly line breakdowns, worker late starts or early quits, worker shortages that change the ideal crew size, etc. However, it is doubtful that they have as much non-productive time and support time in their work process as does construction.

Impact of Improvement on Profitability of a Project

Non-productive or support time can be viewed either as a problem or an opportunity. The construction industry and the supervisor should view non-productive and support time as an opportunity to improve. Every construction firm has access to the same tools, the same equipment, the same bank or money, the same weather. In a manufacturing industry such as construction, the only way to successfully compete with competition is to be more productive with labor and equipment than one's competition.

Given the typical financial composition of the construction process, a small increase in productive time or productivity can have a significant impact on the profitability of the project.

Consider the cost breakdown of the two project estimates shown below; one for a $1 million building construction project, and one for public works for a $1 million highway project. The data below represents an estimate for both types of projects.

Building Project	Cost	%	Public Works Project	Cost	%
Labor cost	$ 400,000	40	Labor cost	$ 200,000	20
Material cost	320,000	32	Material cost	200,000	20
Equipment cost	100,000	10	Equipment cost	400,000	40
General conditions	80,000	8	General conditions	80,000	8
Company overhead	80,000	8	Company overhead	100,000	10
Profit	20,000	2	Profit	20,000	2
Total	$1,000,000	100	Total	$1,000,000	100

Note: Only a small increase in the number of work units put in place per person hour can have a multiplying effect on project cost, profits and time.

The cost components shown assume all the work is done by one firm. Even if the firm subcontracts a portion of the work, somebody has to do the work. Consider the above cost breakdowns either representative of the work a firm self-performs or the total cost to the project owner.

The competitive nature of the construction process (numerous firms competing for the same work) and the fact that the firms engage in a competitive bidding process, has forced the pure profit margin down to around 2%. Some firms do better, some do worse; the numbers shown above should be viewed as typical.

One does not require a major increase in jobsite productivity to realize a significant increase in project profitability. Often just a small percentage increase can have a significant impact on job profitability. Consider the example in the data shown below. It illustrates what a 5% increase in productivity for labor and/or equipment would do for the above two projects.

BUILDING PROJECT	
Premise:	*Result:*
Assume a 5% increase in labor productivity	Decrease in labor cost of 5%
	= (5% times $400,000) = $20,000
	Conclusion:
	= Doubles the planned profit of $20,000
Premise:	*Result:*
Assume a 5% increase in labor productivity and a 5% increase in equipment productivity	Decrease in labor and equipment cost of 5% = (5% times $400,000) = $20,000 = (5% times $100,000) = $ 5,000
	Conclusion:
	= A $25,000 increase in profits
Additional Benefits:	Decreased project time and decreased general conditions

Introduction to Productivity Improvement

PUBLIC WORKS PROJECT	
Premise:	*Result:*
Assume a 5% increase in equipment productivity	Decrease in equipment cost of 5%
	= (5% times $400,000) = $20,000
	Conclusion:
	= Doubles the planned profit of $20,000
Premise:	*Result:*
Assume a 5% increase in labor productivity and a 5% increase in equipment productivity	Decrease in labor and equipment cost of 5% = (5% times $200,000) = $10,000 = (5% times $400,000) = $20,000
	Conclusion:
	= A $30,000 increase in profits
Additional Benefits:	Decreased project time and decreased general conditions

It is clear that even a small increase in productivity can have a major impact on the project profits. Certainly a 5% increase in productivity is attainable. The supervisor's monitoring of worker late starts or early quits, improved scheduling to reduce labor and equipment waiting time at the project, attention to efficient material handling to eliminate excess material handling, and a reduction in lost time owing to accidents can all result in increased productivity. It can be argued that weather doesn't dictate the success or a failure of a project. Labor unions don't dictate the success or failure of a project. Designers don't dictate the success or failure of a project. It is the construction supervisor's actions or non-actions that in great part dictate the time, cost, quality and safety of the project!

Themes for Productivity Improvement

Don't Let Past Inefficiencies Become Goals for the Future

Tradition is very strong in the construction industry. Inefficiencies of the past often become the benchmarks or targets for the future. The construction supervisor might take the attitude that "my way is the only way," or "Don't tell me what to do, I've been doing this for 30 years."

Admittedly, experience is a valuable asset for a construction supervisor. However, experience by itself is not the only attribute one needs to be a successful supervisor. If the construction industry were a perfect industry; i.e., if there were no disputes, cost estimates were perfect, the eight-hour construction workday consisted of zero non-productive labor or equipment time, there were no accidents, etc.; then one could argue that experience by itself was the only asset a construction supervisor needed.

The construction process is not a perfect process. The following are only a few of the many problems that provide the supervisor opportunity for improvement.

- Disputed change orders
- Non-productive labor and equipment time
- Accidents
- Theft of materials and/or tools
- Double handling of material
- Redo or punch list work

Shown in Figure 1-3 on page 1-13 is a pie chart depicting the work states of a craftsman at a jobsite. While the work states and percentages shown may not represent the average day, the illustration does represent a "real" day.

SESSION 1

INTRODUCTION TO PRODUCTIVITY IMPROVEMENT

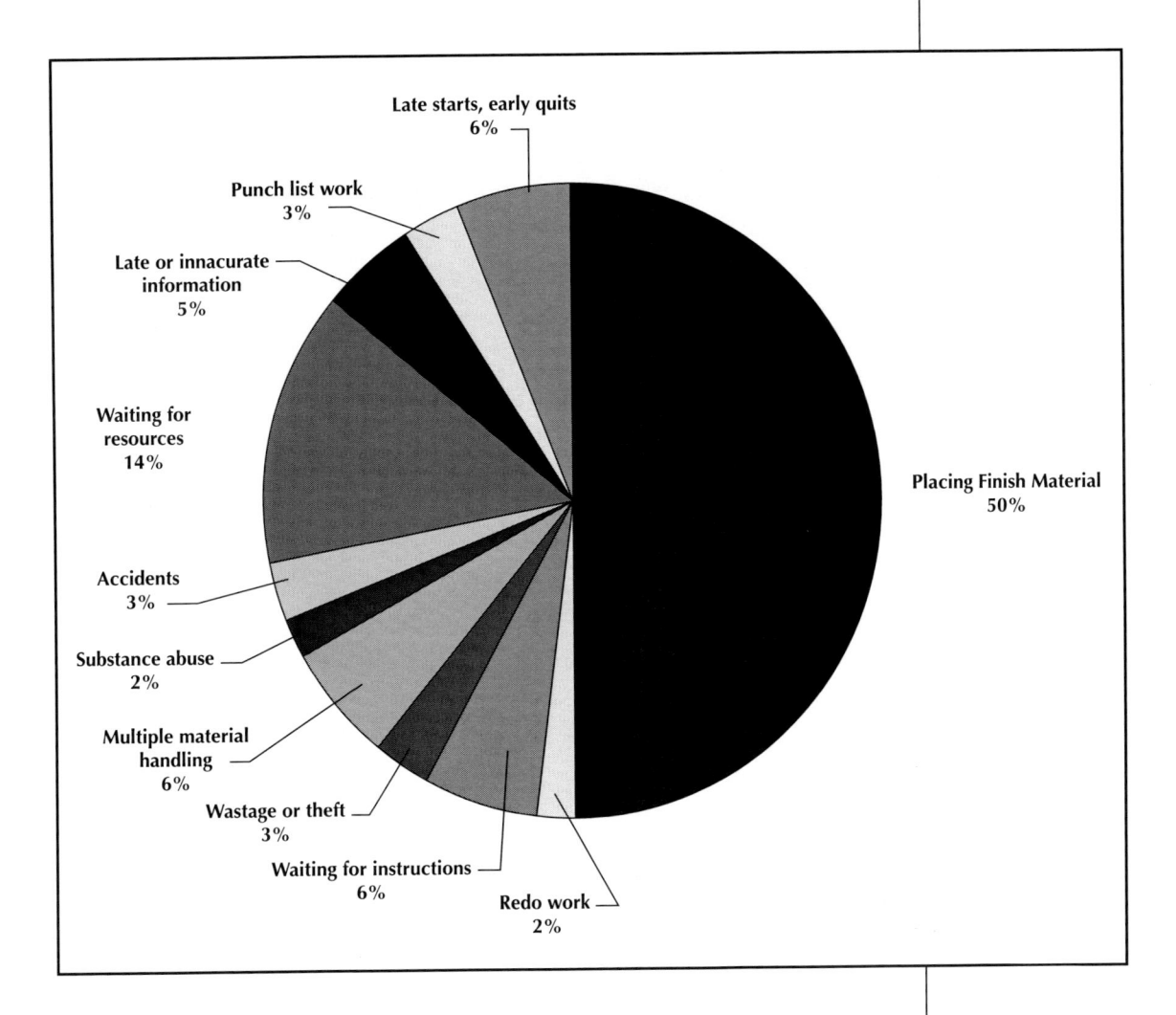

Pie chart segments:
- Placing Finish Material 50%
- Late starts, early quits 6%
- Punch list work 3%
- Late or innacurate information 5%
- Waiting for resources 14%
- Accidents 3%
- Substance abuse 2%
- Multiple material handling 6%
- Wastage or theft 3%
- Waiting for instructions 6%
- Redo work 2%

Fig. 1-3

The example non-productive times shown in Figure 1-3 relate to management issues. Issues such as waiting relate to the failure to properly plan, late starts and early quits relate to not implementing consistent project procedures, etc. The supervisor can make a positive impact on each of these by implementing new management actions.

Not every project has as much non-productive time as that shown in Figure 1-3. However, every project has some non-productive time. The supervisor should view non-productive time as an opportunity to improve.

To improve the workday shown in the figure, the supervisor must "break the mold," "think out of the box" and "use creative thinking." Whatever you want to call it, consider the following ten new themes or supervisor skills as a means of improving the construction process.

Participant's Manual ■ STP ■ Unit 9

Continuous Education

Too often the construction industry, including the construction supervisor, is short sighted. Given the strong traditions of the construction industry, long-term problems cannot be solved with shortsighted vision. Improvement is a marathon, not a hundred-yard dash!

Education can be defined as the short-term commitment of time and/or money to yield long-term benefits. Education is similar to research and development (R&D). Without R&D, companies do not invent new products, new procedures; i.e., they become stagnant.

There is evidence that the construction industry spends less money and time providing ongoing education to its supervisors than most if not all industries. Does the best construction supervisor have a college degree or a degree from the "school of hard knocks;" i.e., experience? A strong argument can be made for both; college-educated supervisors and supervisors who come from the trades.

Independent of the supervisor's formal educational background, the following is proposed:

The supervisor should be required to obtain 40 hours of continuing education a year. This education can include attending seminars, going to trade shows, or reading books.

Every year there are new materials available for construction, new equipment, new methods of construction, new technology, etc. How can the supervisor be effective over the long-term if he or she doesn't get out of the fire drill of being a supervisor and look for new ideas?

Process versus Results Management

The traditional role of the construction supervisor can be viewed as a "results" driven manager. Examples of being focused on results are:

- Getting serious about a subcontractor's failure to complete in 21 days what he promised would be complete in 20 days.

- Obtaining a bonus for beating the budget or estimate.

- Getting serious about a dispute or claim when the project is complete.

- Getting worried about not meeting a liquidated damage date a few days before the date.

The following is proposed:

The supervisor should shift his or her focus to managing/ monitoring the process rather than focusing only on the result.

An example of process management would be the supervisor requiring a subcontractor to set out the manpower required to get something done, as well as setting out that it will be done in 20 days. For example, the subcontractor might determine that eight workers are required. The supervisor would then monitor the process; i.e., monitor the presence and work effort of the eight workers. If the effort is not there, the results will not be attained. Monitoring process or effort enables the supervisor to identify problems more quickly so that solutions can be implemented.

Consistent Procedures and Practices

The construction supervisor can be viewed as an entrepreneur. The supervisor is empowered to make numerous decisions each day that affect the project time, cost, quality and safety of the project. However, when it comes to following company procedures to include required paperwork, how to start and finish the workday to eliminate late starts and early quits, procedures to control tool usage and equipment usage, etc.; there is no room for entrepreneurship.

Quality and productivity improvement can best be obtained by having each and every supervisor in the same firm follow set procedures consistently. Perhaps there is no bigger "black hole" in the construction industry than the inconsistent practices of supervisors in the same firm. It is common to see two supervisors in the same firm filling out daily reports differently or following different policies on when the workers on a project have to be at their work location at the start of the day, etc. The following is proposed:

A detailed project procedures manual should be given to each supervisor in a firm. The supervisor should be evaluated and rated (and rewarded) for his or her compliance with the set procedures.

Jobsite reviews or audits should be made to evaluate supervisors at work, rather than merely rate the supervisor by results. Supervisors that are in compliance should be commended and/or rewarded. If you fix the process by requiring consistent correct procedures, favorable results will occur.

Proactive versus Reactive Management

The traditional construction supervisor can be viewed as a reactor to problems, a policeman and an auditor. Every day, problems arise at the construction jobsite that require an action on the part of the supervisor. The construction supervisor is constantly putting out fires.

It is important that the supervisor serve in the role of a reactor to problems. He or she must be a policeman or auditor to see that everyone is working, that everyone is abiding by company policies and procedures. Most construction supervisors serve this objective well; they monitor construction methods and workers.

However, given an industry that offers opportunity for improvement, the supervisor needs to be proactive; i.e., to look for better ways to do things, not just enforce the inefficient ways of the past. Past inefficiencies should not become the targets for the future. Working hard does not necessarily mean working smart.

The following is proposed:

Once a month, the supervisor should be required to close the trailer door, brainstorm and write up a better way (a best practice) to do something at the jobsite that will improve time, cost, quality or safety.

One way of challenging a work method to seek an improved work method is to ask oneself the following questions when analyzing a construction work process:

- What is the work method?
- What are we trying to achieve?
- How are we currently doing the task?
- Why are we doing it this way?
- Who is best able to do the task?
- Where is the best place to do the task?
- When is the best time to do the task?

While there can be no guarantee that the supervisor will come up with a great idea each and every month, the mere fact that it becomes a monthly effort to try, will make the supervisor proactive as well as reactive. Working smarter, not harder, should be the objective.

Measurement and Analysis of a Defect

Construction supervisors have traditionally monitored the progress of a project by tracking labor hours and cost, material quantities and cost, and equipment hours and cost, against budgeted quantities for specific defined cost codes. Examples of cost codes are forming walls, placing concrete block, erecting pipe, installing ductwork, etc. These types of cost codes can be considered "productive" cost codes.

However, when one visits a construction jobsite, one witnesses workers in a non-productive state; e.g., waiting for materials, doing redo work, looking for tools, etc. The supervisor seldom measures or quantifies this non-productive time. Instead the time expended during these non-productive times is assigned to productive cost codes.

The construction supervisor cannot effectively improve a defect unless

1. the defect is measured,
2. the causes of the defect are identified and
3. new ideas or procedures are implemented to reduce the cause of the defect.

The construction process contains many defects, including:

— Redo work

— Waiting on materials

— Workers waiting for instructions

— Punch list work

— Double handling of materials

— Accidents

— Theft

— Lost or misplaced tools

The following is proposed:

The construction supervisor should select one defect per year and make it his or her objective to reduce or eliminate the defect; e.g., incidents of redo work.

Once the defect is selected, the supervisor should set out a program for measuring the defect. For example, assume the supervisor measures the number of incidents of redo work on three similar projects. One project may have 15 incidents, one might have ten incidents, and one might have only five incidents of redo work.

Introduction to Productivity Improvement

The reasons or causes for the variation in the number of incidents of redo work should be investigated. By focusing on the cause of the variation and reducing the negative factors, the number of incidents of redo work can be reduced. Such a continuous improvement program should strive for zero defects.

Risk or Variation Analysis

The construction industry has a history of focusing on averages. For example, cost books are published that print average productivities (e.g., place 2 cubic yards of concrete per person hour) for various construction work tasks. Similarly, weekly or monthly job cost reports are prepared that summarize average productivity achieved for the time period. At the end of the workday, the supervisor accumulates concrete yardage tickets and divides them by the labor hours expended for the day to yield average productivity for the day.

Focusing on averages for a process subject to variation does not optimize one's ability to improve the process. Let us assume a construction supervisor collects data about the productivity of placing concrete forms during an example day. The data is shown in Figure 1-4 below.

While the average productivity was 10 square feet of contact area (sfca) per person hour, there were hours when the productivity was as much as 15 sfca per person hour and as small as 5 sfca per person hour. The supervisor needs to focus on how they achieved the 15 sfca and what caused the small productivity of 5. By duplicating the events that resulted in the 15 sfca per person hour and by eliminating the cause of the unfavorable 5 sfca per person hour, the supervisor can improve the average productivity of 10 sfca per person hour.

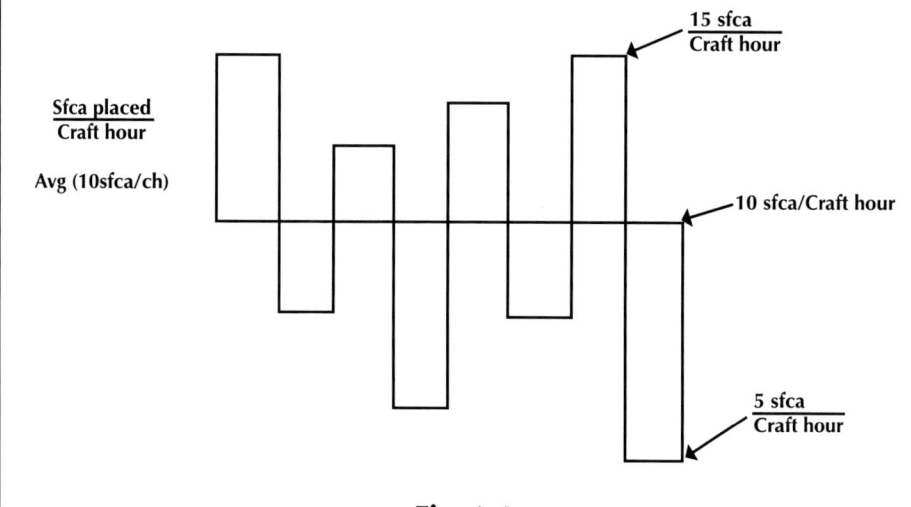

Fig. 1-4

The following is proposed:

The supervisor should focus on a construction operation that has considerable variation in productivity from one time period to the next and analyze the differences as a means of productivity improvement.

Instead of focusing on productivity variation per hour, the supervisor can concentrate on differences in productivity from one day to another day as a means of finding causes for differences.

Vital Few versus Useful Many

The construction supervisor is asked to do more things every day than he or she has time to do. It is therefore important that the supervisor focus on what is important; i.e., the vital few activities or tasks. Let's assume that two construction work activities are going on at the same time, one which costs $100 per unit of work to place and another which costs $20 per unit of work to place. Clearly if the supervisor can only be at one of the two locations, he or she should supervise the more expensive work task. The higher-cost work task can be referred to as a vital activity and the lower-cost work task can be viewed as one of the useful many work activities.

Vital activities need more supervisor attention than useful many work activities. There are at least four criteria for identifying vital work activities.

- High-cost work tasks
- High-risk work tasks (productivity varies significantly from one time period to the next)
- Work tasks that dictate the project duration; i.e., critical path activities.
- Work tasks that the firm has little or no prior work experience performing.

The concept of the vital few and the useful many is comparable to the 80–20 rule that is part of Pareto theory. It states that "an individual should not expend 80% of their effort on the 20 tasks that are least important."

The following is proposed:

Before the project starts, the supervisor should review the estimate and identify vital activities versus the useful many work activities and use this list as a guide in managing his or her workday.

Planning Versus Reacting

There is little question that the construction supervisor works hard. However, more often than not, the supervisor is in a role of reacting to problems; i.e., a policeman. While it is important to be able to react to problems in a construction process in which uncertain events and issues constantly arise, reacting or policing work activities by themselves will not improve the work processes.

Instead of expending all his or her time putting out fires, the supervisor can reduce fires (i.e., problems) from starting by being more attentive to planning. A few minutes preparing formal plans that anticipate problems can reduce the number of problems that occur.

Some people would argue that formalized planning in the construction process doesn't work given the number of problems or uncertain events that occur daily. Actually the reverse is true; the more problems or uncertain events that occur, the greater the need for formalized planning. If uncertain events or problems couldn't occur, there would be little need to plan.

Some supervisors mentally plan things out on a daily basis. While this is a favorable attribute, given the complexity of the construction process, it is important to write out plans. Having a pencil and paper (or a computer) in front of you when you plan helps you to remember all tasks. More importantly, a written plan serves as a reminder list of actions or tasks the supervisor must perform to keep a project productive; i.e., to reduce problems.

The following is proposed:

> *On an ongoing basis, the supervisor should use a written form to plan tomorrow's work today. In addition, the supervisor should use a form to look ahead or plan ahead three to four weeks in the construction schedule.*

Focus on Quality First

The success or failure of every construction project can be measured in terms of four variables:

- Project cost
- Project time
- Project quality
- Project safety

While each of these variables is important, the supervisor should never lose sight of the most important one. If a project is over budget, the construction firm can usually tighten its belt and survive a small cost overrun. In addition, by identifying cost overruns early, the impact of the overrun can be minimized.

If a project is over budget in regard to time or schedule, chances are that the supervisor can accelerate the schedule by working overtime or adding more resources. If work is done improperly and that leads to poor quality, the work can be fixed or repaired, but that means redo work or work performed on the punch list. The point is that while a cost problem, a schedule problem or a quality of work problem are unfavorable project characteristics, there is a remedy or fix for these problems.

This is not the case when one has a safety problem leading to an accident. When an accident occurs, there is no fixing it; there is no turning back. An injury to a worker ruins a project, regardless of a favorable project time, cost and quality.

The following is proposed:

The supervisor should always make safety his or her first priority. He or she should start the day by being proactive, anticipating potential safety problems and taking steps to eliminate the potential for an accident to occur.

Pride and a Positive Attitude

Effective supervisors are always proud of what they do. If the supervisor is a whiner, always complaining and blaming people, or if he projects an image that he doesn't like what he is doing, this negative approach negatively impacts the attitudes and productivity of the supervisor's subordinates and the overall project.

The construction supervisor and his or her workers have every right to be proud of what they do. The construction industry is the backbone of the U.S. economy. Annually in the range of 8% to 12% of the gross national product is new construction; the industry employs over five million people; and perhaps most importantly, the construction industry "makes things; it doesn't simply trade things." Any economy that is to prosper over the long term has to make things.

The following is proposed:

The supervisor should make a daily effort to turn problems into opportunities. He or she should reduce incidents of blaming people and instead spend more time commending people and telling them what they did right rather than what they did wrong.

Let's take two supervisors that are confronted with the following problems:

- Five days of bad weather in a row
- A subcontractor that is not staffing the job with enough workers
- A project designer that is being slow in making decisions and is holding up the work process.

The first supervisor spends her time blaming these events for project time and cost problems. When she speaks to her boss about these problems, she speaks in terms of "them or they" for project overruns or problems. Everything out of her mouth seems to be negative.

The second supervisor is subjected to the same problems. However, she uses her creativity to minimize the impact of the problems. The supervisor uses schedule floats to reduce the impact of the weather. The supervisor works with the subcontractor and shows the subcontractor that if the firm puts more people on the project that the subcontractor as well as the project will benefit. The supervisor works with the designer in an effort to speed up the designer's decision making for the project. The second supervisor takes a positive approach to problems; she speaks in terms of "we."

Problems will always occur in construction. Taking a negative approach will never keep them from occurring or minimize the impact of the problems. Just as there is "no crying in baseball," there should be "no whining in construction."

Session 1 Review

Look back over Session 1 and review these key points to be sure you understand them

- Productivity is defined as units of work placed per person or craft hour of work effort.

- A worker or a machine is in one of three work states at any given point in time:
    - Productive work state
    - Non-productive work state
    - Support work state

- It takes only a small percent increase in productivity (say 5%), to have a significant increase in project profitability.

Using on the Job What You Learned Today

Jobsite Assignment

On your current project, try to think of how you could implement one idea or procedure for each of the "new themes" 2 through 10 that were presented in the previous section. (Note: theme 1 was the commitment to ongoing continuous education, which is more of a long-term commitment than something you can apply tomorrow at a jobsite.)

To Get Ready for Session 2

Read the Participant's Manual for Session 2, *Increasing Productivity Through Pre-Planning*.

Session 2

Improving Productivity Through Pre-Planning

Learning Goals for Session 2

After this session, you should recognize the importance of pre-planning to the productivity of the construction phase of the project. You will learn the importance of interfacing the pre-planning phase of the project with the estimate to include:

1. Identifying important or "vital" project work tasks,
2. Identifying base bid work versus change order work,
3. Identifying potential "killer" clauses in the supplementary conditions and
4. Preparing production budgets for crews from the estimate.

Learning Objectives

To accomplish the learning goals, during this session you will:

- Identify the four phases of the construction project and recognize the importance of the time period between the estimate and the start of the project
- Identify vital work tasks from the estimate and specifications
- Identify the difference between base bid work versus extra or change order work
- Prepare a list of unique "killer" clauses contained in the supplementary conditions
- Transpose the estimate into daily or hourly production goals for the work crews
- Prepare and use a checklist for performing tasks in the pre-planning phase of the project

To Get Ready for Session 2

Reading: Read the pages in this session prior to class. Try to think of non-productive time expended at your jobsites that could have been reduced via more attention to pre-planning.

Major Activities for Session 2
- Understand the four phases of the construction project and the importance of the pre-planning phase.
- Interface the pre-planning phase of the project with the estimate.
- Do an exercise that identifies the "vital" activities for an example project.
- Review contract clauses to determine base bid work versus change order work.
- Review supplementary conditions to identify project killer clauses.
- Do an exercise that will require you to identify unique supplementary condition clauses.
- Learn how to break the estimate into jobsite production goals for crews.
- Do an exercise in preparing daily or hourly crew production budgets.
- Prepare a generalized checklist for pre-planning a project.
- Review this session.

A Review of Session 1

In Session 1, you learned how to measure productivity and why it is important to increase productivity. A small increase in construction productivity can have a significant impact on the project profitability and project duration. By using new themes or approaches, the supervisor can make a significant impact on construction jobsite productivity.

Here are some of the facts that you learned in Session 1:

- Productivity is measured as units of output produced per unit of craft hour expended.

- Construction productivity can be increased by working smarter, not necessarily harder.

- Construction productivity has increased more slowly than productivity in non-construction industries.

- Ways to increase productivity over the long run include:
  — Continuing education
  — Focusing on process, not just results
  — Measurement of productivity defects and their cause
  — Openness to new ideas

- A 5% increase in productivity can more than double the profits of a project.

- New themes or approaches are needed by the supervisor to increase productivity. Past inefficiencies should not become benchmarks for the future.

Increasing Productivity Through Pre-Planning

The Four Phases of the Construction Process

From the constructor's view, a project is successful if the project meets the following four criteria:

- Constructed on the financial budget
- Constructed according to the project duration schedule
- The project meets quality objectives
- The project is completed safely (i.e., free of injuries)

To meet the four criteria, the construction supervisor must be attentive to what might be considered the four phases of the construction project. These phases are shown in Figure 2-1 below.

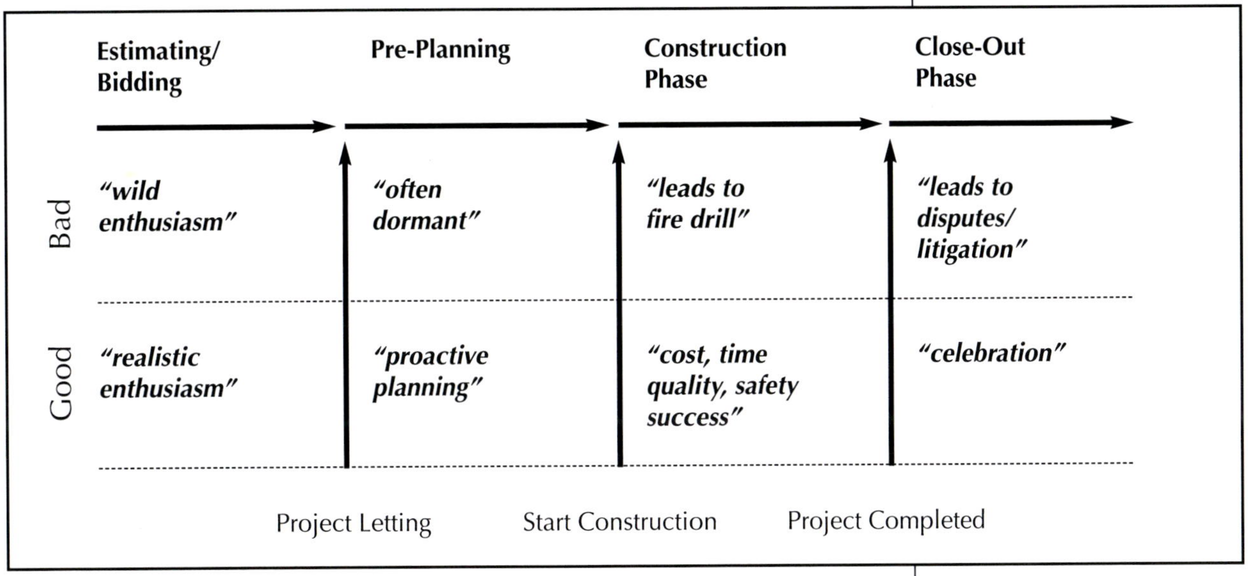

> The time spent by the supervisor between when the constructor is awarded a project and when the firm actually starts construction is critical to the success of a project in the construction phase. The tasks performed during this time period are referred to as **pre-planning**.

	Estimating/Bidding	Pre-Planning	Construction Phase	Close-Out Phase
Bad	"wild enthusiasm"	"often dormant"	"leads to fire drill"	"leads to disputes/litigation"
Good	"realistic enthusiasm"	"proactive planning"	"cost, time quality, safety success"	"celebration"

Project Letting — Start Construction — Project Completed

Fig. 2-1. The Four Phases of the Construction Process

Much emphasis is given to the estimating phase of construction. Given that most construction contracts are awarded based on a "low bid" bidding process, the importance of the estimate is obvious.

[handwritten note: LOWEST QUALIFIED BIDDER]

The importance of the construction phase stems from its visibility. The construction supervisor operates out in the open. The visibility of labor and equipment at a project puts the construction phase and the supervisor under a magnifying glass.

However, the success of a project when it comes to time, cost, quality and safety is in great part dependent on what the supervisor does or does not do prior to the construction phase. All too often the construction firm puts a project to rest during the time period between when they get the contract and when the firm starts construction. The firm and the supervisor do very little during this time period. In fact, the supervisor may not even get assigned to "manage" the project until a few days before the project starts. The result is that there may be little to no pre-planning of project tasks such as planning production budgets, pre-ordering long lead material items, or organizing the paper flow for the project. In effect, the project becomes dormant between project letting and the start of construction. As noted in the figure above, this leads to a fire drill mode, a process of reacting to problems that could have been prevented through pre-planning. These problems can lead to project disputes, claims, cost overruns, time overruns, etc.

As illustrated in the figure above, pre-planning can lead to a more productive construction phase and a more desirable project closeout. The point is that productivity improvement starts before the construction phase; it starts with getting the supervisor involved in pre-planning prior to the start of the construction phase.

The pre-planning phase of a project should focus on two objectives:

- Interfacing the construction supervisor with the estimate
- Planning the construction phase

Suggested pre-planning tasks for each of these objectives are presented in this session.

Interfacing the Supervisor with the Estimate

Most construction firms structure the estimating function as a decentralized process. By this we mean the firm establishes a separate department and assigns individuals to this function. These individuals become full-time estimators. This centralized estimating process is illustrated in Figure 2-2.

```
              Construction Company Owner
                         |
        ------------------------------------
        |                |                 |
Accounting and    Estimating/Marketing   Construction/Supervision
   Finance
```

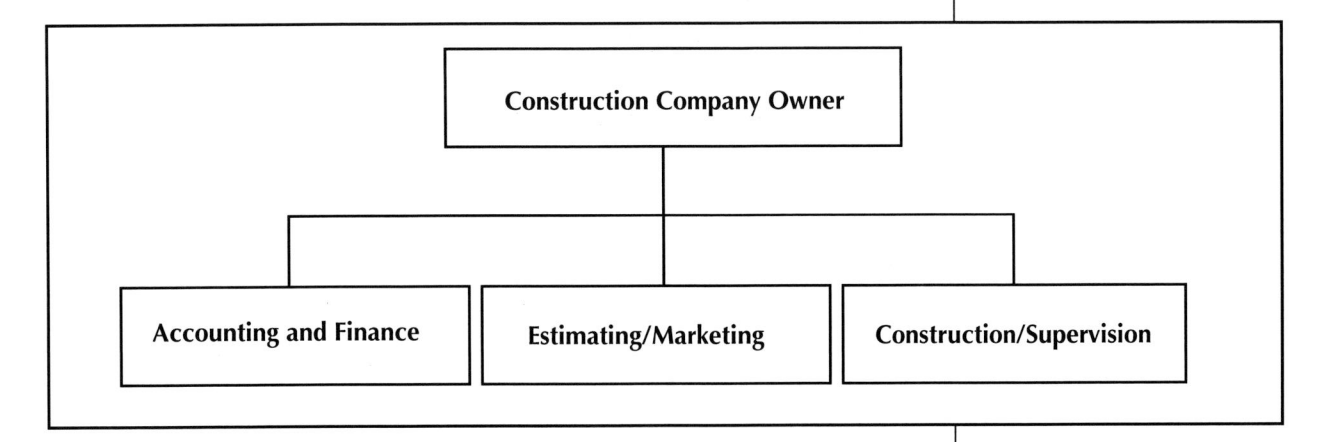

Fig. 2-2

The benefit to the construction firm of the decentralized estimating process is that the estimators become specialized in costing work, securing subcontractor bids, buying out materials, etc. The construction supervisor becomes focused on the constructing of the project. However, there is also a major disadvantage to the process. If the bid/estimate prepared by the estimator is successful, the project is "handed off" to the supervisor. For one, the supervisor may not get the opportunity to provide valuable construction experience knowledge to the estimator. Secondly, the construction supervisor gets very little information about the estimating assumptions and contract documents. This puts the supervisor at a disadvantage in regard to planning and carrying out the construction process.

One of the purposes of the preplanning phase of the project is to interface the construction supervisor with the project estimate; to provide input to the estimate, and to learn valuable information from the prepared estimate and accompanying contract documents.

A recommended structured process for interfacing the project supervisor into the estimating phase of the project is shown in Figure 2-3.

Note: In most construction firms, estimating and construction supervision are two separate departments and two separate groups of individuals. Therefore, it is critical that they be interfaced and important information passed to the supervisor from the estimator prior to starting the project.

SESSION 2

IMPROVING PRODUCTIVITY THROUGH PRE-PLANNING

INTERFACING THE SUPERVISOR WITH THE ESTIMATE

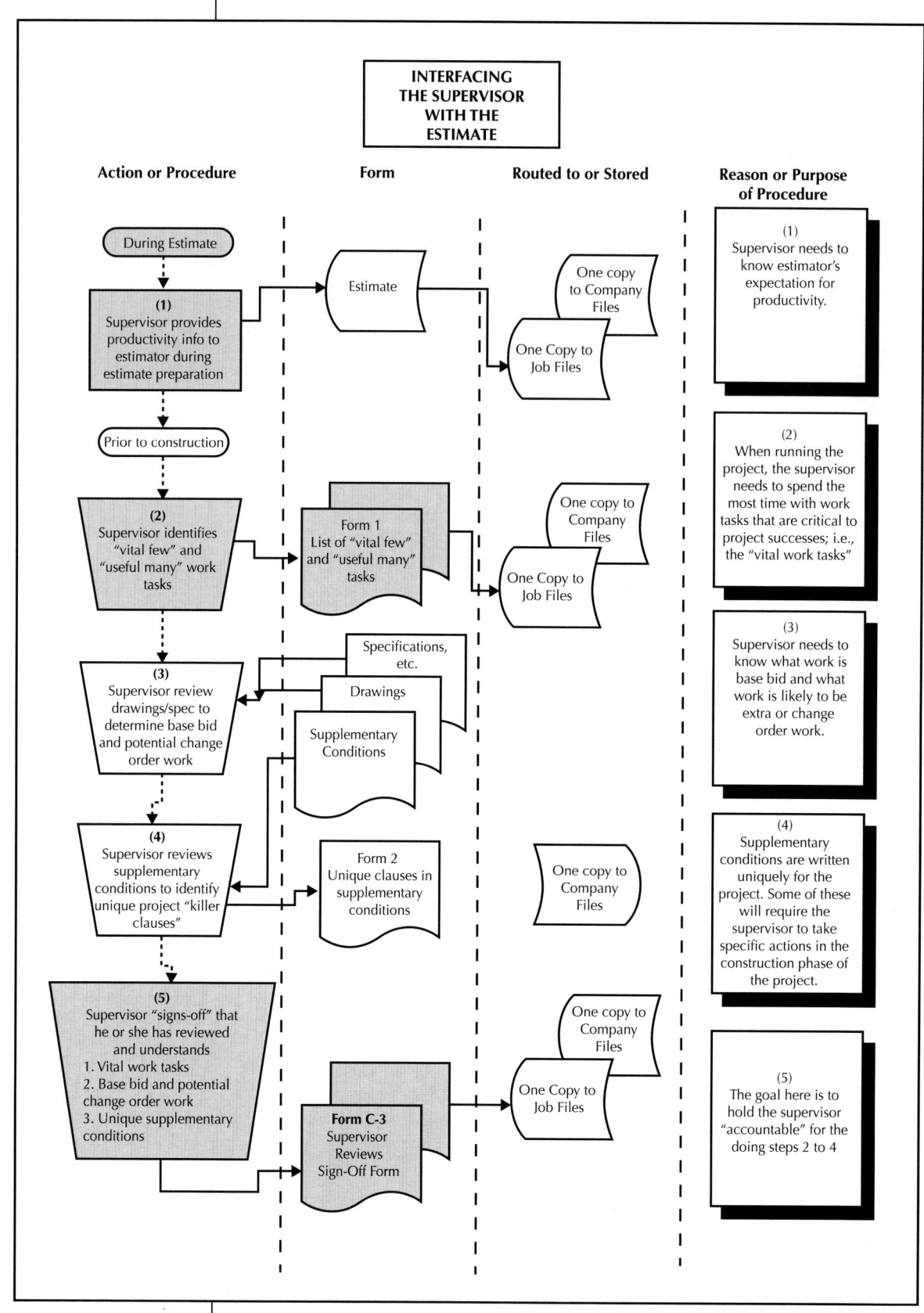

Action or Procedure	Form	Routed to or Stored	Reason or Purpose of Procedure
During Estimate → **(1)** Supervisor provides productivity info to estimator during estimate preparation	Estimate	One copy to Company Files; One Copy to Job Files	(1) Supervisor needs to know estimator's expectation for productivity.
Prior to construction → **(2)** Supervisor identifies "vital few" and "useful many" work tasks	Form 1 List of "vital few" and "useful many" tasks	One copy to Company Files; One Copy to Job Files	(2) When running the project, the supervisor needs to spend the most time with work tasks that are critical to project successes; i.e., the "vital work tasks"
(3) Supervisor review drawings/spec to determine base bid and potential change order work	Specifications, etc.; Drawings; Supplementary Conditions		(3) Supervisor needs to know what work is base bid and what work is likely to be extra or change order work.
(4) Supervisor reviews supplementary conditions to identify unique project "killer clauses"	Form 2 Unique clauses in supplementary conditions	One copy to Company Files	(4) Supplementary conditions are written uniquely for the project. Some of these will require the supervisor to take specific actions in the construction phase of the project.
(5) Supervisor "signs-off" that he or she has reviewed and understands 1. Vital work tasks 2. Base bid and potential change order work 3. Unique supplementary conditions	Form C-3 Supervisor Reviews Sign-Off Form	One copy to Company Files; One Copy to Job Files	(5) The goal here is to hold the supervisor "accountable" for the doing steps 2 to 4

Fig. 2-3

2-6   Participant's Manual ■ STP ■ Unit 9

The process shown above includes the following five steps:

1. **Supervisor should meet with the estimator during bid preparation and provide construction productivity information to the estimator.**

   The construction estimator often comes under attack as not having enough sufficient knowledge or experience in the construction process to properly estimate labor and equipment cost and productivity. By reviewing the project drawings and specifications with the estimator, the supervisor can provide valuable insights regarding unique work difficulties and suggest work methods that influence the costing of the project work. The purpose here is to have the estimator and supervisor merge their knowledge into an estimate / bid that reflects what the project will cost when it is built under the direction of the supervisor.

   It is important that the supervisor input his or her knowledge into the estimate and that the estimator and supervisor agree as to what methods of construction will be used when construction starts.

   Secondly, if a project goes over the time or cost budget in the construction phase of a project, it is common for the estimator to blame the construction supervisor, and for the construction supervisor to blame the estimator. By having the supervisor provide input to the estimate during the estimate preparation, the issue of who is responsible is removed, in that the estimate phase becomes more of a team effort. Everyone gains from this team effort rather than blaming one another.

   Some of the input the supervisor can provide to the estimator during the bidding phase of the project includes the following:

   - Information as to what methods of construction should be used; for example, what forming systems should be used. If the estimator assumes one forming system and the supervisor uses a different forming system to construct the project, surely the cost of doing the work will be different from the bid.

   - Knowledge about unique construction difficulties that may influence the costing of the project.

   - Knowledge about likely labor, material or equipment shortages that may influence the costing of the project.

   - Suggestions regarding the project time schedule (e.g., how it might be shortened) that may influence the costing of time related costs to include general conditions costs.

   One of the problems of formalizing the process of having the supervisor meet and provide input to the estimator during the bidding phase of the project is that some construction firms may not assign a specific supervisor to manage a project until after the estimate is bid and the contract awarded. This organizational problem can be alleviated by having the construction firm identify the likely supervisor early in the four-phase process shown earlier. Even if a supervisor is working on another project at the time, the supervisor could be called in to meet with the estimator for a few hours. The purpose of the meeting is not to prepare the estimate but rather to provide input to it. This is not a major time-consuming task.

2. **The supervisor should review the estimate to identify the "vital few" work tasks and the "useful many" work tasks.**

    As pointed out in section one, the construction supervisor seldom has enough time to do everything expected of him or her once the project starts. They can't be everywhere every minute of the day. For example, once the project starts, there are likely several work tasks happening simultaneously at the project; forming walls at one location, placing rebar in columns at another location, pouring a slab at another location, etc.

    Since the supervisor can't be everywhere every minute of the construction workday, he or she must pick and choose. To optimize the supervision function the supervisor should be more attentive to supervising important work tasks; i.e., the vital few activities. On any one project the supervisor may have to monitor hundreds of work tasks or cost codes. However, it is likely that only a handful of these work tasks dictate the project time, cost, quality and safety.

    Four criteria are suggested for identifying project vital work tasks

    - Cost of the work
    - Risk or variation in the production process
    - Work tasks that dictate or drive the project schedule
    - Work tasks the firm and supervisor have seldom done previously

    a. **Cost of work**

        If the supervisor cannot be in two places at the same time, he or she should be supervising the more expensive work task. For example, all other things being equal, if a work task such as excavation work costs $6.00 per cubic yard to perform, and the placing of concrete costs $60.00 per cubic yard to perform, the supervisor should spend more of his or her time managing the $60.00 item.

        When considering the cost of an item, it is also important to focus on the number of units that have to be performed. For example, one item may have a unit cost of $100 per unit,

---

Note: Some work tasks are more important and need more supervision than other work tasks. The more important work tasks can be referred to as the "vital" work tasks. Criteria for identifying the vital work tasks are:

- Cost of the work
- Risk or variation in the productivity
- Tasks that dictate or drive the project duration
- Work tasks that the supervisor has not done previously

whereas another item may have a unit cost of $30 per unit. However, there may be 100 units of the $30 per unit item and only five units of the $100 per unit item. In that case it is important that the supervisor focus on the item with more units.

b. Risk or variation in the production process

Risk simply means variation from an expected estimate or average. Assume a supervisor is using two different forming systems to form concrete walls at two different locations at a project. Assume further that the construction firm has gathered hourly productivity data about each of the work methods as shown in Figure 2-4.

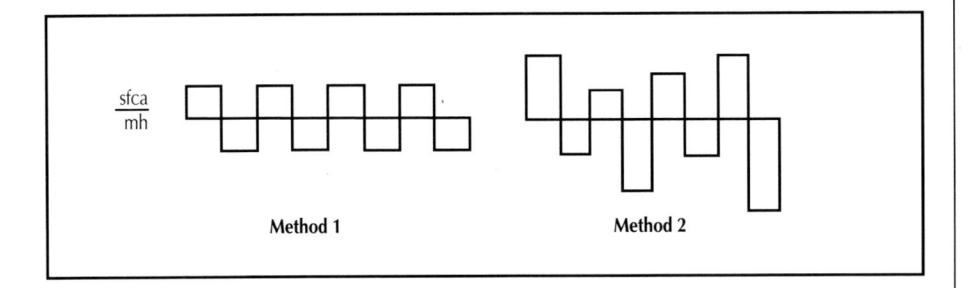

Fig. 2-4

Observation of the data shown above indicates that on average the workers using the two different forming systems are obtaining the same average productivity (square feet of contact area placed per man-hour). However, there is considerably more variation in the hourly productivity for method 2. There were hours when the crew did very well (above average), and hours when the crew did very poorly (below average). Given a choice, the supervisor should spend more supervision on work method 2.

Consider the two work tasks of forming concrete walls and placing the concrete into the walls with a ready-mix truck and a chute. A review of project results would indicate that actual craft-hours expended to form the walls often vary considerably from the estimated craft-hours; i.e., it is a high-risk function. On the other hand, a review of project results would indicate that the actual craft-hours taken to place the concrete is very close to the budgeted or estimated craft-hours. However, more often than not, the placement gets more supervision time than the concrete forming work task. Supervisors need to assess how they spend their limited supervision time.

Note: Work tasks that dictate or drive the project duration are often referred to as "critical" activities.

c. Work tasks that dictate or drive the project schedule

One of the purposes of preparing an overall project schedule (such as a bar chart or critical path schedule) is to determine which work tasks or activities dictate or drive the project duration; often referred to as the critical path. Clearly these work tasks or activities should get more of the supervisor's attention than so called non-critical activities; i.e., work tasks that have time "float." While focusing on critical path activities is important, it should be noted that it is only one of the four criteria for identifying "vital" work tasks. A later section focuses more on the use of planning tools, such as the critical path method, to increase productivity.

d. Work tasks the firm and supervisor have seldom done previously

Typically on each and every project a supervisor manages, he or she has to monitor one of two types of work:

— work the firm and the supervisor have frequently performed on other projects,

— new work tasks that the firm and the supervisor have not done before.

The supervisor needs to be more attentive to work of which he or she has little prior experience.

For example, some general contractors do their own masonry work, and others subcontract this work. If a general contractor decides to take on the masonry work as a means of being more competitive, the supervisor needs to pay more attention to this work on the project in question. The new work, and lack of experience performing it, is likely to provide more potential for surprises (good or bad) than work the firm has performed previously.

Using these four criteria, the construction supervisor should identify these "vital" work tasks before starting the project, i.e., pre-plan. These vital work tasks need more attention in regard to planning and control. For example, the supervisor might decide to monitor the above-mentioned masonry work on a daily basis by measuring the blocks or brick put in place per crew. On the other hand, the supervisor might rely more on a weekly or monthly job cost report as a means of monitoring the useful many work tasks.

Review of Contract Documents for Identifying Vital Few Work Tasks and Useful Many Work Tasks

Exercise

This is a group project. You will be teamed up with three or four participants. Use the four criteria listed in this section as a guide in identifying your "vital" work tasks — for example, projects your team members have constructed. Also list five to ten work tasks that you view as the "useful many"; work tasks that your group determines need less of your attention.

Be prepared to give your reasons for identifying the work tasks as vital or useful.

> If the supervisor does not have a clear understanding of the base bid work requirements, he or she might do change order work and believe it is base bid work. The result is that the firm would not bill the extra work nor get paid for the extra work performed.

3. Supervisor reviews contract drawings and specifications to determine base bid work and potential change order work

The typical gap between the estimating and supervision functions can lead to extra construction work and failure to bill the work (let alone collect money for it). The construction industry performs thousands, if not millions, of dollars of work every year for free owing to the fact that the supervisor may not thoroughly understand the scope of the base bid work before starting the project. The supervisor may end up doing work that he or she believes is base bid work when in fact it could be billed as extra or change order work. The supervisor can best prevent this by thoroughly reviewing the project drawings and specifications prior to starting construction.

Change order work typically does occur during the construction work; i.e., work not required as base bid work and not included in the contractor estimate. Change order work can be disruptive to the construction process. Poorly administered change order work is one of the leading reasons for construction disputes between the contractor and the project owner and/or designer. The change order work process is typically a three-step process:

- Project owner and/or designer issues a requests for change
- Contractor prepares a cost proposal (CP) for performing the extra work
- Project owner (through designer) issues a change order for the work

Unfortunately each of these three steps does not always go smoothly. Sometimes the project owner and the contractor cannot agree that the work in question is actually extra or change order work; the owner/designer may take the position that the work should be considered base bid work and the contractor argues that it is extra work. Secondly, they may not be able to agree as to a fair price for the work. Disputes may develop as a result.

The contractor and supervisor need to be proactive in regard to change orders. If the supervisor can identify change order work early, he or she is in an improved position to negotiate a fair price for the work and also take appropriate management actions to minimize the potential impact on project productivity and the project schedule.

The supervisor should review project drawings and specifications to identify potential work difficulties and potential extra work areas. Rather than reacting to extra work situations during the construction process, a supervisor should attempt to identify them before the project.

As part of the contract document review of drawings and specifications, it is recommended that the supervisor write down on a form potential work difficulties and potential extra work that may evolve. This will serve as a good reminder once the construction process starts.

4. **Review project supplementary conditions to identify unique project clauses that may cause the supervisor difficulties if they are overlooked. Given the potential detrimental impact of these clauses, they are often referred to as "killer clauses."**

   When a construction contract is signed, the contractor agrees to abide by the following six legal contract documents:

   ■ Drawings

   ■ Specifications

   ■ General Conditions

   ■ Agreement Form

   ■ Addendum

   ■ Supplementary Conditions

   The **drawings** essentially indicate the quantity of work that must be performed by the contractor, cubic yards of excavation, square feet of contact area of wall forms that must be erected, linear feet of pipe to install, pounds of ductwork to be installed, etc.

   The **specifications** focus more on the quality of work that has to be achieved; compaction of the excavation work, concrete strength, etc. Obviously it is important that the supervisor understand both the drawings and specifications such that the quantity and quality of the work is performed according to the contract.

   The **general conditions** are, by definition, rather general. They state the roles and responsibilities of the general contractor, the subcontractor, the designer, etc. For the most part the general conditions are the same on each and every project.

   The **addendum** represents changes that are made in the contract documents prior to the letting of the contract. They are like change orders, except they are prior to the letting as opposed to change orders being after the contract letting.

There are six legal contract documents:

■ Drawings
■ Specifications
■ General Conditions
■ Supplementary Conditions
■ Addendum
■ Agreement Form

SESSION 2

IMPROVING PRODUCTIVITY THROUGH PRE-PLANNING

The **agreement form** is the piece of paper on which the contractor and the project owner agree to a dollar amount for which to complete the contract work.

The supplementary conditions can contain unique clauses that can prove detrimental to the interests of the construction firm and the supervisor. These clauses are often referred to as "killer" clauses. The clauses should be identified prior to starting construction (ideally while the project is being estimated).

It is the **supplementary conditions** that are often overlooked (not read) by the contractor and construction supervisor. The supplementary conditions are sometimes referred to as "special conditions."

It is critical that the supervisor become acquainted with the supplementary conditions prior to starting the construction process. It is in the supplementary conditions that the project designer writes contract administration clauses that may be detrimental to the supervisor's ability to manage the construction process.

The project designer may attempt to overprotect the project owner client with various protective clauses. Given the existence of these clauses, the supervisor may need to take specific actions to minimize their potential impact. A few of these clauses that need the supervisor's attention are:

Supplementary conditions clause	*What it is*	*Implication for supervisor*
Liquidated damage clause	Indicates financial damages ($s per day) the contractor will be assessed if the project is not completed on time.	Needs to be especially attentive to completing project on time. Needs to document any and all delays that are caused by project owner or designer.
Notification clause	Requires the supervisor to put the project owner and/or designer on notice within a specific time period (e.g., 14 days) of an event if the contractor is to have any financial remedy for issue.	Supervisor must be more attentive to writing letters and notifying project owner and/or designer about a problem sooner than he or she may have been in the past.
No damage for delay clause	If significant change orders occur, the contractor will likely be given added project time (liquidated damages not assessed) but will not be given financial remedy for added general condition costs.	Needs to be especially attentive to completing project on time. Needs to document any and all delays that are caused by project owner or designer.

There may be several additional supplementary condition clauses that the contractor and supervisor need to know about to manage the construction phase of the project. The point is, because some of these clauses are unique to a specific project, they have the potential to "surprise" the supervisor managing the construction phase of the project.

The use of the company supplementary clause checklist can minimize the possibility of overlooking one of these clauses. Using such a checklist, the supervisor looks for the existence of such a clause when reviewing the supplementary conditions, records the existence or non-existence, and takes appropriate actions when necessary. Obviously it is possible that a new clause appears on a project. However, once it does, even if it is overlooked the first time, it should be added to the checklist so that it isn't missed a second time.

Just as it is important for the estimator to "take-off" project quantities from the drawings to determine required construction tasks, it is also important that the supervisor "take-off" unique supplementary conditions. A small amount of time pre-planning the project can greatly minimize difficulties in the construction phase of the project.

5. **Supervisor should "sign off" that pre-planning tasks have been performed.**

    Given the many tasks that the supervisor has to do, it is possible that he or she may forget to do something; e.g., overlook an important pre-planning task. The best way not to forget something is to use a checklist as a reminder list. Such a reminder list is illustrated in the last section of this session.

Exercise

Review of Supplementary Conditions

In this section, emphasis was on the supervisor's review of the project supplementary conditions so that the unique and the possibly detrimental clauses are identified prior to starting a project. If this is done, the supervisor can ready himself or herself to take the appropriate action prior to or during the construction phase of the project.

Shown on the following page is a checklist for identifying various unique supplementary conditions. The three clauses discussed in the section are listed as well as why the clause is important, and a suggested supervisory action to take. In addition, three columns on the left of the form have been added. The supervisor can initial these to indicate that he or she has looked for the existence of the clause; indicate whether the clause is present, and indicate the date the supervisor looked for the clause.

It is intended that the participant remove the completed checklist and use it for review of the supplementary conditions for actual projects. The purpose is twofold:

1. It serves as a reminder list,

2. By using the checklist, all supervisors are required to do the same thing.

In effect, the supervisor becomes accountable. More often than not, accountability ensures responsibility, which in turn ensures performance.

Before using the checklist, you are asked to do the following:

■ For the additional supplementary condition clauses that are included as number 4 and 5, indicate why the clause is important, and what action is needed by the supervisor.

■ Given your experience and the type of work you supervise, list an additional five supplementary condition clauses that you should look for when reviewing the supplementary conditions. Also list why the clause is important, and what action, if any, is needed by the supervisor.

#	Supplementary conditions clause	What it is	Implication for supervisor	Name	Yes	No	Date
1	Liquidated damage clause	Indicates financial damages ($s per day) the contractor will be assessed if the project is not completed on time.	Needs to be especially attentive to completing project on time. Needs to document any and all delays caused by project owner or designer.				
2	Notification clause	Requires the supervisor to put the project owner and/or designer on notice within a specific time period (e.g., 14 days) of an event if the contractor is to have any financial remedy.	Supervisor must be more attentive and prompt in writing letters and notifying project owner and/or designer about problems.				
3	No damage for delay clause	If significant change orders occur, the contractor will likely be given added project time (liquidated damages not assessed) but will not be given financial remedy for added general condition costs. Needs to be especially attentive to completing project on time.	Needs to document any and all delays caused by project owner or designer.				
4	Scheduling clause						
5	Arbitration clause						
6							
7							
8							
9							
10							

Note: The craftsperson and the foreman often go to work without being given a daily or hourly production goal. The result is that they seldom know for sure if they did a good job or a bad job. Not sharing production goals leads to mistrust and the development of a we-they attitude.

Pre-Planning Production Budgets

Supervisors and their workers are more productive if they know what is expected of them in regard to production, quality and safety. The construction foreman and his crew often go to work and are told what to do without a goal or budget. Having a production goal enables an individual to take pride and satisfaction when meeting a goal. Without a goal, an individual has no measuring system by which to measure his or her effort.

The gap between estimating and construction in many construction firms has resulted in an estimate not being broken down into daily production goals. During the pre-planning phase of the construction process, the estimate should be broken down into daily or hourly production goals for the supervisor. The supervisor should be part of the team that makes these calculations so that he or she can agree to the production goals and become aware of what is expected. As simple a thought as this is, many construction firms and supervisors do not do this. Instead, the supervisor is simply assigned to the project and told to construct it. He or she is expected to do the best he or she can. Goal setting and production goals can go a long way to increasing productivity and giving the supervisors and crew members work satisfaction.

The estimate that is prepared for purposes of bidding the project should be broken down into daily (perhaps hourly) production goals for the supervisor and his or her crew. Supervisors and crewmembers think more in terms of units of work placed per time period rather than units placed per person hour (i.e., productivity). The transformation of the estimate into daily production goals is made somewhat confusing by the fact that estimates and productivity are often typically expressed in units of work per person hour as opposed to work per crew hour or time period. Most construction tasks are performed by crews that are made up of more than one worker.

The transformation of the estimate into daily production goals is not complicated; it merely involves taking the time to do it. It should be done as part the pre-planning process. The determining of production goals from the estimate will now be illustrated by example.

The estimate for a project is often prepared and summarized on an estimating form similar to the following:

IMPROVING PRODUCTIVITY THROUGH PRE-PLANNING

Work task	Units	Quantity	Labor productivity	Labor hours	Labor Dollars ($)	$/unit of material ($)	Material Dollars Total	Dollars ($'s)
Form walls	sfca	20,000	0.1 mh/sfca	2,000	$60,000	$0.80/sfca	$16,000	$76,000
Form columns	sfca	5,000	0.3 mh/sfca	1,500	$45,000	$1.00/sfca	$5,000	$50,000

As an example of preparing production goals for specific work tasks, let us focus on the work task "form walls." The estimator has estimated the following:

Quantity of work = 20,000 square feet of contact area (sfca)

Estimated labor productivity = 0.1 craft-hours per sfca

Therefore, the craft hours are estimated as follows:

(20,000 sfca) x (0.1 craft-hours/sfca) = 2,000 craft-hours

The production rate the estimator has used (0.1 craft hours/sfca) is actually the reciprocal of productivity in that productivity is expressed in units of work per craft hour. The 0.1 craft hours per sfca is equivalent to 10 square feet of contact hour per craft hour. Many estimators prefer to think in terms of craft hours per unit rather than units per craft-hour.

The production rate of 0.1 craft-hours per sfca (or productivity of 10 sfca per craft-hours) comes from the estimator's best estimate or forecast of productivity based on past history of doing previous projects. Published cost books such as R.S. Means can also be used as guides in estimating the productivity.

The labor cost estimate or budget is estimated as follows:

(2,000 craft hours) x (labor rate) =

Assuming an average labor rate of $30.00 per hour:

(2,000 craft hours) x ($30.00) = $60,000.00

This information above is the format of most construction estimates. It should be broken down into crew or worker production goals per day or per hour. To determine production goals, one of two pieces of information is needed; how long the supervisor has to do the work (activity duration in days), or the size of the work crew(s). One determines the other.

The estimate should be the basis for setting out hourly or daily production work goals. It is important that this transformation be made in the pre-planning phase of the construction project.

More often than not, the contractor and supervisor either knows or is given the duration for the work and therefore must determine the crew size to do the work. Let us assume that the "forming of concrete walls" has to be done in 10 construction days so that other work can proceed as scheduled. It follows that the supervisor must do 2,000 sfca area per day:

1. Calculate needed production per day

Quantity of work to perform	20,000 sfca
Divided by number of work days	10 days
Equals	2,000 sfca/day

While the number of workers on a crew can vary, the contractor typically knows the best sized crew to use. Work rules may also dictate the composition of the crew; e.g., two laborers for every three carpenters. Let us assume the contractor plans on using a five-person crew to erect the concrete forms. Therefore, every crew hour will result in five craft-hours of work. To determine the number of crews that will be required, the estimated productivity and the sfca/day need to be considered.

In the estimate, a production rate of 0.1 craft-hour per square foot of contact area was assumed. This is equivalent to a productivity of 10 sfca per craft-hour. It follows that, using a five-person crew, the sfca placed per day is estimated as follows:

2. Calculate production rate performed per crew-hour

$$\frac{(5 \text{ craft-hours})}{(\text{crew-hour})} \times \frac{(10 \text{ sfca})}{(\text{craft-hour})} = \frac{(50 \text{ sfca})}{(\text{crew-hour})}$$

Assuming an eight-hour day, one crew is estimated to place the following sfca per day.

3. Calculate production performed by the crew per day

$$\frac{(8 \text{ crew-hours})}{(\text{day})} \times \frac{(50 \text{ sfca})}{(\text{crew-hour})} = \frac{(400 \text{ sfca})}{(\text{day})}$$

So if the planned duration is such that the work must be done in days, which can only be accomplished if 2,000 sfca of forms are placed per day, five crews will be needed.

4. Calculate number of crews required

$$\frac{(2,000 \text{ sfca})}{(\text{day})} \div \frac{(400 \text{ sfca})}{(\text{day/per crew})} = 5 \text{ crews}$$

If the contractor or supervisor cannot use five crews, the supervisor has to consider one of the following:

- Have the smaller number of crews work overtime
- Increase productivity over the 10 sfca / per hour estimated
- Take longer than the planned 10 days to do the work

It should be noted that the above calculations assume that the 10 planned workdays are all available. Should the supervisor estimate that on average there is one day of rain for every 10 work days, then the production rate of 10 sfca per craft-hour and five crews will fall short of getting the work done in 10 days. A larger number of crews, overtime or a higher production rate would be needed, given one day of rain.

The point to be made is that these production calculations for the crew should be made from the estimate prior to starting the work; i.e., the calculations should be made during the pre-planning phase of the project.

In the above calculations, a crew production rate of 400 sfca per day was determined. The supervisor (and his or her crew) should know this production rate so that they have a goal; i.e., what is expected of them. As soon as the crew production rate falls below this 400 sfca per day, the supervisor should identify the cause of the problem and implement actions to achieve the 400 sfca per day. If the supervisor waits until the tenth day to see if the planned progress was met, it is too late to address the productivity problem.

Production goal-setting for the crew and workers enables the supervisor to plan and monitor the process rather than attempting to solve the problem when it is too late.

Pre-planning to include determining crew and craft production rates takes time. However, the supervisor cannot afford *not* to take the time to plan. The above calculations yielded the following information, which is critical to the supervision plan:

Number of crews needed = 5

Crew production rate per hour = 50 sfca / hour

Crew production rate per day = 400 sfca / hour

Ideally, each and every work task that is estimated in the bidding phase is broken down into production goals for the construction phase. At the very minimum, key or "vital" work tasks are broken down into production goals. An example form for this purpose is on page 2-23.

Exercise

Pre-Planning Production Rate Goals

Shown below are example estimates and work duration schedules for various construction work tasks for a project. For the work tasks that you perform in the firm for which you work, calculate the following information. Do the calculations assuming the following:

- assuming one bad day of weather per five working days (no work performed on bad weather days).

a. **Concrete work**
   500 cubic yards of concrete placement
   production rate per person equals 1.0 craft-hours per cubic yard
   crew 2 finishers, 2 labor, 1 carpenter, 1 ironworker
   required duration 10 days

b. **Masonry work**
   4,000 standard 8" x 8"x 16" masonry blocks
   production rate per person equals 0.1 craft-hours per block
   crew 3 bricklayers, 2 laborers
   required duration 5 days

c. **Electrical work**
   80 clf of aluminum #6 wire
   production rate per person equals 2.0 craft-hours per clf
   crew 2 electricians
   required duration 5 days

d. **Duct work — mechanical**
   9,600 sf of blanket type fiberglass
   production rate per person equals 0.05 craft-hours per sf
   crew size 2 asbestos workers
   required duration 10 days

e. **Structural Steel**
   33,600 lf of W 8x10 structural steel members
   production rate per person 0,10 craft-hours per lf
   crew 5 steel workers, 2 operators
   required duration 20 days

1. Required production per day

2. Required crew production rate per hour

3. Required crew production rate per day

4. Number of crews required

A Pre-Planning Checklist

Just as a checklist can aid the supervisor in identifying "killer clauses" in the supplementary conditions, a pre-planning checklist can aid the supervisor in making sure that he or she doesn't overlook an important pre-planning task. An example pre-planning checklist appears on page 2-25.

It is important that the supervisor use such a checklist on each and every project; he or she should not use it on some projects, and not use it on other projects. Similarly, all the supervisors in the construction firm should use it (or if the firm decides not to use it, nobody should use it).

The construction firm has to address the practice of using different forms and different procedures within the same firm. In many construction firms, some foremen are very attentive to keeping good timecards, while other foremen do a poor job of filling out the timecards. Their cards will have cost code errors, or be illegible or incomplete. In contrast, some supervisors do a good job of completely filling out a daily report regarding work performed, weather, number of workers present, instructions given, etc. However, a few supervisors in the same firm may choose to be sloppy and tardy in filling out daily reports.

Quality can be defined as consistency. Once a firm sets out defined practices and procedures, then they should be followed consistently by everyone. That is one of the advantages of using standardized forms and checklists such as the checklist shown on the following page.

Why should the construction firm be concerned about pre-planning? If a supervisor is a good motivator and gets his workers to work hard, so what if he or she doesn't follow set-out procedures such as using the pre-planning checklist on the following page? The answer is it *does* matter. Inconsistent practices lead to a lack of accountability, an increased possibility of losing a lawsuit or claim, and perhaps most importantly, reduced construction productivity.

The first five pre-planning tasks shown on the following page were discussed in earlier pages of this section. While the list is not complete (it should be custom designed to the type of work the participant performs), additional suggested pre-planning steps are also listed in the checklist shown.

Consistent practices lead to quality and productivity improvement. By using a pre-planning checklist, the supervisor can help reduce forgetting an important pre-planning action or task and can utilize consistent procedures from one project to the next.

Pre-planning Checklist

Task	Name	Title	Date	Action to Take
1 Supervisor reviews drawings and specifications to determine base bid work, areas of difficulty and potential change order work				
2 "Vital few" and "useful many" work tasks selected				
3 Review of supplementary conditions to identify unique or "killer" clauses				
4 Scheduling requirements				
5 Work coordination requirements				
6 Added safety requirements				
7 Added reporting requirements				
8 Unique meeting requirements				
9 Partnering requirements				
10 Clean-up requirements				
11 Long lead items/materials				
12 Special equipment to requisition				
13 Change order process				
14 Utility interface requirements				
15 Unique labor requirements or rules				
16				
17				
18				
19				
20				
21				
22				
23				
24				

Exercise

Additional Pre-Planning Tasks

This session included a suggested reminder checklist for use by the supervisor for performing pre-planning tasks. After reviewing the checklist, suggest five to ten additional pre-planning tasks that you would suggest be added to the checklist, considering the type of work you supervise and the firm for which you work.

Pre-Planning Task	Name	Title	Date	Action to Take
1				
2				
3				
4				
5				
6				
7				
8				
9				
10				

Session 2 Review

Look back over Session 2 and review these key points to be sure you understand them:

- The importance of the time period between when a construction firm learns that it will construct a project and when construction is actually started.
- The importance of the supervisor's knowledge to the construction estimate.
- The importance of the supervisor identifying the "vital" work tasks to be done during the construction phase of the project.
- The importance of the supervisor identifying base bid work before he or she starts the project.
- The importance of the supervisor reviewing the supplementary conditions to identify troublesome "killer" clauses in the project contract.
- How to prepare daily or hourly production goals for the crewmembers.
- The importance of using a detailed checklist for pre-planning.

Using on the Job What You Learned Today

Jobsite Assignment
While at your project, identify problems that could have been prevented via improved pre-planning. List the pre-planning tasks that could have reduced or eliminated the problem.

To Get Ready for Session 3
Read the Participant's Manual for Session 3.

Session 3

"MORE"—Four New Skills for the Effective Supervisor

Learning Goals for Session 3

After this session, you will learn how to become a proactive supervisor by continually working on the four new skills:

- **M**easurement or benchmarking
- **O**pportunity for improvement through challenging the work process
- **R**isk analysis for productivity improvement
- **E**stimating costs to improve focus on improvement

The four skills, referred to by the acronym MORE, will put the supervisor in a role of being a proactive supervisor with the objective of productivity improvement.

Learning Objectives

To accomplish the learning goals, during this session you will:

- Compare the traditional approach to monitoring construction versus a more proactive approach known as "MORE"
- Measure production by focusing on the means of improving productivity
- Challenge construction work methods by seeking ways of working smarter, not harder
- Measure production risk and variation as a means of continuous improvement by eliminating poor productivity and duplicated actions
- Allocate proper supervision time according to cost factors

To Get Ready for Session 3

Reading: Read the pages in this session. Think of how your attention to an improved work method could have led to higher productivity on a past project.

Major Activities for Session 3

- Discuss the difference between traditional monitoring of work processes versus a more proactive approach referred to as "MORE."
- Do an exercise that shows how historical accounting data can be used to improve productivity.
- Review examples of how measurement can be used to improve a work process.
- Do an exercise in which you will use measurement to improve productivity.
- Discuss means of challenging work to seek improvement.
- Review examples of how data that quantifies productivity risk can be used to improve productivity.
- Do an exercise for which you will quantify productivity risk.
- Discuss how knowing the cost of items or methods of construction is as important as knowing what they are.
- Do a follow-up jobsite assignment that focuses on identifying the cost of materials and work processes.

A Review of Session 2

In Session 2, you learned the importance of pre-planning prior to the start of construction. Attention to pre-planning between the time the construction firm receives a project (e.g., at the letting) and the start of construction can have a significant positive impact on construction time, cost, quality and safety.

Some of the facts that you learned in Session 2 are:

- Given the fact that the supervisor's time is limited and he or she cannot be everywhere during the construction phase of a project, it is important that the supervisor identify important or "vital" work tasks that will be performed in the construction phase of the project. The supervisor will then focus more on these work tasks in the construction phase than he or she will on the "useful many" work tasks.

- The supervisor needs to familiarize himself or herself with the estimate and contract documents so that he or she knows the required base bid work requirements.

- The supervisor should identify unique clauses in the supplementary conditions that may require added supervisor time or actions. These unique clauses are sometimes referred to as "killer" clauses.

- The supervisor should know how to break project estimates into daily or hourly production goals or standards for work crews.

- It is beneficial if the construction firm and the supervisor use a detailed checklist to remind them of pre-planning tasks that should be performed prior to the start of construction.

The Traditional Approach to Supervising Construction Versus MORE

The traditional role of the construction supervisor is often viewed as one of monitoring or policing the construction project and the various work tasks that make up the project. As part of this monitoring role, the supervisor performs the following:

- monitors onsite workers to make sure they are doing work;
- monitors materials flows to make sure material is delivered to the proper locations when needed;
- monitors the project schedule to compare actual progress against planned progress;
- monitors and reviews job cost reports to update unit costs and productivity as the work progresses;
- monitors equipment use to make sure that the equipment is used efficiently and is in proper working order;
- monitors quality of work performed;
- monitors the work process to ensure that the work is performed safely.

Another way of viewing the supervisor's traditional role as a monitor or policeman is the traditional job cost preparation and review process shown in Figure 3-1.

Traditional supervision entails using an accounting approach to monitor project budgets.

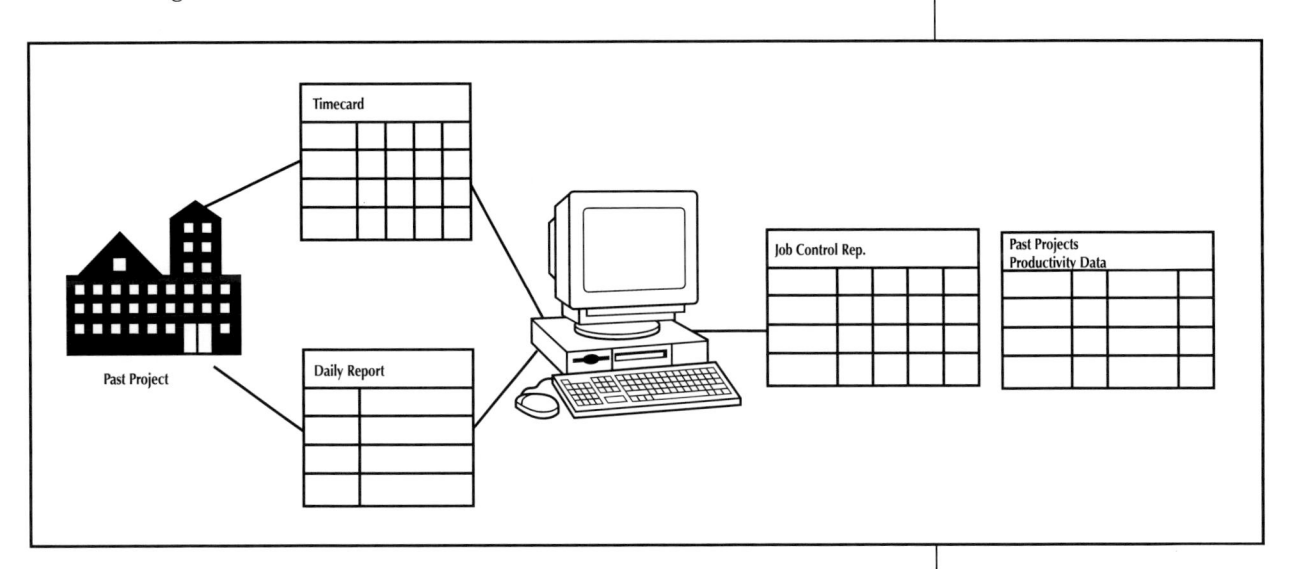

Figure 3-1. Traditional Monitoring Role of the Construction Supervisor

When using the job cost control process illustrated in Figure 3-1, the supervisor monitors labor hours against the budgeted labor hours relative to percentage of work put in place at the time. For example, if the report indicates that 25% of the labor hours have been expended but only 20% of the work is in place, the supervisor must pursue a proper correction. After completion of the project, the results are summarized and become part of the data base that is used by the estimator for future bids on new projects.

The traditional monitoring role of the supervisor shown in Figure 3-1 can also be viewed as the "accounting cycle" approach to productivity. Time cards, quantity reports and the job cost report are the core of the approach. Such an approach focuses on preserving or maintaining the labor productivity budget. Past performances become the target for future projects.

The traditional or accounting approach is critical to being a good supervisor. The supervisor needs to be well versed in the process and should be schooled in providing proper input to the process and should be able to interpret and use various reports produced by the process. We will address the importance of the accounting cycle and accurate and timely jobsite recordkeeping in a later session.

While the traditional or accounting approach is an excellent process of control, this approach does little to stimulate increased productivity. The traditional or accounting approach to supervision would be all that is necessary if the typical project were near or at optimal productivity. However, as referenced in Session 1, this is not the case. Every construction project and every construction work task typically has significant potential for productivity improvement.

> The "MORE" approach requires the supervisor to be proactive as well as reactive. Both approaches are needed.

To significantly increase construction productivity, the supervisor needs to take a new and more proactive approach to supervision. One of these approaches is referred to as MORE. The letters MORE represent the following four skills or approaches to supervising construction.

- **M**easurement or benchmarking
- **O**pportunity for improvement through challenging the work process
- **R**isk analysis for productivity improvement
- **E**stimating costs to improve focus on improvement

"MORE"—Four New Skills for the Effective Supervisor

The MORE approach attempts to put the supervisor in a more proactive role by challenging the work process. Unlike the traditional approach to supervision that uses time cards, quantity reports and job cost reports, the MORE approach can be viewed as using the tools shown in Figure 3-2.

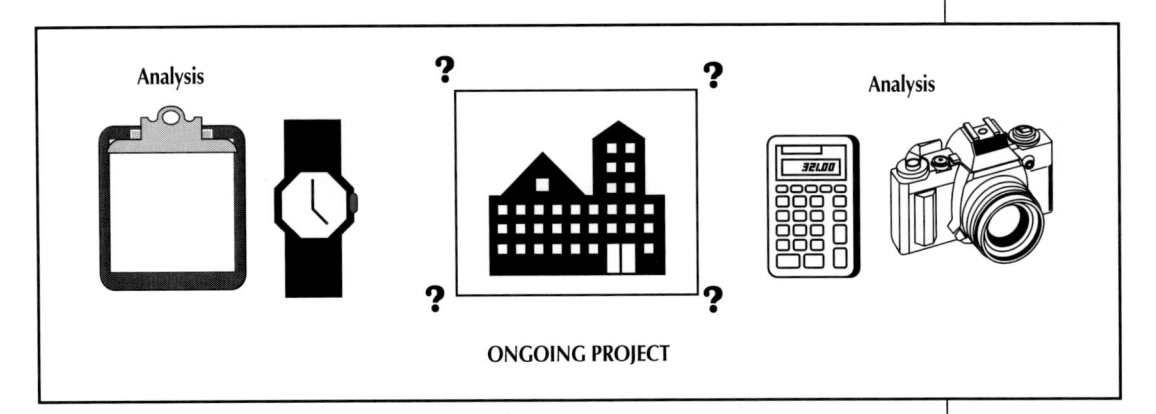

Fig. 3-2. Tools for Implementing MORE

MORE does not entail "time and motion" studies of workers. Admittedly such an approach might intimidate the supervisor's workers. However, the supervisor does have a right to critique, to analyze, and to look for better ways to do things. The following sections address the four skills of MORE individually.

Session 3

"MORE"—Four New Skills for the Effective Supervisor

Exercise

Using Past Project Accounting Cycle Data for Productivity Improvement

If past project data for a work task for good projects and bad projects are merely averaged, then it follows that the average by itself does not promote improvement. Normally the average is used for estimating future projects. However, the past project data collected can serve the productivity improvement task if the data is analyzed rather than merely averaged. Consider the following historical data a supervisor collected while erecting job-built concrete wall forms:

Past project	Quantity of work	Craft-hours	Units / craft hour	Craft-hours/unit	Crew size	Notes
School-1	2,400 sfca	384	6.25	0.16	5	Job clean, tools and parts well managed
Office-1	3,800 sfca	532	7.14	0.14	4	Excellent supervisor, job clean, tools and parts well managed
Warehouse	4,200 sfca	504	8.33	0.12	5	Few wall blockouts
School-2	4,800 sfca	1,247	3.85	0.26	7	Trade disrupted, waiting on materials and parts
Office-2	5,200 sfca	1,143	4.55	0.22	8	Unclean jobsite, worker congestion

a. What was the average productivity for all five past projects (units placed per craft-hour)? Note: this is the productivity that the estimator will likely use for future projects and that the supervisor is likely to target as the productivity standard.

b. What was the best productivity and worst productivity achieved on projects?

c. Is the best productivity a realistic benchmark or goal for estimating? For the supervisor to try to attain on each and every future project?

d. What do you believe should be identified as a realistic achievable productivity on all future projects given the data shown? State your reason as to why you have set out this productivity standard.

Implementing MORE

Measurement or Benchmarking

The premise of the measurement component of MORE is that measurement is fundamental to improvement. The measurement component will draw one's attention to inefficiencies and improvement potential.

- How many labor hours were expended on the construction project for punch list work?
- How many hours was a laborer in a non-productive work state versus that of a mason on the same project?
- How many instances were there of double handling of materials on a specific project?
- Do we get more square feet of contact area of wall forming done in the morning or afternoon?
- Do we get higher productivity for placing sheet metal ductwork on Tuesday or on Wednesday?
- How many picks do we get per hour with a crane?

The above are examples of questions that the supervisor cannot normally answer. The reason he or she cannot answer the above questions is that the construction supervisor typically does not pay attention to measuring things. Instead he or she monitors or polices the work process. As long as the productivity is similar to that proposed in the budget, the supervisor likely feels satisfied. If the above issues were measured, the supervisor would likely find variations and causes that could lead to improvement.

The Measurement approach is to draw the attention of the supervisor to improvement potential. It is difficult to improve something unless it is measured.

Measurement is not proposed as a means of "placing blame," nor simply to gather data. Measurement is a means of focusing on causes of variation and low productivity. For example, there has to be a reason why two similar projects have a different amount of redo hours expended per labor hour on the project. Something must have been done right on one project that was not done on the other project. By measuring the occurrences of redo work on the two projects, the reason or cause for the variation can be studied and addressed for overall improvement.

There are many things the supervisor can measure; e.g., how much work is done on Tuesday versus Wednesday, how many production cycles are made in a given hour, etc.

In the MORE approach, the construction supervisor is asked to measure things or events that he or she has taken for granted. Things or events as simple as how far material is moved, the number of times foremen are waiting for material, the number of times work is done twice (redo work), the number of incidences of theft, or anything that affects productivity. The measurement can be done by timing things or events with a wristwatch, by taking random visual samples or via new reporting.

The key is to force the supervisor to become proactive by encouraging the measurement process. This attention to measurement will not require significant added personnel or added time for the supervisor. Instead of merely monitoring or watching, the supervisor can pick something to measure and make it part of his or her normal routine.

Let us consider a few examples:

Example 1: Studying a tower crane operation

A construction supervisor has concluded that much of the reason his vertical building project schedule has slipped relates to the use of the tower crane. The project progress is very closely tied to the productive use of the tower crane. The supervisor therefore undertook the measurement of the number of "picks" of material the crane was making per hour over a two-day period.

# of picks	Day 1 (Comments)	# of picks	Day 2 (Comments)
5	Waiting for person to hook pick	4	Difficult to reach material
12		10	
6	Moved water bucket and scrap material	14	
15		4	Waiting for person to hook pick
4	Operator took short break	6	Waiting for person to hook pick
12		5	Operator took short break
6	Waiting for person to hook pick	9	
6		12	
Avg. =	8.25	Avg. =	8

The average number of productive picks per hour was averaging a little over eight for the two days. However, by observing and measuring the pick cycles, it was obvious that the total production output was being significantly curtailed by not having a worker on the floor elevation where the material had to be hooked. Instead, the crane operator (and the crew waiting for material) frequently waited while an individual climbed a ladder to the elevation where the crane pick needed to be hooked.

It also became obvious what the impact would be if the operator should take a break at an inopportune time or if the crane were used to do tasks not assigned to it, such as move the water bucket.

The supervisor figured out his crew cost per hour and concluded that every time the crane made one fewer pick per hour it had the impact of costing the work $240 in crew time and productivity. It became obvious to the supervisor that he was justified in hiring a worker at $30 per hour just to manage and hook the crane movements. The supervisor also implemented a policy that the crane was not to be used for work such as moving the water bucket when work was in progress.

One might suggest that all this should have been obvious to the supervisor without having to "measure" pick placements. The opposite may be true; if you don't stop to measure and look, inefficiencies are more likely to become standards.

Example 2: Minimizing Material Handling

A sheet metal construction supervisor observed that her project was losing a considerable amount of time and money moving material from one location to another. While some of the material movement was the fault of other contractors getting in her way, she felt this was not the only reason. She undertook a random process of tagging delivered material, and asked anyone who moved the material to initialize the tag and describe the material being moved. She explained to everyone that she was not doing this to blame anyone; she simply wanted to find out what was going on so that she and the workers could assess it.

After developing the measuring system for a month, she concluded that a piece of ductwork material on the project was moved an average of 3.2 times before it was installed. This was excessive.

More importantly, the movement of the material could not always be placed with another trade. By measuring the material movement and the causes for the movement, she concluded the following:

- 24% of extra movements related to another trade being in the way.
- 26% of the extra movements related to the fact that their own support staff delivered or stored the material at the wrong location.
- 18% of the extra movements were related to the fact that the material was delivered too early and had to be moved because it got in the way of things.
- 12% of the extra movements related to the fact that the wrong material was delivered to the site.
- 8% of the extra movements related to the fact the material was not properly protected from adverse weather that occurred.
- 12% of the extra movements could only be traced to normal construction operations.

She noted that less than one-fourth of the extra or non-productive material movements could be blamed on another trade. She also concluded that 64% of the extra non-productive movements were in great part controllable by her own workers and her firm's actions or non-actions. She immediately took steps to reduce these causes. The result was a significant increase in productivity and decrease in project duration.

In both of the examples presented, the supervisor's taking the time to measure rather than merely monitor or police was the difference between productivity improvement and letting inefficiencies become standards. The job cost report by itself did not disclose this potential productivity improvement. Until the supervisor got out a clipboard, pencil and paper and calculator, productivity improvement was not addressed.

Productivity Fade

Group Exercise

Your company, an industrial piping contractor, has observed two productivity phenomena that are troublesome to overall project profitability and schedule. The firm performs heavy work such as concrete work and steel erection.

The normal workday is from 7:30am until 4:00pm (30 minutes lunch). The supervisors believe that there has been a significant dropoff in overall crew and worker productivity in the afternoon.

The average project takes approximately eight months to complete. Profit margins and productivity seem to be fairly steady through the first eight to eight and one-half months of the project. However, during the last few weeks of a project, the profit margins seem to slide dramatically.

The supervisor was asked to measure data to help the firm get a handle on the situation. The measured data regarding morning/afternoon productivity follows.

Time period	Productivity (lf/craft-hr)	Time period	Productivity (lf/craft-hr)
Monday morning	8.33	Monday afternoon	7.00
Tuesday morning	10.0	Tuesday afternoon	6.52
Wednesday morning	8.33	Wednesday afternoon	6.82
Thursday morning	7.14	Thursday afternoon	5.84
Friday morning	8.33	Friday afternoon	5.84

The supervisor determined the above numbers by measuring the number of linear feet of pipe placed per hour and dividing by the number of craft-hours worked that hour.

The measured data proved the supervisor's hunch to be correct.

a. Based on your group's work experience, list possible reasons for the measured lowered productivity in the afternoon.

b. Brainstorm how you could measure or obtain data to prove or disprove the causes you listed in part a.

c. If your identified causes prove to be the actual causes, what actions, if any, can be taken to reduce them and thereby increase productivity in the afternoon?

Data regarding the productivity and profit fade has also been collected:

Project	Productivity during first 80% of earned labor hours	Productivity drop in last 10% of earned labor hours	Productivity drop in last 5% of earned labor hours	Labor hours of cleanup in last 10% of earned labor hours (% of total hrs)	Labor hours of punch list in last 10% of earned hours (% of total hrs)	Apparently worker slowing up; i.e., less productivity	Other possible factors
School 101	20 units/hr	4%	12%	1.5%	1.8%		
Office Bldg.	30 units/hr	6%	7%	1.8%	2.2%		
School 102	24 units/hr	1%	1%	0.2%	1.0%		
Hospital	16 units/hr	8%	12%	1.7%	1.6%		

a. Discuss what factors other than those shown above could be the reason for the lower productivity near the end of the projects.

b. Brainstorm, given the data shown above, how the supervisor might be able to determine the lower productivity that is due solely to the worker slowing up because the worker sees the end of the job in sight.

c. Based on the data shown and your answers to parts a and b, what management actions can the supervisor take to increase overall productivity in the last 10% of each project they construct?

Opportunity for Improvement Through Challenging the Work Process

The second component of MORE is the focus on challenging the work process for the opportunity to improve. Almost always, there is more than one way to accomplish a work task. Different crew sizes, the use of varying types of equipment, the use of alternative work methods, the substitution of different materials and even the alternative times when a work task can be performed enable the construction supervisor to choose between several ways of accomplishing a work task. Each of the alternative ways of doing the work function will result in a different time and cost. In addition, depending on how a work task is performed, work tasks that come after it may be affected positively or negatively. The process of challenging a work process looking for an opportunity to improve is a three-step process:

1. Familiarize yourself with existing methods.

2. Conceptualize an alternative method. Sketch the proposed method on a pad of paper to better describe it.

3. Make total cost, unit cost and duration calculations to compare the alternative methods.

Making the above analysis on an ongoing basis forces the supervisor to become conscious of looking for better ways to do things. His or her ability to determine a better work method is not guaranteed. However, the mere fact that the supervisor will take the time to consider alternatives will likely result in finding opportunity for improvement.

Several modeling techniques, such as time study and work sampling, can be used by the supervisor to analyze and challenge a work process. However, the supervisor can also effectively challenge a work process by merely observing it and asking himself or herself a few questions. The supervisor should look at the current work process and ask the following questions.

- *What is the work method?*
- *What are we trying to achieve?*
- *How are we currently doing the task?*
- *Why are we doing it this way?*
- *Who is best able to do the work?*
- *Where is the best place to do the work?*
- *When is the best time to do the task?*

> The key to finding a better or improved way of doing something is to force oneself to analyze, not just police or watch.

Asking these questions as you view a work process can lead to ideas for improving the work method. It helps to make notes and write down answers to each of these questions. It often requires several observations of several factors to understand or discover an opportunity for improvement. Observe the process, write down your observations and then analyze the results.

An Example: A Framing Operation

A supervisor is in charge of a carpentry framing operation. Because of the design of the structure, the framing members must be cut to a variety of specific lengths. In the current method, the lumber is stored by the side of the building and carried by a laborer (L) to a cutting location where a carpenter (C) cuts the studs to length on a cutting table. From the cutting location, two laborers carry the studs to carpenters (F) who nail the framing members into place. The current work process is shown in Figure 3-3.

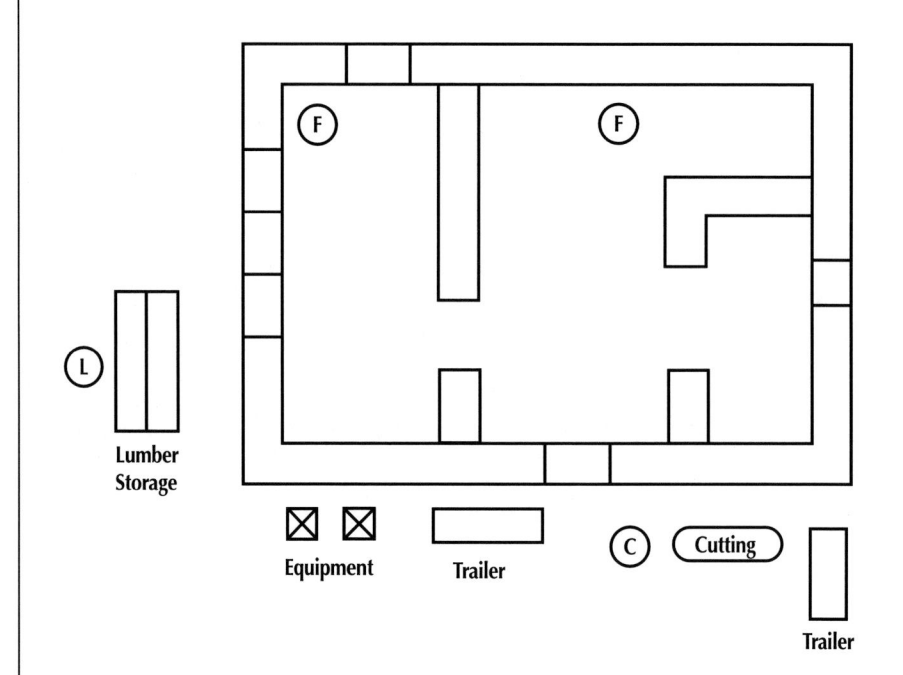

Fig. 3-3. Existing Method for a Work Task

Let us assume that the supervisor has noticed a significant amount of non-productive time in the current work process. His first action is to observe the work process, then ask himself the seven questions noted above, and then writing down his observations and answers.

- **What is the work method?**

    Stored lumber is carried to an onsite fabricating location, cut to length, then carried to two framing locations.

- **What are we trying to achieve?**

    The objective is to erect the framed structure quickly with a minimum of waiting time and material waste.

- **How are we currently doing the work task?**

    By cutting the studs at an onsite fabrication location, then carrying them to carpenters.

- **Why are we doing it this way?**

    Studs must be cut to a variety of specific lengths.

- **Who is best able to do this task?**

    This is a carpenter task; laborers carry the studs to the cutting site and to the carpenters.

- **Where is the best place to do the task?**

    Quality and cost effectiveness would improve if the studs were cut in the carpentry shop at the home office, or if they were precut before delivery from the supplier.

- **When is the best time to do the task?**

    There should be a supply of cut studs at the framing location before framing starts and throughout the framing operation.

By means of observing the work process, answering the questions, and analyzing his or her observations, the supervisor in our example discovered the following production delays or inefficiencies.

- Carpenters waiting for studs from laborers
- Laborers waiting for carpenters cutting studs
- Carpenters cutting studs waiting to receive material from storage
- Studs cut to wrong length; carpenter gives to laborer to take back to cutting location.
- Considerable material wastage because of incorrect lengths.
- Excessive walking to and from storage area and around equipment.

The supervisor then developed and implemented several changes to the current method:

- Cut the lumber at the company's home office carpentry shop
- Color code the cut lumber by length
- Deliver cut lumber to the site
- At the site, store the cut studs at two locations that are near the framing operations
- Reduce the crew from two laborers to one laborer

The changed work method is illustrated in Figure 3-4.

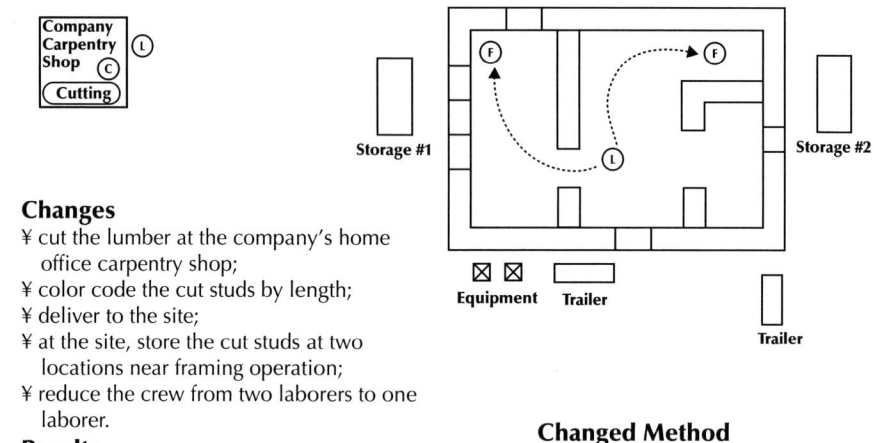

Changes
- cut the lumber at the company's home office carpentry shop;
- color code the cut studs by length;
- deliver to the site;
- at the site, store the cut studs at two locations near framing operation;
- reduce the crew from two laborers to one laborer.

Results
- framing operators no longer wait for studs;
- there is no waiting at the onsite fabrication location;
- fewer pieces are returned to storage;
- number of laborers and waiting time are reduced.

Changed Method

Fig. 3-4. Improved Method Determined Via Challenging the Work Process

The changes resulted in the five significant productivity benefits:

- Framing carpenters no longer wait for studs because an inventory or pre-cut, color-coded studs is nearby and available for delivery by a laborer (previously delay #1);

- There is no waiting at the onsite fabrication location because it has been eliminated (previously delays #2 and #3);

- Fewer pieces are returned to storage after being rejected for incorrect length at the framing location (previously delay #4);

- Material waste is reduced because quality control at the home office carpentry shop is better than at the on-fabrication location (previously delay #5);
- Number of laborers and walking time is reduced because the inventory of cut studs is closer to the framing locations and there are fewer rejected material pieces to be returned to storage.

Significant productivity improvement resulted in the changed method illustrated in Figure 3-4. This improvement resulted from simply challenging the work method.

The carpenters and laborers in the original method (Figure 3-3) did not choose to be non-productive. They may well have been hustling from one location to the next. The improved method results in the workers working smarter, not harder.

It should be noted that before the supervisor makes the changes shown, he or she should also evaluate the cost of the new method. For example, the cost for transporting the studs from the carpentry shop, the reduction in the crew size and waiting time, and the reduction in the material waste are among factors to be considered.

The supervisor should challenge himself or herself weekly, if not daily, to look for opportunity to improve the work process. If the supervisor gets into the habit of looking for opportunity, he or she will become a proactive supervisor rather than merely being reactive.

Monitoring or policing a work method can be viewed as a means of maintaining productivity. It is the challenging of the work process for opportunity that enables increased productivity.

Group Exercise

Critiquing a Proposed Project Layout for a Highway/Bridge Project

Shown below is a proposed jobsite layout for a new highway project and two new bridges. The new highway is approximately 1 mile long. Critique the proposed jobsite layout and make changes that will accommodate productivity improvement and other concerns relating to the layout of an effective project. The fabrication area is used to prepare the lumber for forms for the bridge abutments.

Rework the suggested revised layout for the project to include material storage areas and restrooms (shown as RRs) on the enclosed worksheet and list changes you have made and why the changes have been made.

Right of Way Fence

Trailer

RR

Borrow Pit

Fabrication Area

New Bridge #1

New Bridge #2

Lumber Storage

Storage Reinforcing

RR

Equipment Storage

Right of Way Fence

Haul Road & Entrance

Risk Analysis for Productivity Improvement

The construction process is subject to considerable uncertainty and risk. The productivity, cost and duration of a work process is dependent on variable and unpredictable weather, variations in worker skills and attitudes, unexpected equipment breakdowns, changes in the difficulty or scope of work, etc.

Risk can be thought of as possible variation from expected or average results.

Example:

Consider the two construction methods illustrated in Figure 3-5. Assume that a supervisor has collected past project productivity data regarding two alternative ways of placing concrete (for example, using a concrete pump versus placing the concrete with a crane bucket). The points shown under the bell-shaped curves represent the amount of concrete placed per worker-hour on past projects. While the past project data implies that both methods of placing the concrete have the same expected average productivity, the past project data implies that the past data samples for Method 1 have varied more from the average than those for Method 2. Method 1 has more productivity risk.

> Risk can be thought of as a variation from the average. By measuring risk, one can focus on variation as a means of improvement.

Comparison of Productivity Risk

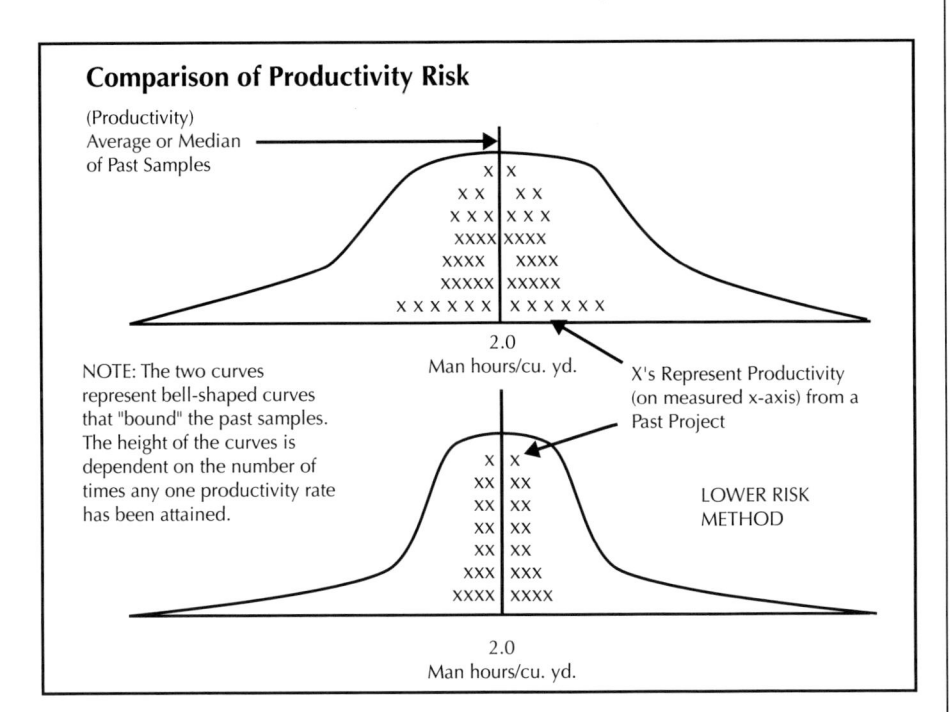

(Productivity) Average or Median of Past Samples

2.0 Man hours/cu. yd.

X's Represent Productivity (on measured x-axis) from a Past Project

NOTE: The two curves represent bell-shaped curves that "bound" the past samples. The height of the curves is dependent on the number of times any one productivity rate has been attained.

LOWER RISK METHOD

2.0 Man hours/cu. yd.

Fig. 3-5. Past project production rate samples

One point to observe about measured risk is that the construction supervisor should pay added attention to risk, as well as cost of production, when managing construction. As an example of the misdirected effort of a supervisor, consider the following steps necessary to construct a concrete foundation wall.

- Form the wall
- Place reinforcing
- Place concrete

Most everyone would agree that the work task above with the most variation in units placed per time period or worker hour (productivity) is the forming of the walls for the concrete. Owing to the difficulty of such tasks (placing the forming ties, releasing the forms from the wall in the stripping operation and bracing the forms), the square footage of contact area of forms placed varies significantly from one time period to the next.

While most construction supervisors would agree that the forming operation has the most variation in the work process and is therefore the riskiest work task, it is the placement of the concrete itself that gets most of the supervisor's attention. The day the concrete is being placed will be the day that everyone at the jobsite is watching the concrete fall from the concrete chute into the wall. On the other hand, the forming operation often goes unsupervised! An analysis of the job cost reports for the project would illustrate that the risk in the project schedule and the risk of the project cost is much more with the forming work task than with the concrete placement work task.

The supervisor should focus on productivity risk as well as production itself. Productivity data can be gathered and printed in the job cost reports that track productivity variation as well as average productivity. As a guide for the supervisor, the work tasks in the estimate might be categorized and prioritized by productivity risk. The intent is to draw the supervisor's attention to work tasks that must be closely planned and supervised. As part of his or her daily planning, the supervisor should use a worksheet to prioritize the risk of work tasks to be done during the day.

On a positive note, productivity variation or risk can be viewed as setting out the potential to improve.

Example:

Let us assume that the construction firm has kept data regarding the average number of craft-hours required to place 100 square feet of contact area (sfca) for two different forming methods. Assume the data is illustrated in Figure 3-6.

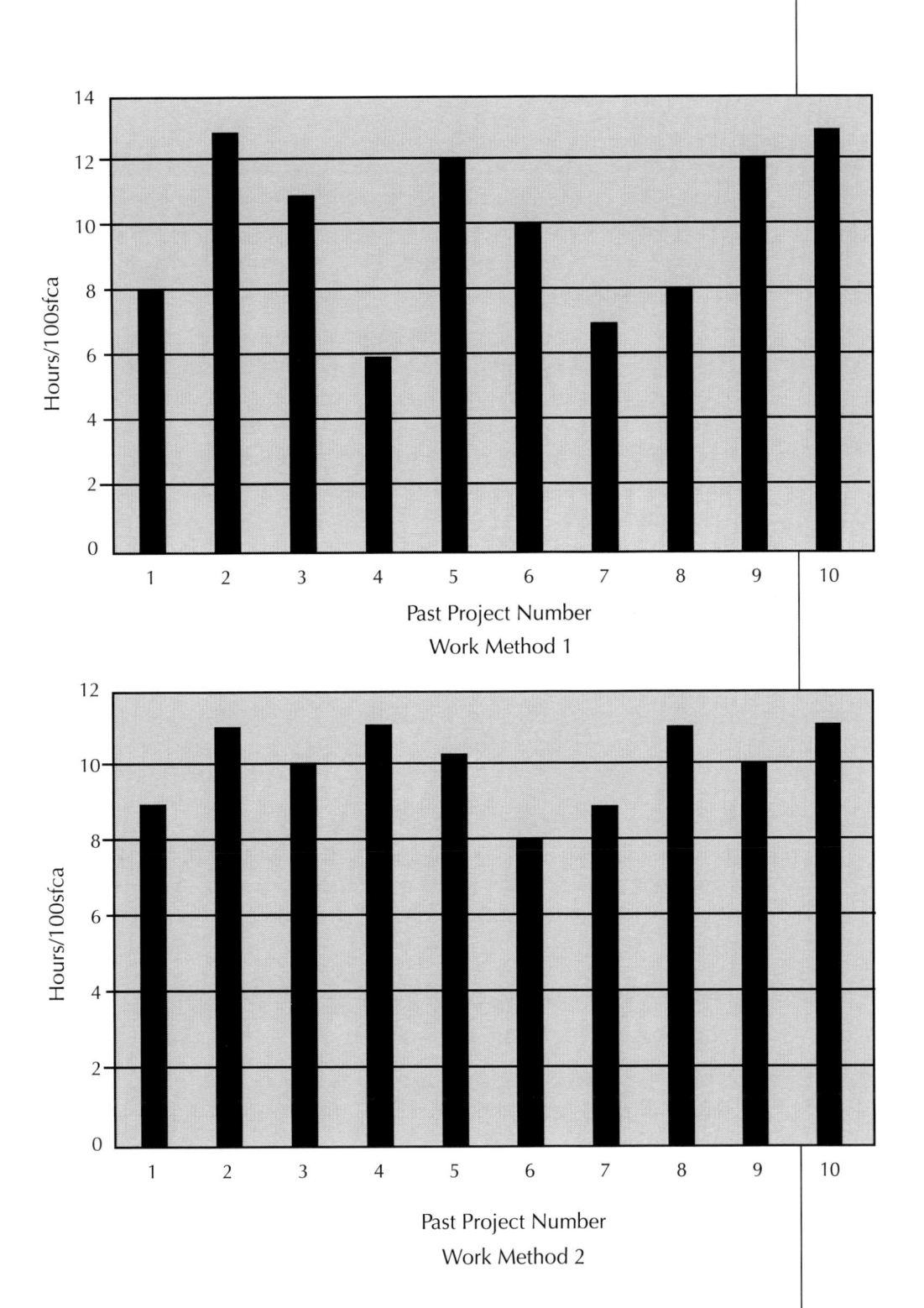

Fig. 3-6. Variation in Production Rate for Two Methods

The variation in productivity from job to job is larger for Method 1 than it is for Method 2. The fact that variation in productivity for Method 1 is greater than for Method 2 may indicate the following:

1. Method 1 is risker than Method 2 as to productivity as a function of time. As such, Method 1 likely needs form supervising.

2. Method 1 may result in more variation in quality of the finished work. One can usually assume that if productivity is more variable, the resulting quality of the finished construction is also more variable. For example, it may be that the quality of the wall finish is more variable.

3. From a productivity improvement point of view, the fact that Method 1 has more productivity variation, or risk, leads one to the conclusion that this method has more potential for improvement. Inspection of the past productivity results for the two methods indicates that a production rate of 6 craft-hours per 100 sfca was attained when using Method 1. This was better than any production rate attained when using Method 2. By studying how this production rate was achieved, and by implementing the improved method, it may be that Method 1 can be improved to the point that the average production rates fall in the range of 6 to 9 craft-hours per 100 sfca — better than the current average of 10.

By studying variation or risk, and by focusing on the production cycles that were better than average, it may be possible for the supervisor to improve the productivity rate for the method in question. Improvement may entail a reduction in the average craft-hours required and/or a reduction in productivity risk or variation.

Many examples can be given whereby the study of productivity variation or risk can lead to the improvement of a work process. For example, the data shown in Figure 3-6 could also represent the following:

- Productivity attained in the morning versus afternoon

- Number of items on the punch lists for two different types of projects

- Number of occasions upon which workers must wait for material at two different projects

In summary, the supervisor should focus on the risk of work processes so that he or she can supervise tasks correctly; the more risk in the work process, the more time the supervisor should expend. Secondly, the supervisor should view risk as an opportunity to improve. By studying work conditions when productivity was good and studying work conditions when productivity was bad, the supervisor can improve productivity. This can be done by duplicating the good conditions and reducing or eliminating the bad conditions.

Using the Job Cost Report to Measure and Monitor Productivity Risk

Exercise

With the objective of measuring and properly supervising production risk, a construction firm has added a few columns of information onto their weekly labor reports. This additional information is to measure risk. The collected data for the three work tasks or codes from an in-process project are as follows:

Week One:

Work task	Units	Budgeted quantity	Budgeted productivity	Quantity this week	Productivity this week	Productivity to date	Productivity variation/risk
Form walls	sfca	4,000	7 sfca/craft-hr	1,000	6 sfca/craft-hr	6 sfca/craft-hr	
Place rebar	pounds	6,000	130 lbs/craft-hr	800	125 lbs/craft-hr	125 lbs/craft-hr	
Place concrete	cu yds	60	1.0 cy/craft-hr	15	1.0 cy/craft-hr	1.0 cy/craft-hr	

Week Two:

Work task	Units	Budgeted quantity	Budgeted productivity	Quantity this week	Productivity this week	Productivity to date	Productivity variation/risk
Form walls	sfca	4,000	7 sfca/craft-hr	1,000	10 sfca/craft-hr	8.00 sfca/craft-hr	
Place rebar	pounds	6,000	130 lbs/craft-hr	2,000	120 lbs/craft-hr		
Place concrete	cu yds	60	1.0 cy/craft-hr	15	0.9 cy/craft-hr.		

Week Three:

Work task	Units	Budgeted quantity	Budgeted productivity	Quantity this week	Productivity this week	Productivity to date	Productivity variation/risk
Form walls	sfca	4,000	7 sfca/craft-hr	1,000	4 sfca/craft-hr		
Place rebar	pounds	6,000	130 lbs/craft-hr	1,600	110 lbs/craft-hr		
Place concrete	cu yds	60	1.0 cy/craft-hr	10	1.1 cy/craft-hr		

Week Four:

Work task	Units	Budgeted quantity	Budgeted productivity	Quantity this week	Productivity this week	Productivity to date	Productivity variation/risk
Form walls	sfca	4,000	7 sfca/craft-hr				
Place rebar	pounds	6,000	130 lbs/craft-hr				
Place concrete	cu yds	60	1.0 cy/craft-hr				

Exercise

a. Fill in the productivity to date for the three work tasks for weeks two and three (note: the productivity to date has been calculated for the "Form wall" through the second week).

b. Based on the productivity obtained from week to week, place a narrative description (e.g., high risk) in the right column (to describe the productivity risk).

c. Based on the productivity data collected to date, where should the supervisor spend most of his or her time in week four? Where should he or she spend the least supervision time? (Caution/Note: The supervisor also has to consider how many of each unit he or she has to perform; risk is only one of the factors the supervisor should consider.)

d. What factors other than productivity risk might be considered by the supervisor in determining where he or she should spend most of their supervision time in week four?

Estimating Costs to Improve Focus on Improvement

The observer of the construction process may view it as the process of using different types of trained workers to place materials like block and brick. However, another view is that everything being done in the construction of a project is a process of handling and placing money. Labor, materials and equipment can be viewed in terms of dollars. In fact, one might propose that the supervisor is not managing concrete or steel placement, he or she is really managing money.

The supervisor's need to know the cost of materials and resources such as labor is critical to his or her ability to properly manage. Consider two construction work tasks that may be scheduled for the same work day; one that has a unit cost of $5 per unit placed and one that has a unit cost of $50 per unit placed. Risk aside, if the supervisor can be in only one of two places, he or she had better be at the more expensive operation.

> It is important that the supervisor remember that he or she is managing costs or money, not just things.

The above example of the supervisor being at the more expensive of the two operations appears obvious. However, sometimes it is not so obvious. The supervisor must know the cost of things if he or she is going to allocate his or her supervisory time.

Example:

Consider a construction work method being observed. The supervisor might observe that two or three workers have a cigarette and he or she might become very upset with the non-productive time of these workers. Assume the following worker wage rate:

Wage rate without fringe benefits for
sample worker   = $28.00/hr.

Wage rate with fringe benefits for
sample worker   = $38.00/hr.

Given the fact that the observer views the three workers as costing anywhere from $28 to $38 dollars an hour, when the observer sees the workers taking a 15-minute cigarette break, the observer sees the following non-productive time or cost.

Non-productive cost = (3 workers) x (1/4 hour) x ($38/hr) = $285.00

This is a considerable sum of money. However, right next to the three non-productive workers may be a crane or another type of equipment that hasn't moved or been productive for two hours. The crane likely rents for $150.00/ hour. Why doesn't the idle equipment get the same attention as the idle workers?

The answer is simple. Most observers of the construction process look at the equipment as metal, not money. The idle equipment, while wasting $300.00 in the above example, gets off easy at the expense of labor.

If the contractor in the above example were to paint the hourly rental or ownership cost of the crane on the equipment, perhaps the observer and supervisor would be more dismayed when they saw it sitting idle. Until the supervisor knows what everything costs on a project — materials, equipment, tools and labor — the supervisor may be misallocating his supervision time.

Consider this second example of why it is important to know costs of things as well as knowing what the item is.

Example:

An owner of a construction firm comes to a project and notices that there are concrete wedge bolts lying all over the jobsite. The concrete wedge bolts cost $1.00 each and are used to connect concrete modular forms at the jobsite.

The contractor, to get the supervisor's attention, went to the grocery store and purchased 20 fifty-cent pieces. After lunch, the contractor asked the supervisor to walk around the jobsite with him and he dropped the 20 fifty-cent pieces at various locations on the site.

At the end of the day the contractor asked the supervisor to walk the job again. Together they found one of the fifty-cent pieces (apparently overlooked by the workers). However, each and every wedge bolt was exactly where it had been in the morning!

The above example merely points out that until people (including the supervisor) view things as money, they often are not attentive to them — or they mismanage them.

All too often there is a gap between the office and the supervisor when cost information is passed along. The supervisor may not have reviewed the estimate to determine what things cost and what the high cost risk tasks are for the project. In the MORE approach to supervising productivity, the supervisor's attention is focused on the cost of things and the cost of work tasks. For one, the cost estimate should be shared with the supervisor (this was discussed in the previous session).

Secondly, the supervisor is well advised to carry an estimating book that sets out what things cost. An example is the RS Means Cost Data book, published commercially. Example cost data from one of the cost books is shown below:

Item	$	Work Method	$
Carpenter	$30/per hr.	Bulk excavation (labor, equipment)	$6.00/cubic yd
Concrete	$70/cubic yd	Place concrete (labor, material, equipment)	$180.00/cubic yd
Crane	$160/hr.	Place electrical conduit (labor, material, equipment)	$12.00/linear ft
Steel beam	$1,500/ton	Place concrete block (labor, material, equipment)	$8.00/sq ft
Modular forming panel	$180/panel	Place structural steel beam (labor, material, equipment)	$4.00/dfca

The vocabulary of the construction industry tends to be in terms like carpenter, concrete, crane, beam or forming panel. However, effective supervisors should expand their vocabularies to know what things cost, not just what they are. Given the requirement to be at more work task places than he or she can be every minute of the workday, the supervisor should be where the money is!

Session 3 Review

Look back over Session 3 and review these key points to be sure you understand them.

- The difference between monitoring work versus the application of MORE.
- Measurement is a fundamental component of improvement.
- Challenging for opportunity means analyzing a work method to determine a means of working smarter, not harder.
- How to measure production risk and how to use the quantified risk as a means of improvement.
- Why it is important to know what things and methods cost rather than merely to know what they are.

Using on the Job What You Learned Today

Jobsite Assignment

Use a cost book and on a sheet of paper write down the cost of at least 10 "things" (e.g., worker, material, machine) that you have onsite, and the cost of five work methods you are performing at the project (e.g., cost of erecting carpentry framing, etc.) You should consider getting this information from the estimator of the project.

To Get Ready for Session 4

Read the Participant's Manual for Session 4.

Session 4

Personnel Management: Making a Job Look Like a Firm

Learning Goals for Session 4

After this session, you should know the following:

- The importance of the onsite worker and his or her attitude and motivation regarding the productivity of the project.

- The four needs of every worker and how the supervisor can provide these four needs.

- The importance of groups and how they affect construction productivity.

The above learning goals all have the focus of aiding the supervisor in managing onsite workers in a productive manner so that the workers in effect "manage themselves."

Learning Objectives

To accomplish the learning goals, during this session you will:

- Motivate the onsite worker to be productive
- Make a job look like a firm to the workers
- Identify the four needs of workers and how to provide these needs
- Recognize the importance of people working as a group

To Get Ready for Session 4

Reading: Read the pages in this session. Try to think of ideas on how to motivate the construction team to include the craftsperson and foreman.

Major Activities for Session 4

- Discuss the importance of labor productivity and the motivation of the worker to the overall productivity of a project.
- Do an exercise that focuses on the difficulties of motivating the onsite worker.
- Discuss the importance of "pride" as a means of motivating the worker.
- Do an exercise that focuses on giving the worker pride in his or her work efforts.
- Discuss the importance of providing the worker a measure of his or her performance.
- Do an exercise that requires "brainstorming" to identify new means of providing the worker measurement.
- Discuss the importance of communication, both written and oral.
- Do an exercise that illustrates effective oral communication.
- Discuss the role monetary benefits have to the worker.
- Discuss various classical personnel management theories.
- Discuss the importance of understanding how workers work in groups and the types of groups that are formed.
- Do an exercise that discusses problems and/or opportunities of workers working in groups.

A Review of Session 3

In Session 3, you learned the importance of acquiring new supervisory skills. You learned that the acronym "MORE" represents four new supervisor skills for improving jobsite productivity.

Some of the facts that you learned in Session 3 are:

- The difference between monitoring work versus the application of MORE.

- Measurement is a fundamental component for improvement.

- Challenging for opportunity means analyzing a work method to determine a means of working smarter, not harder.

- How to measure production risk and how to use quantified risk as a means of improvement.

- Why it is important to know what things and methods cost rather than merely know what they are.

The Importance of Onsite Workers to Project Productivity

The construction process is very dependent on the efforts of the construction workers. Typically on projects the direct labor cost component may be in excess of 35% to 40% of the total project cost (the other cost components being material, equipment, job overhead and company overhead).

The contractor may employ construction workers directly (i.e., do self-performed work), or may in fact employ subcontractors to employ construction workers (often called tradespeople). In many cases the contractor will do both; do some self-performed work, and subcontract to do other work. The point remains that, no matter whether they are employed directly by the supervisor or through subcontractors, onsite workers determine whether the project can be built on time and on budget.

While considered a manufacturing industry, the construction industry can also be thought of as a service industry, given the high dependence on onsite labor efforts. The high dependence on labor is compounded by the fact that many construction workers may view themselves as "working for a job rather than a firm." Whereas a tool and die worker in a factory, a retail clerk at a merchandiser, or a receptionist at an office may work for a firm their entire working life, a construction craftsman may work for several contractors in a given year.

The end result is that the contractor and the construction supervisor are very dependent on the work attitude and motivation of the construction worker. A worker may have the attitude that he helps the firm by being productive when he doesn't have to, or he may have the attitude that he won't be productive unless he has to. For example, if a worker completes work assigned to him, does he or she go looking for more work to do, or does he stand idle, waiting for more work to be assigned to him? The difference between his or her attitude is in great part the difference between a productive job and a profitable job and a non-productive low-profit or loss-of-profits job. If the worker views himself as working for a firm, he is more likely to be productive.

Labor costs typically are on the order of 40% of the overall project cost. In some cases the supervisor might be supervising his or her own labor. In other cases, the labor is provided by the subcontractor(s).

Because workers may only work with a specific contractor or a specific supervisor on a single project, the worker will likely view himself or herself "working for a job, rather than working for a firm."

Exercise

Difficulties of Motivating the Onsite Construction Worker

The supervisor has a major challenge when attempting to keep her workers motivated all the time. Construction is hard, physical, demanding work. In addition the worker may be working for a specific supervisor only once; i.e., on the current project. The worker may view himself or herself distanced from the owner of the construction firm and the overall project profit objective. For these and other reasons, the supervisor must be creative in his or her approach to motivating the onsite workers. In this exercise, you and your group members are to discuss some of the particular problems associated with motivating construction jobsite workers and how these problems might be addressed.

1. When a project is near its end, the onsite construction worker might feel that the end of the project will result in his either getting laid off or having to go to another project. In other words, unlike a firm, construction projects have a relatively short life. The result is that the worker might "slow-up" her work effort in the last few weeks of the job and therefore curtail overall project productivity.

    Discuss examples of this slowdown (sometimes referred to as an "artificial restraint") on your projects and make suggestions as to how this slowdown can be avoided or reduced.

2. On some construction projects many different labor crafts are required; for example, laborers, carpenters, ironworkers, plumbers, sheet metal workers, etc. In a factory environment, there is often one or only a few trades.

    Discuss how this "multiple trade" characteristic of the construction process can lead to personnel and productivity problems. Suggest solutions to resolve the problems or issues.

3. In recent years the number of young people entering the construction trades has been on a steady decline. Discuss the reasons for this and offer up suggestions or solutions on how this issue can be addressed.

The Four Needs of Every Worker

Because of the large ratio of onsite construction workers relative to the number of supervisors at a project, the construction worker is often unattended or not directly supervised. The supervisor cannot be everywhere. This is not to say that the construction supervisor should not attempt to visit and check up on the foreman and the workers on the crews. The supervisor should be especially attentive to monitoring important or "vital" work tasks. However, given the many things that the supervisor has to do on a daily basis, it can be argued that the only person who can effectively monitor the individual construction worker is the worker himself. The worker must be motivated to want to do work.

The supervisor must promote a work site environment that motivates workers. The fact that construction workers may view themselves as working for a job versus a firm compounds the personnel management efforts of the supervisor. In his or her attempt to develop positive worker attitudes and align the worker with the construction firm as well as the job, the supervisor must pay attention to the following four needs of each worker.

- Pride in work
- Measuring system of performance
- An effective communication channel
- Monetary benefits and incentives

The supervisor should view himself or herself as a mentor to workers. If the supervisor portrays a positive approach to work and problem solving, and does not blame others for problems, the workers are more likely to have a positive work attitude and be more motivated about the work process. Supervisors set the example for workers; they are mentors.

The supervisor must motivate the onsite worker so that the worker motivates himself or herself.

(1) Pride in Work

Pride in work in great part includes recognition and giving the workers a sense of accomplishment. Personnel management actions such as a mere pat on the back, placing the names of workers on a sign at the jobsite, asking workers for suggestions and work ideas, and having a day when the worker is able to bring his children or friends to view the jobsite can all be actions in a long-term commitment to productivity improvement. While some of these and other personnel management actions are limited by the short-term nature of some jobs and by other constraints, such as insurance requirements, failure to give workers pride in their work is likely to yield negative results.

One way to give workers pride is to keep reminding workers what is good about their work activity, not what is bad. Normally an individual is called on the carpet when he or she is doing something wrong and is over budget. It is equally as important to call out good deeds. Consider having an "emergency" meeting when an individual has done something right or is under budget. Not only can causes of the good actions be identified and duplicated, but such an action can also have a positive impact on the individual and the overall project.

One cannot be an effective supervisor or worker unless he is proud of what he does. If the supervisor is a whiner, always complaining, always blaming people, or projects an image that he doesn't like what he is doing, it negatively impacts the attitudes and productivity of the supervisor's subordinates and the overall project.

The construction supervisor and the construction worker have every right to be proud of what they do. The construction industry is the backbone of the U.S. economy. Annually in the range of 8% to 12% of the gross national product, the industry employs over five million people; and perhaps most importantly, the construction industry "makes things; it doesn't simply trade things." Any economy that is to prosper over the long term has to make things.

The following is proposed:

The supervisor should make a daily effort to turn problems into opportunities. He or she should reduce incidents of blaming people and instead spend more time commending people and telling them what they did right rather than what they did wrong.

Let's take two supervisors confronted with the following problems:

- Five days of bad weather in a row.
- A subcontractor that is not staffing the job with enough workers.
- A project designer who is slow in making decisions and is holding up the work process.

The first supervisor blames these events for project time and cost problems. When he speaks to his boss about these problems, he speaks in terms of "them or they" for project overruns or problems. Everything out of his mouth seems to be negative.

The second supervisor is subjected to the same problems. However, he uses his creativity to minimize the impact of the problems. The supervisor uses schedule floats to reduce the impact of the weather. The supervisor works with the subcontractor and shows the subcontractor that if the firm puts more people on the project, the subcontractor as well as the project will benefit. The supervisor works with the designer in an effort to speed up the designer's decision making for the project. The second supervisor takes a positive approach to problems; he speaks in terms of "we" instead of "they."

Problems will always occur in construction. A negative approach will never keep them from occurring or minimize the impact of the problems. Just as there is "no crying in baseball," there should be "no whining in construction."

The supervisor should take a "we" approach rather than a "they" approach when it comes to placing the blame and problem solving.

SESSION 4

PERSONNEL MANAGEMENT: MAKING A JOB LOOK LIKE A FIRM

Exercise

Motivating the Onsite Construction Worker

A recent article in the monthly periodical *CONSTRUCTOR*, entitled *Ten Reasons to Convince your Son or Daughter to Become a Construction Supervisor*, lists ten reasons or good aspects of being a construction supervisor.

	Reasons to be a Construction Supervisor
1	A supervisor normally makes over 50 decisions a day; he or she can make a difference.
2	The supervisor gets to deal with people, which makes every day a new day.
3	Construction is a growth industry.
4	The supervisor is mobile; his or her skills are needed from city to city.
5	Salaries and benefits are above average; you get paid for your knowledge and experience.
6	Supervisors can be entrepreneurs and start their own firms if they choose.
7	The construction project offers many problems; however, problems can be viewed as opportunities.
8	The industry is going through a significant change with new technology.
9	Construction supervisors build things, they don't trade things.
10	Every day is a new challenge; it is seldom repetitious; it is hard to get bored.

As a means of motivating the jobsite worker (i.e., the craftsperson), you are to identify a similar list of ten reasons or "good things" about being a construction worker. List them in the table on page 4-9. The objective is to identify a list of favorable attributes that can be brought to the attention of the worker(s) to help them feel proud about their project.

Reasons to be a Construction Craftsperson

1.
2.
3.
4.
5.
6.
7.
8.
9.
10.

(2) Measuring System of Performance

An effective measuring system entails giving a worker a basis of measuring her own individual performance. This includes communicating what is expected of her, and communicating as to how she is doing relative to the plan. The plan and subsequent performance system should be communicated both at a job level and at an individual worker level. Leaving the worker in the dark as to what is expected and how the project is to progress and how it is proceeding does not cultivate a positive worker attitude. Consider the case of a coach of a basketball team. What would happen if the coach told three of the players to go to the locker room while he explained the game plan to two players. Clearly this would cause discontent, a divided team, and a less-than-positive attitude for three of the players. This is what a supervisor is doing when he keeps the construction workers in the dark. It is often beneficial to give the workers a goal so that they can measure their results.

The supervisor should give thought to sharing information such as person-hour budgets and expected productivity for specific work tasks, projected project schedules, and project progress with the workers. The alternative is to assume that the workers don't care. This negative assumption promotes a "we" versus "they" attitude that is sure to result in less than satisfactory productivity.

Supervisors and their workers are more productive if they know what is expected of them in regard to production, quality and safety. The construction foreman and his crew often go to work and are told what to do without a goal or budget. Having a production goal enables individuals to take pride and satisfaction when they meet a goal. Without a goal, an individual has no measuring system by which to measure his or her effort.

The gap between estimating and construction in many construction firms has resulted in an estimate not being broken down into daily production goals. During the pre-planning phase of the construction process, the estimate should be broken down into daily or hourly production goals for the supervisor. The supervisor should be part of the team that makes these calculations, so that he can agree to the production goals and become aware of what is expected of him.
As simple a thought as this is, many contractors and supervisors do not do this. Instead, the supervisor is simply assigned to the project and told to construct it. He or she is expected to do the best they can. Goal setting and production goals can go a long way to increasing productivity and giving the supervisors and crewmembers work satisfaction.

Personnel Management: Making a Job Look Like a Firm

The estimate that is prepared for purposes of bidding the project should be broken down into daily (perhaps hourly) production goals for the supervisor and his or her crew. Supervisors and crewmembers think more in terms of units of work placed per time period rather than units placed per person hour (i.e., productivity). The transformation of the estimate into daily production goals is made somewhat confusing by the fact that estimates and productivity are typically expressed in units of work per person hour as opposed to work per crew hour or time period. Most construction tasks are performed by crews that are made up of more than one worker.

The transformation of the estimate into daily production goals is not complicated; it merely involves taking the time to do it. It should be done as part of the pre-planning process. The determining of production goals from the estimate will now be illustrated by example.

> The project estimate should be broken down into daily production goals for the foreman and workers.

The estimate for a project is often prepared and summarized on an estimating form similar to the following:

Work task	Units	Quantity	Labor productivity	Labor hours ($)	Labor Dollars	$/unit of material	Material Dollars ($)	Total Dollars ($s)
Frame stud walls	MBF	10	20 ph/mbf	200	$6,000	$600/mbf	$6,000	$12,000
Frame beams	MBF	5	30 ph/mbf	150	$4,500	$800/sfca	$4,000	$8,500

As an example of preparing production goals for specific work tasks, let us focus on the work task "frame stud walls." The estimator has estimated the following:

    Quantity of work   = 10 MBF

    Estimated labor productivity   = 20 person-hours per MBF

Therefore the craft hours are estimated as follows:

    (10 MBF) x (20 ph/MBF)   = 200 craft hours

The production rate the estimator has used (20 ph/MBF) is actually the reciprocal of productivity, in that productivity is expressed in units of work per craft hour. The 20 ph/MBF is equivalent to 0.05 MBF of contact hour per craft hour. Many estimators prefer to think in terms of craft hours per unit rather than units per craft hour.

The production rate of 20 ph/MBF (or productivity of 0.05 MBF craft hours) comes from the estimator's best estimate or forecast of productivity based on past history of projects. Published cost books such as R.S. Means can also be used as guides in estimating the productivity. It is an estimate.

The labor cost or budget is estimated as follows:

(200 craft hours) x (labor rate) =

Assuming an average labor rate of $30.00 per hour:

(200 craft hours) x ($30.00) = $6,000.00

This information above is the format of most construction estimates. It should be broken down into crew or worker production goals per day or per hour. To determine production goals, one of two pieces of information is needed; how long the supervisor has to do the work (activity duration in days), or the size of the work crew(s). One determines the other.

More often than not, the contractor and supervisor either know or are given the duration for the work and therefore must determine the crew size to do the work. Let us assume that the "form stud walls" must be done in three construction days so that other work can proceed as scheduled. It follows that the supervisor must do 3.33 MBF per day:

1. Calculate needed production per day

Quantity of work to perform	10 MBF
Divided by number of work days	3 days
Equals	3.33 MBF/day

While the number of workers on a crew can vary, the supervisor typically knows the best size crew to use. Work rules (union) may also dictate the composition of the crew; e.g., one laborer for every two carpenters. Let us assume that the supervisor plans on using a three-person crew to do the work. Therefore every crew hour will result in three craft hours of work. To determine the number of crews that will be required, the estimated productivity and the MBF/day need to be considered.

In the estimate, a production rate of 20 person-hours per MBF was assumed. This is equivalent to a productivity of 0.05 MBF per person hour.

2. Calculate production rate performed per crew-hour

$$\frac{(3 \text{ craft-hours})}{(\text{crew-hour})} \times \frac{(0.05 \text{ MBF})}{(\text{craft-hour})} = \frac{(0.15 \text{ MBF})}{(\text{crew-hour})}$$

Assuming an eight-hour day, one crew is estimated to place the following MBF per day.

3. Calculate production performed by the crew per day

$$\frac{(8 \text{ crew-hours})}{(\text{day})} \times \frac{(0.15 \text{ MBF})}{(\text{crew-hour})} = \frac{(1.20 \text{ MBF})}{(\text{day})}$$

If the planned duration is such that the work must be done in three days, which can only be accomplished with 3.33 MBF per day, then three crews will be needed.

4. Calculate number of crews required

$$\frac{(3.33 \text{ MBF})}{(\text{day})} \div \frac{(1.33 \text{ sfca})}{(\text{MBF per crew})} = 3 \text{ crews}$$

If the supervisor cannot use three crews, the supervisor has to consider one of the following:

- Have the smaller number of crews work overtime
- Increase productivity over the 0.05 MBF per person-hour estimated
- Take longer than the planned three days to do the work

It should be noted that the above calculations assume that the ten planned workdays are all available. Should the supervisor estimate that on average there is one day of rain for every 3.3 work days, then the production rate of 0.05 MBF per person-hour and three crews will fall short of getting the work done in three days. A larger number of crews, overtime, or a higher production rate would be needed, given one day of rain.

The point to be made is that these production calculations for the crew should be made from the estimate prior to starting the work; i.e., the calculations should be made during the pre-planning phase of the project.

In the above calculations, a crew production rate of 1.2 MBF per day was determined. The supervisor (and his or her crew) should know this production rate so that they have a goal; i.e., what is expected of them. As soon as the crew production rate falls below this 1.2 MBF per day, the supervisor should identify the cause of the problem and implement actions to achieve the 1.2 MBF per day. If the supervisor waits until the third day to see if the planned progress was met, it is too late to address the productivity problem.

Production goal setting for the crew and workers enables the supervisor to plan and monitor the process rather than attempting to solve the problem when it is too late.

Pre-planning, including determining crew and craft production rates, takes time. However, the supervisor cannot afford not to take the time to plan. The above calculations yielded the following information, which is critical to the supervision plan:

Number of crews needed = 3

Crew production rate per hour = 0.15 MBF / hour

Crew production rate per day = 1.2 MBF / hour

Ideally each and every work task estimated in the bidding phase is broken down into production goals for the construction phase. At the very minimum, key or "vital" work tasks are broken down into production goals.

Preparing Production Budgets for Crew Members

Exercise

Based on a project take-off and estimate for an upcoming project, the construction supervisor has determined the following information:

Concrete blocks to place:	45,000 blocks
Productivity of a worker:	15 blocks / person hour
Typical crew:	4 masons, 2 laborers
Work duration:	Work must be completed in 20 days

Determine the following:

1. The number of crews that will be required each day in order to complete the work in 20 days.

2. The number of concrete blocks that each crew will have to place per day and per hour.

(3) An Effective Communication Channel

Poor communication at jobsites leads to unnecessary redo work, poor worker attitudes and an inability to properly monitor the work progress. There are two types of communication that are critical to a productive jobsite: oral communication and written communication.

Effective and productive communication at a jobsite is complicated by the fact that communication is carried out in the open and during a relatively noisy job process. The individuals communicating may have different vocabularies and different communicating skills. A construction craftsperson, foreman, superintendent, project manager and architect may all speak and interpret various phrases and words differently.

Effective communication entails listening as well as talking.

Effective communication entails listening as well as talking. All too often the contractor or supervisor only talks *at* the worker instead of asking the worker for ideas or listening to his concerns. On occasion the person who knows how to form the concrete or place rebar may not be the supervisor but instead the craftsworker. Failure to take advantage of the worker's knowledge runs the risk not only of missing an improved construction method, but also may adversely affect the work attitude of the craftsman. Knowing a better way to do something, but not being asked one's ideas, tends to promote an "I don't care attitude."

Effective supervisor communication also entails taking the time to properly explain the work process to the worker. The construction craftsworker may think he is supposed to know how to do something even if he doesn't. Confused as to what to do, rather than ask for an explanation, the worker may proceed to do the work incorrectly. The result is that the supervisor will have to correct the work later; a non-productive work process.

The construction industry has been characterized for many years as an industry with inadequate written communication at the jobsite. Inaccurate time cards, late reports, failure to give the worker or supervisor written feedback, and lost or misplaced documents are typical of the construction jobsite. Part of the reason for these written communication inadequacies relates to the decentralized nature of the work process. Unlike most industries, which create and monitor their written communication system and cost accounting process at the same place they make their product, the construction industry's written communication is often created at the jobsite, transferred to the contractor's main office, and hopefully communicated back to the jobsite. This process results in untimely and sometimes incorrect reports.

The supervisor often complains about bad record keeping at the jobsite; but in fact he himself may promote bad record keeping. The use of a weekly timecard that requires foremen to keep track of workers' hours charged to specific work tasks is likely to be filled out weekly rather than daily. The result will be that the foreman cannot remember on Friday what the worker did on Monday. Perhaps a daily timecard would ensure more accurate data. Preprinting timecards with work codes may improve proper charging of labor hours. In addition, the use of daily report forms that require supervisors merely to check items like the weather conditions rather than describe the weather conditions is more likely to be legible and lessen the time for the recording process.

In critiquing his own written communication process or system the supervisor should remember the following three rules for improving the accuracy and timeline of the jobsite record-keeping process.

a. An individual required to fill out a form should be shown where the data goes and how it is used.

b. An individual required to fill out a form should be shown by example that his data was in fact used.

c. Any individual who fills out a form or inputs data should be given subsequent feedback.

Given these rules, consideration might be given to posting at a very visible worker location a sign that flowcharts the information system being used at the jobsite. Also post a sign or report that charts project progress against planned progress, so workers can measure their progress. This aids communication as well as making the job look like a firm. In summary, the supervisor should work at improving the oral and written communication process at the jobsite with a two-fold objective:

- more timely and accurate data and reports

- a means of using the communication process to align all personnel with the company goals for the project.

Sidebar:

Three rules for achieving accurate and timely record keeping are as follows:

a. An individual required to fill out a form should be shown where the data goes and how it is used.

b. An individual required to fill out a form should be shown by example that his data was in fact used.

c. Any individual who fills out a form or inputs data should be given subsequent feedback.

Exercise

Designing a Weekly Report for Workers to Improve Communication

Assume you and your group members have been assigned the task of designing a weekly job report that is to be given to workers when they leave the jobsite at the end of a workweek. The form is to be used on projects greater then $10 million or which have a project duration of more than one year. The information on the form or report is to be given to every worker and has the objective of improving communication on the jobsite and improving the communication between the contractor/supervisor and the workers.

With your fellow group members, discuss and list the types of information that should be reported on the form/report.

(4) Monetary Benefits and Incentives

Some would suggest that workers are only in it for the money. If that is the case, why do workers take days off with no pay? Why do workers with sufficient wealth continue to work? Yes, money is important, but it is not the only need of workers. Pride, a measuring system, and a communication channel are also important needs.

Some of the classic studies on why workers produce indicate that money or financial gain is only one of several worker needs. One theory resolves around what is referred to as the motivational-maintenance model. Money is defined as a maintenance factor or need. In this theory, if a maintenance factor such as money is taken away from a worker it will take away worker motivation and negatively impact productivity. On the other hand, it is not a motivational factor, which means giving more of it will not necessarily result in greater productivity.

It follows that every worker is different. Some are driven by the need for money and security, others are driven by pride, and yet others are driven by measurement data, or the ability to communicate. It is therefore important that the supervisor recognize what motivates and what does not motivate each and every worker. No two workers are the same when it comes to what motivates them.

Incentives as a Motivational Tool

Similar to using monetary benefits as a means of motivating workers are incentives. Incentives can be in the form of gifts or awards for performance, time off for having met production goals, added money for increased production or for beating budgets, and use of piece work as a means of compensation. Examples of incentives used by various construction firms are:

- Each foreman who attains a minimum number of hours of work without a worker accident for a defined time period has his or her name put into a pool. Subsequently the construction firm selects randomly one of the names from the pool and the person is given a brand-new pickup truck.

- A crew assigned to do roadway paving work is given a production goal in terms of linear feet or square feet of roadway surface expected in a day. If the production goal is met in less than eight hours, the crew can go home and still is paid for the eight-hour workday.

- Work hour and cost budgets are established for specified work tasks. If the work crew completes the work in less time than the specified budgets, the cost savings are shared by the firm and the work crewmembers, using a specified sharing formula.

Another example of incentives is the use of piecework. In such a process, workers are compensated by how much work they perform. For example, roofers would be compensated a specified dollar amount for each square foot of roofing placed as opposed to getting compensated by the hour.

Incentives have proven to be an effective means of motivating workers. This is especially the case when there is a significant potential for production increases without jeopardizing quality or safety issues. The supervisor needs to be careful in applying the incentives so that he or she does not achieve increased production at the expense of another project variable such as safety or quality. For example, a work crew placing masonry units might place more bricks or blocks in a defined time period by means of a work process that jeopardizes safety or diminishes quality.

In deciding whether or not the use of an incentive is appropriate for a specific work task or project, the supervisor should consider the pros and cons set out in the table below:

Advantages of Incentives	Disadvantages of Incentives
Can be used to meet increased performance if there is potential for improvement.	Could result in another project variable being jeopardized to meet the incentive.
Distinguishes the good worker from the poorer worker in that the good worker gets rewarded.	Need to be careful that the method used for measuring the incentive is fair; otherwise could cause worker discontent.
Develops an environment of worker competition that may stimulate performance.	Could possibly discriminate against an older worker that could not keep up owing to the demanding physical nature of the work.
Can be a win-win process in which the workers and the firm benefit.	Could be in conflict with labor work rules; for example, a labor union might take issue with piecework as a method of worker compensation.

As with many other management practices in regard to productivity improvement, there is no single cure-all for all situations. Incentives have proven beneficial in select instances and should be considered by the supervisor; especially when the following work characteristics are present:

1. There is significant potential for improvement
2. A monitoring system is in place so that non-incentive variables can be monitored
3. The work is repetitive, so meaningful goals can be specified easily
4. There is no conflict between the incentive and labor work rules
5. Safety is not jeopardized by the use of the incentive.

Classical Personnel Management Theories

There are classical personnel management practices or philosophies that the construction supervisor should know in his or her attempt to motivate workers.

Theory X and Theory Y

Theory X and Theory Y represent two different theories as to why workers are motivated to work. According to Theory X, an individual has an inherent dislike for work and will avoid it if possible. The theory also assumes that people shun responsibility, have little ambition and desire a high degree of security.

Several supervisor management approaches to motivation spring from the acceptance of Theory X. For one, it implies that the supervisor must be strong and responsibility should be concentrated with the supervisor; that is, the individual worker merely wants to be directed. The supervisor motivates the worker by coercion, using either a positive or negative approach. That is, to motivate the Theory X worker, the manager might offer extra pay (a positive approach) or threaten the worker with punishment (a negative approach).

In contrast with Theory X, Theory Y assumes that human beings derive both external and internal satisfaction from the performance of work, and assumes that the average person does not inherently dislike work. Theory Y holds that if workers are committed to the objectives of the work, that they will in fact accept work as they do play or rest. The key is to make the worker's objectives consistent with the firm's objectives. Unlike Theory X, Theory Y assumes that people can learn to accept responsibility, and have the capacity to be creative and imaginative in solving work objectives.

Maslow Theory

Another classic personnel management theory was founded by A. H. Maslow. Maslow identified the five worker needs shown in Figure 4-1. The physiological needs shown in the illustration include needs for food and shelter. These and the safety and security needs shown are often referred to as physical needs. Social needs, esteem and status needs, and self-realization and fulfillment needs are often referred to as personal-satisfaction needs (sometimes called inner or higher order needs).

```
        Self-realization
         & fulfillment

       Esteem and Status

    Belonging and social activity

      Basic psychological needs
```

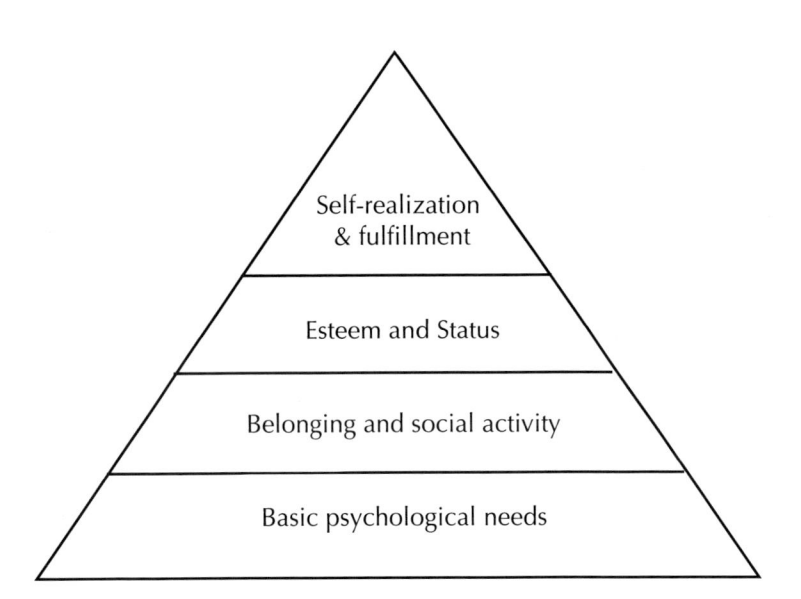

Fig. 4-1

Maslow's people management theory is that individuals start at the bottom of the triangle shown. At first the worker is motivated by basic physiological needs (food and shelter). The theory is that as long as an individual has not satisfied a need (or obtained an adequate amount of it) then the worker can be motivated by offering him or her more of this need. However, once the worker considers himself or herself to have obtained an adequate amount of the need, he or she goes on to the next higher need shown in Figure 4-1. At that stage, the worker can be motivated only by the next higher need. For example, once a worker has obtained what he or she believes is adequate food and shelter, safety and security have to be offered to motivate the worker.

Motivational-Maintenance Theory

Frederick Herzberg described two independent sets of factors that influence a worker's satisfaction and performance. This motivational-maintenance theory holds that a worker or group's job satisfaction comes from both maintenance and motivational factors. The motivational and maintenance factors are shown in Figure 4-2.

% of workers with negative feelings towards their work   % of workers with positive feelings towards their work

40   30   20   10   0   10   20   30   40

MOTIVATIONAL FACTORS

Achievement

Recognition

Responsibility

Advancement

MAINTENANCE FACTORS

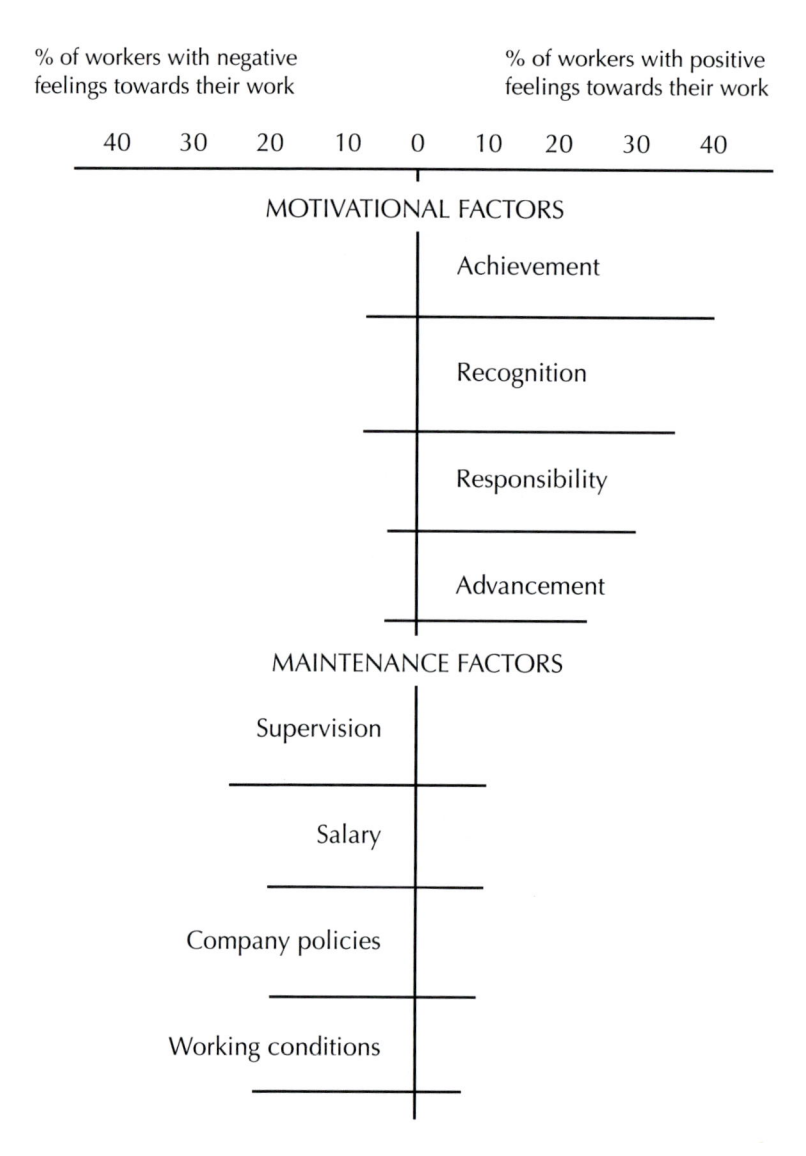

Supervision

Salary

Company policies

Working conditions

Fig. 4-2

The motivational-maintenance theory holds that maintenance factors are needed to "maintain" productivity. If maintenance factors are taken away from a worker or diminished, then the worker(s) will be less productive; i.e., they will lose their motivation. On the other hand, providing a worker more of the maintenance factors will not result in an increase in productivity. To increase productivity, motivational factors have to be provided to the worker. Similarly, if the motivational factors are not provided, it does not follow that productivity decreases; it only follows that productivity does not significantly increase.

The supervisor should be attentive to these overall management theories in attempting to motivate the workforce. However, it is equally important that the supervisor recognize each worker as an individual. What motivates one worker may not motivate another worker.

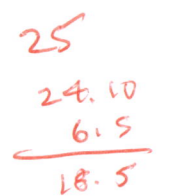

Group Behavior

Much of the behavior of the individual employee can be understood only in the context of the group in which he or she works. Commitment to production goals, acceptance of leadership, satisfaction with work and effectiveness of performance all tend to depend on the way a person relates with his or her co-workers. The effects of group behavior and the work environment on the individual worker are especially important with regard to construction productivity and personnel management.

Very little construction work is done by an individual in isolation. Instead, several laborers representing more than one type of craft interact in the building process. Labor unions often require that several types of craftspeople work together. For example, many union agreements require the use of a laborer to help two carpenters. Even if individuals are not mixed together for a particular type of work, they still interact with fellow workers during lunch or non-work hours. As time goes on, groups of workers begin to share common goals and values.

From a sociological point of view, a group is more than just a collection of individuals working together in one location. A group is formed only as a result of interpersonal relations. Researchers describe the process of group formation as the result of the following four essential characteristics.

1. A motivational base shared by individuals and conducive to recurrent interaction among them.

2. An organization (group structure) consisting of roles differentiated in some degree from those of nonmembers.

3. A shared set of norms (values, rules and standards of behavior).

4. More or less consistent effects, produced by the group, on the attitudes and behavior of individual members.

A construction union, which includes all construction labor in a given craft, is itself a group. It has traits that are similar to the four characteristics just listed. Smaller groups of individuals within a union and employed at a particular project site also share these characteristics.

Groups are often classified by type. One broad classification identifies groups as either formal or informal. Examples of formal groups include business organizations and professional associations. Although formal groups influence individual workers with their policies, informal groups are often more difficult to control and as such have a greater influence on personnel management. Informal groups result when

> A group can be defined as a collection of individuals working together in one location.

individuals with common social interests come together. These groups can be further classified as one of the following three types.

1. Large groups that arise because of internal politics. These types of groups are often referred to as "gangs" or "crowds."

2. Groups formed on the basis of common jobs. Members are often intimate and work, talk and even dine together. This type of group is often referred to as a "clique."

3. Small groups consisting of a few (two or three) close friends. This type of group is often referred to as a "sub-clique."

Groups can be positive or negative in regard to productivity.

Each of these three types of informal groups can be observed in the construction industry. Union workers gathering for a labor strike or forming a group to protest nonunion work can be classified as a gang or crowd. Cliques are common on a construction project. Often several workers may share a sport or hobby that brings them together. Cliques can prove beneficial or detrimental to productivity, depending on their goals and values. Smaller groups of two or three workers who live close to one another are typically friends who share common interests and may prefer to work together. Generally this type of group presents few problems with regard to personnel management.

Even if the supervisor can prevent the existence of cliques, it may not be advantageous to do so. If the goals of the clique are consistent with those of the firm, the firm will reap the benefits; however, a clique may prove to be a productivity constraint if its goals or values differ from those of the firm. With proper leadership, the goals and values of clique and firm can be made compatible.

It is the supervisor's duty to encourage meaningful group goals. Without them, group members are unlikely to share common work objectives. If group goals are so vague that workers interpret them differently, the possibility of increased productivity is lessened. The supervisor must also see that workers in a group understand the relationship between their personal objectives and group goals. Group values favoring higher productivity are likely to develop when workers understand group goals, understand how their own objectives relate to those of their group or clique, and find meaning and satisfaction in the work they do.

Supervising Various Types of Work Groups

Exercise

For each of the situations described below, write down 1) what you perceive to be the problem and 2) what you as a supervisor would do to alleviate the problem. Be prepared to discuss your results with the group.

a. You have noticed that on one of your ironworker crews, two of the workers are continually arguing. While the arguing appears to have some positive effects, in that they are typically arguing about the best way to do the work, the constant arguments appear to disrupt the other three workers on the crew. You have noticed that the two individuals who argue appear to be good friends and that they drive to and from work together.

b. Several of the concrete finishers on your jobsite appear to be good friends and spend considerable time after work hours together. They play on a softball team together and all are on a bowling team. More recently, however, they appear to be continually complaining about the other crafts at the jobsite and the overall management of the project. This damper to your job productivity seems to be instigated by two troublemakers among their group.

Session 4 Review

Look back over Session 4 and review these key points to be sure you understand them:

- Labor costs account for approximately 40% of the project cost.
- It is important that the supervisor motivate the worker in such a way that in effect the worker monitors and supervises himself or herself.
- To motivate a worker, the supervisor must be attentive to the four needs of a worker: pride, measurement, communication and monetary compensation.
- Construction workers typically work in groups. Group behavior should be monitored by the supervisor to enable improved jobsite productivity.

Using on the Job What You Learned Today

Jobsite Assignment
At your jobsites, identify five actions you can take to improve personnel management or motivation.

To Get Ready for Session 5
Read Session 5 of the Participant's Manual.

Session 5

Equipment Management for Productivity Improvement

Learning Goals for Session 5

After this session, you will recognize the importance of the need to manage equipment as well as manage labor. You will learn that there are essentially two ways to improve project time and cost:

1. improve labor productivity,
2. improve equipment productivity

[handwritten: GOOD QUESTION]

Often equipment is more expensive than labor, and is non-productive more often than labor. You will learn how the supervisor can improve overall project productivity by being attentive to a ten-point program for equipment productivity improvement.

Learning Objectives

To accomplish the learning goals, during this session you will:

- Identify the differences between labor and equipment
- Implement a ten-step program of improving equipment productivity

To Get Ready for Session 5

Reading: Read the pages for this session in your Participant's Manual. Try to think of ways to keep construction equipment more productive.

Major Activities for Session 5
- Learn the many types of equipment that are used in construction.
- Learn to view equipment as money, not just metal.
- Do an exercise that requires you to know what things cost, not just what they are.
- Learn to weigh the benefit of equipment versus labor when selecting a work method.
- Discuss how equipment has limited work capability.
- Do an exercise in which you will discuss the mechanical issues relative to equipment production.
- Learn to view equipment as being in one of three work states.
- Do an exercise in which you will calculate the cost of non-productive equipment time.
- Learn the importance of scheduling work tasks around the availability of equipment.
- Learn the importance of equipment maintenance.
- Discuss the safety aspects of working with equipment.
- Learn the difference between equipment ownership costs and operating costs.
- Do a change order exercise that pertains to ownership and operating costs.
- Learn how to model two pieces of equipment working together.
- Do an exercise that calculates production for the interdependent pieces of equipment

Participant's Manual ■ STP ■ Unit 9

A Review of Session 4

In Session 4, you learned the importance of motivating workers and of personnel management practices. The construction process is such that a high percentage of project cost is onsite labor costs. Given the relatively small ratio of supervisors onsite to onsite workers, it is important that the supervisor motivate workers so that they in effect motivate themselves. The supervisor cannot stand over each and every worker all the time.

Some of the facts you learned in Session 4 are the following:

- Onsite labor costs account for on the order of 40% of the overall project cost.

- The supervisor has a harder time motivating construction workers because the workers may not work for the same firm all the time; many of the workers might view themselves as working for a job.

- Workers have four needs:

    — Pride,

    — Communication,

    — A Measurement System and

    — Monetary Benefits and Incentives

    It is important for the supervisor to be attentive to all the needs of the worker, not just the financial need.

- There are various classical theories as to how to motivate workers.

- It is important for the supervisor to understand group dynamics of workers.

Improving Equipment Productivity

One could properly define the construction firm as a firm that uses labor and equipment to transform material into a construction project. It is important that the construction supervisor be attentive to keeping labor and equipment productive. The difference between constructing a project on budget and on schedule relates to the productivity of labor and equipment.

The dollar amount and type of equipment needed for a specific project varies considerably depending on the type of construction project. For a small commercial type construction project, the only equipment might be a backhoe and a small crane, with the total cost of equipment being only about 10% of the total project cost. On the other hand, for a heavy and highway project such as a new roadway and bridge project, the needed equipment will consist of several earthmoving pieces of equipment, pavers, pile drivers, etc. The sum of the equipment cost for a project of this type may exceed 40% of the total project cost.

> The dollar amount and type of equipment needed for a specific project varies considerably depending on the type of construction project. The total cost of equipment as a percentage of the total project cost may range from as little as 10% to more than 40%.

Just as there are many types of construction labor crafts and skills, there are many types of construction equipment available to the supervisor. While the number of labor types may be less than 20, the different types of equipment available to the supervisor is almost endless.

One category of equipment types is as follows:

- **Earthmoving Equipment**
  - Tractors
  - Scrapers
  - Excavators
  - Graders
  - Dozers, etc.

- **Lifting and Hoisting Equipment**
  - Forklifts
  - Scissor Lifts
  - Mobile Cranes
  - Tower Cranes
  - Gantry Cranes
  - Derricks

- **Foundation Equipment**
  - Pile Hammers
  - Vibratory Drivers

- **Dewatering Equipment**
  — Pumps
- **Conveyors**
  — Bucket Conveyors
  — Belt Conveyors
- **Paving Equipment**
  — Asphalt Pavers
  — Concrete Pavers

Additional equipment relates to specific trades, e.g., electrical and mechanical equipment.

One way to classify the many types of equipment available is to group it by the function it performs, such as equipment that loads, carries and dumps loose material. Another way of classifying equipment is by the type of construction operations in which it is used, e.g., equipment that is used for earthmoving.

In general, construction equipment performs one of the following operations:

- Removal of existing material
- Transporting material
- Processing material
- Moving processed material
- Placing finished material

Productivity starts with the selection of the right equipment for the project in question. Some of the selection factors include the following:

- Specific construction operation
- Job specification requirement
- Condition of the jobsite
- Location of the jobsite
- Time allowed to do the job
- Balance of interdependent equipment
- Mobility required of the equipment
- Versatility of the equipment

Equipment Management for Productivity Improvement

Unfortunately the construction supervisor may not always be assigned the best or most productive piece of equipment for a specific project. The cost of purchasing many of the types of equipment listed above exceeds $200,000. The result is that the construction firm often uses what it has rather than going out and renting or purchasing a new piece of equipment.

Independent of which equipment the supervisor is assigned or uses for a specific project, the supervisor must focus on maximizing the productivity of the equipment to achieve project objectives. The supervisor should be attentive to the productivity guidelines for optimizing equipment productivity at a jobsite that are shown in **Figure 5-1** below.

> The construction firm often uses whatever equipment it has rather than the most productive equipment for the work task in question.

Productivity Consideration	Why	Example/comment
1. View equipment as money, not just as equipment or metal.	Idle equipment is not just idle equipment; it is wasted money. Because the supervisor may not know what a piece of equipment costs on an hourly basis, he or she may not be as attentive to the cost of idle of equipment as they should be.	It is not unusual to be critical of workers having a cigarette for ten minutes. The worker might be making $25 or more an hour. However, equipment costing over $100 a hour might be idle for hours and not be viewed as being a problem or criticized.
2. Plan the logistics of equipment.	Minimize the time it takes for equipment to be moved from one task to another task.	A poor plan may result in a crew standing idle for many minutes awaiting the arrival of equipment from the other side of the building.
3. When determining the best method for a work task, evaluate the benefits of using equipment versus labor.	Typically the supervisor will have a choice between using labor and equipment. The selection of one versus the other dictates productivity and other project considerations.	The supervisor might employ workers to do a task that could be done more safely and more effectively by the use of equipment that could be rented or purchased.
4. Be attentive to the work capacity of a machine.	Just as a worker can produce only a limited amount of work owing to his or her energy-producing capabilities, the same is true for equipment.	If a supervisor attempts to lift too heavy a load or uses the improper boom angle for a machine, the equipment will tip over or collapse, causing a major cost, schedule and safety problem.
5. Be attentive to the percentage of time equipment is working versus being idle or in a "support" state.	The supervisor is only doing added-value work with equipment when the equipment is being used to "place" material.	Measurement is a tool of improvement. If the supervisor does not keep track of productive time for a piece of equipment relative to non-productive or support time, he or she will likely not be attentive to improvement.
6. Be attentive to scheduling work tasks around equipment availability.	Work should be scheduled to take full advantage of equipment at the jobsite.	If work is not scheduled around the availability of equipment, the equipment will sit idle for days at a time. Idle equipment takes away from job profits and also keeps the equipment from other supervisors.

Productivity Consideration	Why	Example/comment
7. Be attentive to proper equipment maintenance.	The supervisor should provide maintenance to equipment when it is idle or in a standby mode so that it does not break down during a work task.	Equipment that breaks down at an inopportune time results in project time and cost increases. The result will be idle labor time and schedule delays while the equipment is fixed or replaced.
8. Always be attentive to working safely with equipment.	Given the size and type of work equipment does, most accidents with equipment lead to severe worker injuries.	The supervisor should make sure that all operators and workers assisting in the use of the equipment are properly trained and are in compliance with safety regulations and provisions.
9. Be attentive to equipment's ownership and operating cost component.	If equipment is sitting idle at a job, there is still a lost ownership cost. If the equipment is used for added work but does not take added project time, there is an added operating cost.	Labor costs are a function of labor use; if the worker is not at a job, he or she normally does not get paid. But equipment, once purchased, has an ongoing ownership cost if unused no matter where it is.
10. Be prepared to model or consider the interrelationship of two or more pieces of equipment working together.	Often two or more pieces of equipment work together and the productivity of one piece is dependent on the productivity of the other piece.	Trucks bring asphalt or concrete to pavers, scrappers are pushed by a bulldozer, excavators load dump trucks. If one of the pieces of equipment is idle, there is no productivity.

Fig. 5-1

A Ten-Step Program for Equipment Productivity Improvement

#1 View Equipment as Money, Not Just as a Machine

Productivity was defined in Session 1 as the following:

$$\text{Productivity} = \frac{\text{Units of output}}{\text{Person-hour of effort or input}}$$

However, productivity can be increased by means other than a person or persons working harder. Providing a worker with a more productive piece of equipment or even replacing the worker with a machine or piece of equipment will likely increase productivity. Perhaps an improved definition of productivity would be the **efficiency by which materials are placed using labor and equipment.**

By focusing only on labor and ignoring equipment, the supervisor does not get a true measure of total productivity or the means to increase productivity. So why do supervisors typically pay more attention to labor productivity than they do to equipment productivity? One of the primary reasons is that equipment is typically viewed as metal or machines, whereas labor is viewed as money.

Most laypersons, let alone the construction supervisor, know approximately the hourly wage rate of a construction worker. For example, even without all the appropriate fringe benefits, the labor rate for a project craftsperson might be $25 per hour. Therefore, if the craftsperson is observed to be in a non-productive state (for example, waiting on materials for 15 minutes), it is easy to calculate that in excess of $6 has been wasted owing to non-productive labor time.

Often next to the craftsperson who was idle for 15 minutes was a machine such as a crane that didn't move or do a productive activity for over an hour. In many cases the hourly rate (rental or ownership) for the equipment is greater than the hourly rate for the worker. Nonetheless, the idle equipment may not be the center of attention when it comes to the layperson or supervisor looking at a means of increasing productivity. The reason is that the equipment is viewed as a machine or piece of metal when in fact it should be viewed as money. In many cases, the hourly rental or ownership cost for a piece of construction equipment is greater than the hourly rate of a worker. For example, the crane noted in the example above may rent for more than $100 per hour.

One might suggest that if the hourly cost of owning or renting a piece of equipment was painted onto the machine, the supervisor would be more attentive to idle equipment time or non-productive equipment

> The supervisor may not be as attentive to non-productive equipment time as he or she is to non-productive labor time. This may be because the supervisor might view equipment as "metal" when in reality it is money.

activities. It is important for the supervisor to view equipment as money, not just as metal. Idle equipment is typically more costly than an idle craftsperson. With the objective of being more attentive to the cost of idle or non-productive equipment, the supervisor should make an effort to learn the hourly cost of equipment at his or her project.

Exercise

Knowing the Hourly Cost of Labor and Equipment

The construction supervisor pays considerable attention to managing "things"; i.e., a craftsperson, a crane, electrical conduit, sheet metal, backhoes, etc. Another view is that the supervisor is actually managing money. Unless the supervisor knows what things cost, he or she may expend too much of his or her supervision time with low-cost items. Listed below are examples of things used at construction projects. Your group is to fill out the requested cost information. In doing this exercise, it is not critical that you are precise in listing the cost; the objective is to draw your attention to the relative cost of the various things the supervisor manages during a project.

Material	*Cost*	*Unit*	*Labor*	*Cost*	*Unit*	*Equipment*	*Cost*	*Unit*
Asphalt			Laborer		Hr.	1 cy Excavator		Hr.
Steel			Carpenter		Hr.	Man Lift		Hr.
Concrete			Supervisor		Hr.	Concrete Paver		Hr.
Wood			Ironworker		Hr.	Concrete Pump		Hr.
			Electrician		Hr.	Pile Driver		Hr.

A Ten-Step Program for Equipment Productivity Improvement

#2 Plan the Logistics of Equipment

The importance of project pre-planning was discussed in Session 2. Pre-planning equipment logistics is part of the pre-planning function. Where equipment is stored at the jobsite and where it is positioned in regard to the work it will perform significantly impact overall project productivity.

Consider the project layout shown in Figure 5-2. The fact that the equipment is stored near the entrance way may create safety issues, logistics issues and productivity issues.

> Where equipment is located on the site will in part dictate the equipment productivity and overall project productivity.

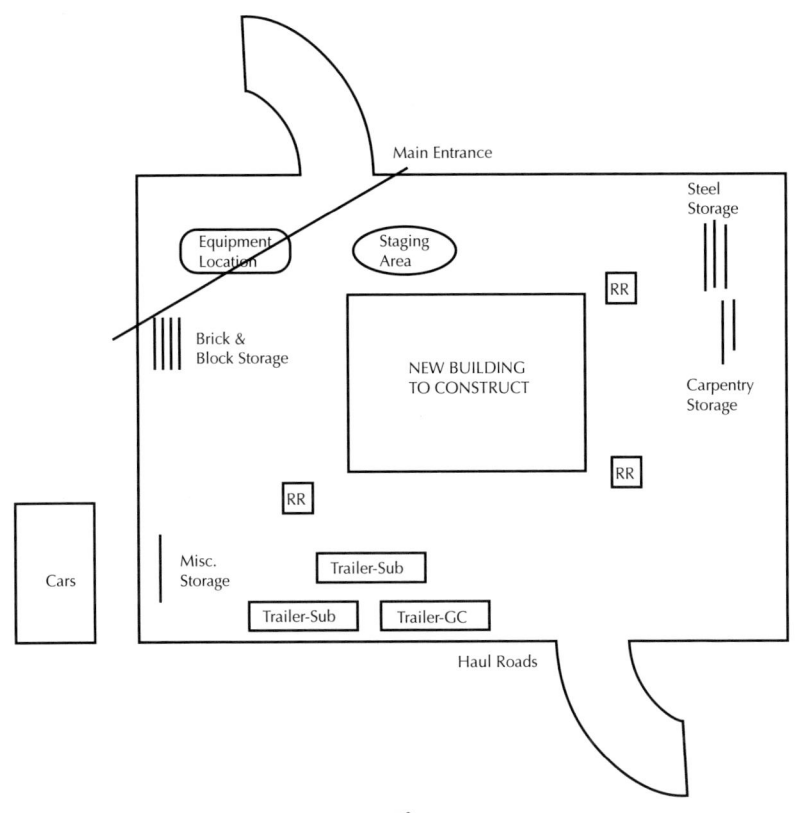

Fig. 5-2

It is important for the supervisor to participate in the pre-planning phase of the project so that he or she can offer their input as to where equipment is to be stored and located for optimal overall project productivity. An example of a non-optimal location would be one where a crane boom has to be stretched beyond its acceptable safety angle, or where its set-up requires moving it several times during a project. The layout and identifying of equipment moves should be planned before the start of the project; it should not be a reaction issue.

A Ten-Step Program for Equipment Productivity Improvement

#3 When Determining the Best Method for a Work Task, Evaluate the Benefits of Using Equipment Versus Labor

There are typically two means of doing construction work:

1) using labor or

2) using equipment.

The supervisor should consider the benefits of using either labor or equipment to do a work task. The supervisor must view the "big picture" when making a choice. For example, it may be appear more costly to rent equipment versus use onsite labor to move material from one location to another at a jobsite. However, if the supervisor considers the big picture, it may be that the equipment can be used to assist in work tasks required at the project. In addition, by using the equipment to move the material rather than using workers, the chance of a worker accident is reduced. In addition, the use of the workers to transport the material may tire them out, affecting their productivity for other work tasks.

The use of labor versus equipment to perform a work task, and vice versa, has benefits and disadvantages. Listed below are some points for the supervisor to consider when deciding upon the use of labor or equipment for performing a work task.

Some of the advantages of using equipment rather than labor are:

- Productivity typically is less affected by weather.

- Productivity may be more predictable (i.e., less varied)

- The unit cost of performing work may be lower (especially if there are many units of work to perform and/or the equipment can be used for additional work tasks).

- The ownership of the equipment may aid marketing and serve as a basis for qualifying for other projects.

- Less use of labor reduces the potential for a worker accident.

On the other hand, relative to the use of equipment, labor also has advantages:

- A worker may be more flexible as to the type of work he or she can do.

- There is a minimal mobilization cost to engaging a worker to do a task on a project versus that of bringing in and mobilizing a piece of equipment for a work task.

- The unit cost of performing work may be lower (especially if there is only a small amount of work to do and the duration is short).

A Ten-Step Program for Equipment Productivity Improvement

#4 Be Attentive to the Work Capacity of a Machine

Just as a worker can produce only a limited amount of work owing to his or her energy producing capabilities, the same is true for equipment. If a piece of equipment is worked beyond its capacity, the result can be catastrophic. A crane tipping, for example, could result in critical injuries. At the very minimum, working a machine beyond its engineering limits will result in added maintenance and operating costs and increase the possibility of equipment breakdowns leading to productivity problems.

The construction supervisor should be familiar with the mechanical and production limits of the equipment on his or her job. These characteristics vary depending on the type of equipment being used. Figure 5-3 lists how these production limits are commonly defined for some examples of equipment used in construction.

Equipment Type	Description of ability to work; production considerations
Excavation equipment with rubber tires	Rimpull Horsepower Resistance of grade Effect of altitude on engine performance Coefficient of traction
Mobil Crane	Lifting capacity Center of gravity Load radius Base boom angle
Paver	Horsepower RPM Mechanical efficiency Drive wheels

Fig. 5-3

The equipment listed in Figure 5-3 represent only three of the many types of equipment the supervisor might use at projects. Other equipment might include scissor lifts, compactors, hauling trucks, etc. The point is, the work capacity of each of these machines is defined by various mechanical characteristics. The supervisor should be acquainted with these characteristics in selecting, using and monitoring equipment performance.

Production Capability of a Machine

In the above session, various mechanical characteristics of three different types of equipment were listed. Your group is to select one of the three above equipment types (or another type of equipment not listed) and describe why various mechanical aspects are relevant to the limitations of the equipment. For example, describe rimpull, what it means and how it is measured.

A Ten-Step Program for Equipment Productivity Improvement

#5 Be Attentive to the Percentage of Time Equipment Is Working Versus Being Idle or in a "Support" State

In earlier sessions, discussion focused on the non-productive work states of craftpersons. Non-productive work states include time waiting, time doing redo work, time expended double-handling material, etc. It was suggested that this non-productive time often approached 50% of a construction workday. Although such a high percentage of non-productive time should be a concern to the supervisor, let's compare this percentage to that for construction equipment.

Many types of construction equipment are metered so that the hours a piece of equipment actually works in a given time period can be tracked. According to several equipment manufacturers and contractors, many construction firms can expect to average somewhere between 800 to 1,000 productive hours from a typical piece of equipment in a given year. Assuming a 2,080-hour work year (52 weeks, with a 40-hour work week), and 800 hours of productive equipment time, construction equipment is non-productive 62% of the time; a percentage greater than that for labor!

One might argue that equipment is more difficult to keep productive. A piece of equipment can only do certain things; for example, a backhoe is used to dig soil. However, the same is true for labor; an electrician only does electrical work, a carpenter does carpentry work, etc. In fact, one might argue that equipment should be easier to manage — equipment does not have an attitude, whereas a worker might.

Idle equipment is a detriment to construction productivity. Given the relatively high cost of equipment, it is important for the supervisor to keep it productive.

Like a worker, a piece of equipment at a jobsite is either working or not working. To improve equipment productivity, the supervisor should consider keeping records of what equipment is doing; not just where or what it is.

> Construction equipment is only adding value to the overall project when it is being used for tasks that must be done; i.e., productive work.

Consider the following data, which summarizes an analysis a supervisor makes regarding the work states of two similar pieces of equipment at two similar projects.

- **Productive** (performing necessary work)
- **Standby** (able to work, but no work available)
- **Non-productive** (not capable of doing the work, broken or doing unnecessary or low-value tasks)

Work states of equipment	Job 1	Job 2
Productive	42%	62%
Standby	28%	22%
Non-productive	30%	16%

By comparing the data, the supervisor can see that the non-productive and standby time for the equipment at Job 1 was greater than it was on Job 2. By investigating the causes for the differences, the supervisor can take steps to improve the performance of the equipment at Job 1. The issue is not one of measuring work states to place blame on one equipment operator or to place blame on the project supervisor. The intent is to draw attention to the cause for the difference in the productive work states so that actions can be taken to improve.

The purpose of the above measurement is not to place blame. The measurement of productive to non-productive equipment hours at a project can be used as an effective measure of rating supervisor performance. Given the high cost of construction equipment at equipment intensive projects, it is important that the construction supervisor keep equipment productive. If the supervisor has idle equipment at his or her project, the equipment is unavailable to another project and supervisor.

Independent of the reason why the work state data is collected, the fact remains that construction equipment is typically in a non-productive work state more often than is labor. This, coupled with the fact that equipment is often more expensive than labor on an hourly basis, should focus the supervisor on what equipment is doing, not just what it is.

Exercise

Calculating Non-Productive Cost

A construction supervisor has analyzed the various work states of labor and equipment that are being used to place material for a work method. After analyzing the work process for several hours, the supervisor judges the typical work states of labor and equipment for a work cycle to be as shown below (note: the listing of work states as a function of time using bars as shown is commonly referred to as a "crew-balance" model). Assuming all work states other than when a worker or machine is placing or handling material are non-productive, calculate the total non-productive cost for each worker and each machine for the entire workday (assuming an eight-hour day).

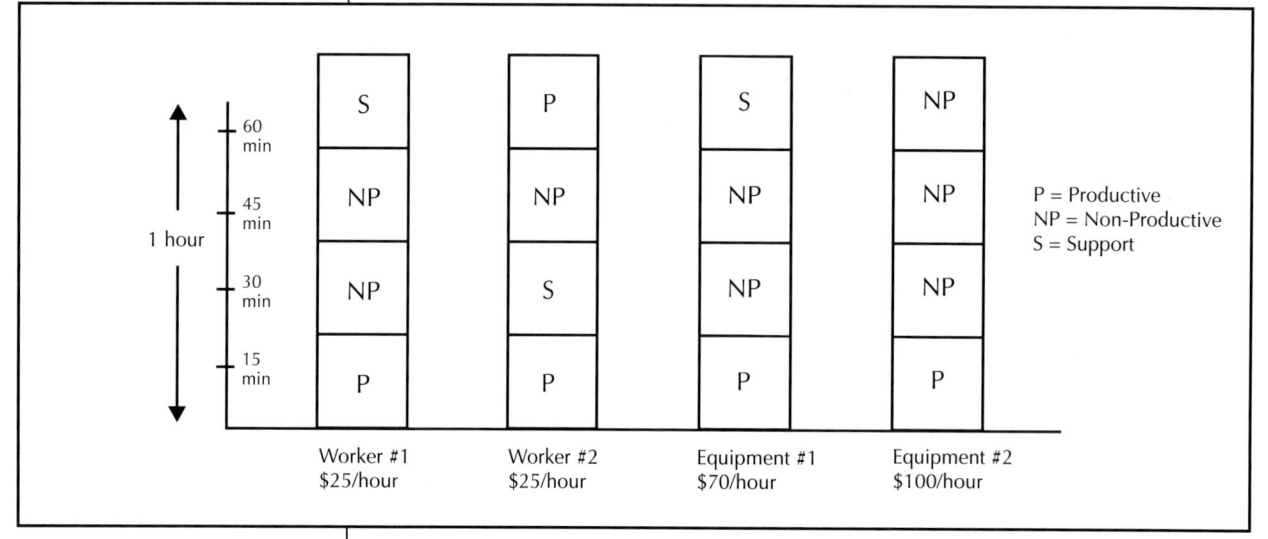

Time	Worker #1 $25/hour	Worker #2 $25/hour	Equipment #1 $70/hour	Equipment #2 $100/hour
45–60 min	S	P	S	NP
30–45 min	NP	NP	NP	NP
15–30 min	NP	S	NP	NP
0–15 min	P	P	P	P

P = Productive
NP = Non-Productive
S = Support

A Ten-Step Program for Equipment Productivity Improvement

#6 Be Attentive to Scheduling Work Tasks Around Equipment Availability

Planning is a key to productivity. Not having a plan leads to non-productive use of resources and project time, plus cost overruns. The topic of the supervisor's planning will be discussed in the next session.

However, typical construction schedules are driven by the technical nature and the sequencing of the work tasks. For example, it is normal to schedule the forming and placement of a concrete foundation wall after the placement of the concrete in the foundation footings is completed. This is how we build!

Given the high cost of equipment, the supervisor should also be attentive to scheduling construction work around the equipment availability, especially if the equipment is very expensive.

For example, assume that three work activities are scheduled, two of which require the use of an expensive piece of equipment; let's refer to them in Figure 5-4 as activities A and C.

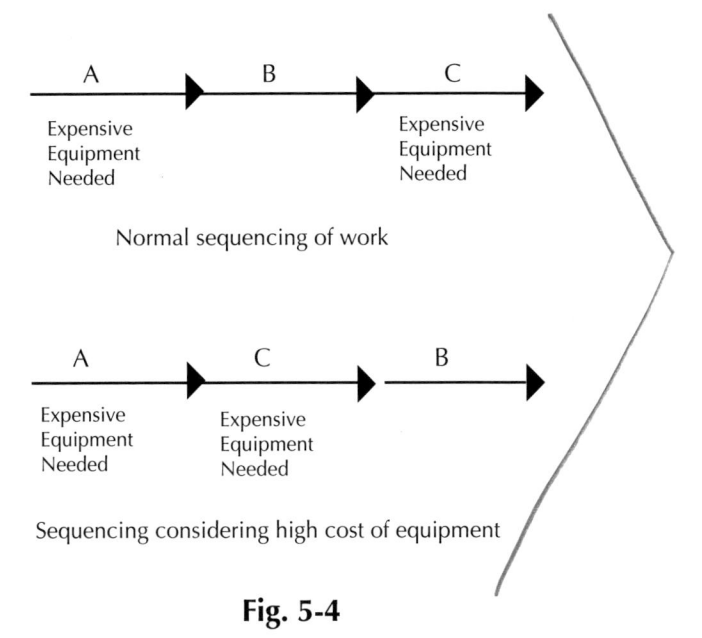

> The supervisor should consider scheduling to accommodate the availability of expensive equipment rather than merely considering the normal sequencing of the project.

A → B → C
Expensive Equipment Needed   Expensive Equipment Needed

Normal sequencing of work

A → C → B
Expensive Equipment Needed   Expensive Equipment Needed

Sequencing considering high cost of equipment

Fig. 5-4

Given the high cost of using the equipment, the supervisor might be well advised to do the activities that require it, and then send it back to the vendor or to another job on which it is needed. The alternative is to keep it idle on the job while activity B is being performed.

A Ten-Step Program for Equipment Productivity Improvement

#7 Be Attentive to Proper Equipment Maintenance

The productivity of equipment is greatly determined by the equipment's **utilization** or **availability** factor. Depending on the type of equipment, the manufacturer, and the age and how well it is maintained, the availability percent for equipment varies. For example, manufacturers of excavation equipment may suggest that on average their equipment is available 85% of the time for use in doing production work. During the other 15% of the time the equipment will be in service or possibly in a breakdown state. The utilization or availability of a specific piece of construction equipment is dependent on the following factors:

- The type and brand of the equipment (i.e., some equipment is manufactured to higher standards).

- The age of the equipment (i.e., like any mechanical device, construction equipment tends to wear out and break more often over time).

- The use of the equipment (i.e., if a machine is operated outside its normal operating mode, it will be damaged).

- The maintenance program used to care for the equipment.

When a piece of equipment breaks down, the construction supervisor is likely to incur an added cost; the cost of an idle crew of workers that is waiting for the availability of the equipment. A crew cost may be well in excess of $100, maybe even as much as $500. If the crew is dependent on the availability of a piece of equipment and the equipment should break down, the construction supervisor may incur this labor crew cost without any offsetting production. Clearly this is a cost that jeopardizes the ability to complete a project on time and on budget.

It follows that if the construction supervisor is to achieve a productive project, he or she must be attentive to the ongoing maintenance of a piece of equipment. This includes attention to such items as oiling the equipment, changing belts, filters, etc.

Given the high cost associated with having a needed piece of equipment break down during the production process, the supervisor should consider a **preventive maintenance** program. A preventive maintenance program essentially means that maintenance expenditures are made on a regular basis to a machine *before* the equipment breaks down. Records are kept on when equipment parts should be changed relative to their typical life.

When equipment breaks down, the supervisor is likely to incur added costs such as the cost of an idle crew of workers waiting for the availability of the equipment.

A Ten-Step Program for Equipment Productivity Improvement

#8 Always Be Attentive to Working Safely with Equipment

Each construction project has four variables by which the overall project can be judged; cost, time, quality and safety. Safety is undoubtedly the most important variable. Non-attention to safety can lead to an accident, which of course jeopardizes productivity as well as causes workers harm. Unlike a cost or time overrun or a quality issue that can be remedied, there is no turning back on an accident; i.e., it cannot be fixed.

Every year there are numerous worker fatalities and thousands of lesser accidents related to the use of construction equipment. A worker getting crushed by a paver, a crane tipping over and killing two workers or a worker falling off a piece of equipment and being injured are just a few examples of issues that arise owing to improper equipment use.

As is true when a worker gets injured, the real cost of a mishap or equipment accident is often overlooked. The idle time related to the accident, the equipment repairs, the impact on the project schedule and the impact on the morale of the workers have to be considered.

Given the high cost and negative impact that an equipment mishap or accident creates, the supervisor should be attentive to the following:

- Being proactive to developing a program for equipment safety.
- Stress working smart, not just hard, with equipment.
- Training all workers that are around equipment to be safe and careful.
- Train workers in how to operate equipment safely.

> Every year there are numerous worker fatalities and thousands of lesser accidents that relate to the use of construction equipment.

SESSION 5

EQUIPMENT MANAGEMENT FOR PRODUCTIVITY IMPROVEMENT

A Ten-Step Program for Equipment Productivity Improvement

#9 Be Attentive to Equipment as Having an Ownership and Operating Cost Component

When a construction craftsperson works at a project for eight hours, he or she gets paid for eight hours. On the other hand, if the craftsperson is not at the project, he or she does not get paid. In other words, hourly labor costs can be viewed as a variable cost; they are paid as a function of activity.

On the other hand, equipment should be viewed as having two hourly cost components; an ownership cost and an operating cost. Even if equipment is not at a project (for example, the equipment might be idle at the company office), there is an hourly cost associated with the equipment. This is our third difference between labor and equipment; i.e., equipment has an ownership hourly cost and an operating hourly cost.

The hourly cost of owning and operating a piece of construction equipment is as shown below:

Hourly cost = Depreciation + Maintenance + Operating + Repair + Finance + Insurance + Tax + Replacement

A cost that increases as time increases is referred to as a cost that is a function of time; a **fixed** cost. When discussing construction equipment, this type of cost is referred to as an **ownership** cost. On the other hand, a cost that increases as the equipment is used is referred to as a **variable** cost. When discussing construction equipment, this type of cost is referred to as an **operating** cost.

A description of each of the above hourly equipment cost components as to type and whether they are a function of time (ownership) or use (operating) is shown in Figure 5-6. Normally, the ownership cost components of a piece of equipment are in the range of 20% to 30% of the total cost.

The knowledge regarding a piece of equipment's ownership and operating cost are relevant to the following issues or decisions that a supervisor may have to make.

- Decisions to work overtime
- Issues as to when equipment should be kept or replaced
- Keeping equipment at a jobsite versus releasing it
- Change order costing

The hourly cost of a piece of equipment includes both an
- Ownership cost and an
- Operating cost

The hourly cost of using a piece of construction equipment includes the following:
- Depreciation
- Maintenance
- Operating
- Repair
- Finance
- Insurance
- Tax
- Replacement

Type of cost	Description	Function of use (operating cost) or a function of time (ownership cost)
Depreciation	The initial purchase cost has to be recovered through depreciation; equipment likely depreciates as a function of time and use (maybe 50% each).	Part Operating (use); Part Ownership (time)
Maintenance	Things like hoses, small repairs	Operating (use)
Operating	Fuel, oil	Operating (use)
Repair	Major expenditures; e.g., undercarriage of a machine	Operating (use)
Finance	Money either has to be borrowed to finance or taken out of investments.	Ownership (time)
Insurance	A small cost component but the contractor would likely carry insurance on a piece of expensive equipment.	Ownership (time)
Tax	Some states have a property tax on equipment.	Ownership (time)
Replacement	Equipment costs continue to increase. The hourly rate should include an inflation rate to replace the equipment.	Ownership (time)

Fig. 5-6

SESSION 5

EQUIPMENT MANAGEMENT FOR PRODUCTIVITY IMPROVEMENT

Exercise

Pricing Change Orders

Assume you are the supervisor on a bridge project that has a planned duration of 200 days. While constructing the piers of the bridge, your firm ran into unknown site conditions, rock dikes that were not shown on the drawings. Because of the need to stop bridgework and excavate the added work, the project was projected to take an extra 20 days.

- Owing to the unknown site conditions, the project owner agreed to issue you a change order to dig out the rock dikes. However, one of the pieces of equipment you used to the perform the work was idle on the river dock awaiting future work on the bridge. Your company provided you the following information regarding the cost of the equipment:

    Depreciation hourly cost = $40 (50% a function of time, 50% a function of use)

    Maintenance hourly cost = $10

    Operating hourly cost = $8

    Repair hourly cost = $13

    Finance hourly cost = $8

    Insurance hourly cost = $2

    Replacement hourly cost = $6

The equipment was used for 100 hours doing work on the rock dike removal. The owner indicated that it was not responsible for paying any cost reimbursement to you for the equipment because it was at the project anyway. Calculate and discuss what amount of money you believe the project owner should reimburse you for the equipment use (minimum and ideal).

Exercise continues on page 5-23

- Owing to the delay to do the extra work, you had to stop bridge-work for 30 days. Because of this, one of your pieces of equipment used to construct the bridge had to be moved and stored. As a result, the equipment was at the project 30 extra days. The hourly cost for the equipment, as calculated by your firm, is as follows:

  Depreciation hourly cost = $60 (50% a function of time, 50% a function of use)

  Maintenance hourly cost = $20

  Operating hourly cost = $8

  Repair hourly cost = $15

  Finance hourly cost = $12

  Insurance hourly cost = $2

  Replacement hourly cost = $8

  Even though you did not do any added work with the equipment than was planned, your boss has indicated you should put together a change order for the extra time the equipment was at the project. Quantify the amount of the request and indicate your justification for the request.

A Ten-Step Program for Equipment Productivity Improvement

#10 Modeling Equipment Production: Two Interdependent Pieces of Equipment Working Together

> Many construction activities require two or more types of construction equipment that are interdependent on one another.

Many construction activities require two or more types of construction equipment that are interdependent on one another. For example, a bulldozer may be used in a borrow pit to help several scrapers load dirt. The scrapers, lacking adequate horsepower, may need a push to load themselves to capacity. Similarly, several trucks may be used to bring dry-batch concrete mix to a single paving machine that is being used to mix and place concrete for a roadway. In both of these construction operations, work cannot be performed unless both types of equipment are used together. If one of the two types of equipment fails to perform its function, the other piece of equipment cannot work. One piece of equipment is dependent upon the other.

The supervisory issue in this interdependent production process concerns the need to balance the two or more types of equipment. Consider our scraper example: one bulldozer is being used to push several scrapers that are moving soil from a borrow pit to a distant location. On the one hand, if too many scrapers are used, they will stand in line, in a non-productive state, waiting to be serviced by the bulldozer. On the other hand, if too few scrapers are used, the bulldozer waits idly in the borrow pit for a scraper to push. The issue of how many scrapers should be used is complicated by the fact that the hourly cost of the scrapers is likely different from that of the bulldozer. Therefore, it is more expensive to have one waiting for the other.

The problem of having two interdependent pieces of equipment working together can be modeled or studied by what is referred to as a queuing or waiting line problem. It is shown in Figure 5-7.

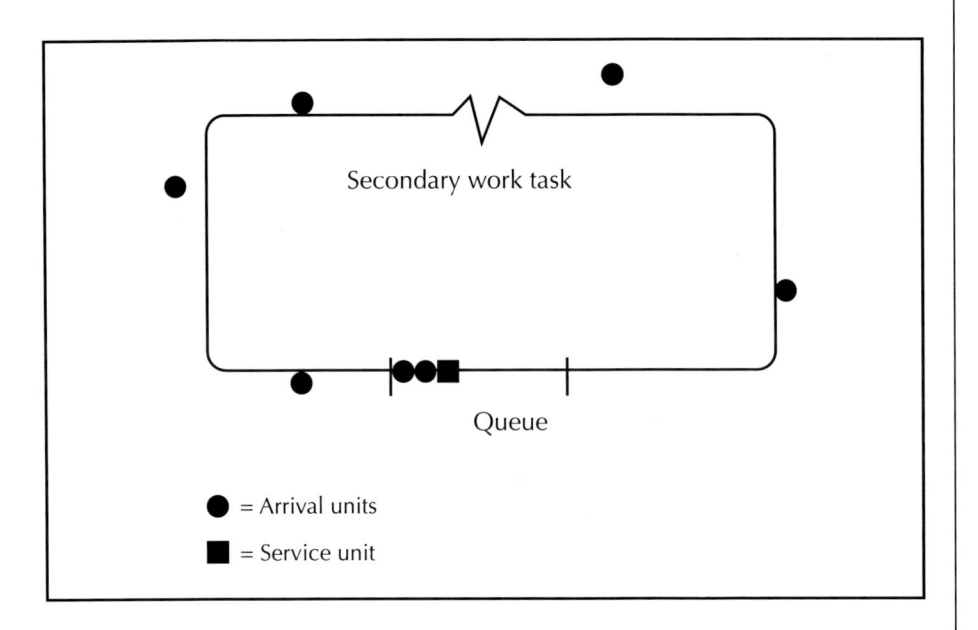

```
┌─────────────────────────────────────────┐
│              ●      ╱╲     ●            │
│           ┌─────────╱──╲──────────┐     │
│           │                       │     │
│        ●  │   Secondary work task │     │
│           │                       │     │
│           │                       │  ●  │
│           │                       │     │
│           │     ┃●●■    ┃         │     │
│        ●  └─────┸───────┸─────────┘     │
│                   Queue                 │
│                                         │
│      ● = Arrival units                  │
│      ■ = Service unit                   │
└─────────────────────────────────────────┘
```

Fig. 5-7

The model shown above shows one service unit and a finite number of what are referred to as "arrival" units. To illustrate why the supervisor must be attentive to this interdependent resource model when planning or monitoring equipment productivity, let us consider the following example:

- Work method: Performing excavation work with an excavator that loads trucks which haul the excavation offsite to a dump area.
- Number of excavators: One
- Number of trucks: To be determined
- Each truck is loaded to a capacity of 6.25 cubic yards
- Time to excavate and load a truck = 15 minutes
- Hourly cost of excavator = $160 / hr
- Hourly cost of a single truck = $50 / hr
- Total distance to dump site when truck leaves excavator = 15 miles
- Total distance to return to excavator after truck leaves dump area = 15 miles
- Average speed of truck when traveling to and from dump site = 30 mph
- Time to unload at the dump site = 20 minutes

- Total cubic yards to be excavated and hauled = 10,000 cubic yards (note: for simplicity we will assume no soil shrinkage or swell factors)
- Typical work day = 8 hours

The construction supervisor should recognize this as a production system that utilizes interdependent equipment. Questions include the following:

- How long will the work take?
- What is the cost of the work?
- How many trucks should be used?

To illustrate how the supervisor might and should analyze the equipment production, we will consider the following three approaches:

- Focus only on a single equipment production unit
- Approximate solution of the interdependent equipment system
- Perform an exact solution to the interdependent equipment system

Focus only on a single equipment production unit

Failing to recognize the problem as an interdependent queuing problem, the supervisor might inappropriately look only at the excavator. The excavator can load 6.25 cubic yards of excavation material into a truck in 15 minutes. This is equivalent to 25 cubic yards in an hour.

Many cost books (for example, R.S. Means Cost books) publish production rates for various equipment tasks such as the one described. Production rates in a cost book for various types of equipment are shown in the following table:

Equipment Type	Hours/CY	CY Per Hour
½ cubic yard excavator	0.067	15
1 cubic yard excavator	0.044	23
½ cubic yard shovel	0.036	28
1 cubic yard shovel	0.017	59

Assume that this is how the supervisor and the construction firm determined that the excavator could excavate and load 25 cubic yards per hour. Focusing only on the production rate of the excavator and the fact that the excavator can load a truck in 15 minutes, the supervisor decides on four trucks to keep up with the excavator.

Accordingly, the supervisor calculates the duration, cost and number of trucks as follows:

Duration:

Production per day based on excavator = (25 cy/hr) times (8 hrs) = 200 cy

Total work to perform = 10,000 cy

Total days required = (10,000 cy) / (200 cy/day) = 50 days

Cost:

Cost per hour:

Excavator	= $160
Trucks 4@ $50 each	= $200
Total cost per hour	= $360
Cost per day = ($360/hr) x (8hrs)	= $2,880
Total Cost = ($2,880) x (50 days)	= $144,000

Number of trucks:

4 to balance the 15-minute load rate of the excavator

This plan, derived by focusing only on the excavator, is quick but it is shortsighted and incorrect. For one, the analysis has overlooked the relative cost of the two pieces of equipment. More importantly, the analysis has failed to recognize the time it takes a truck to return from the haul and dump site. As will be shown below, a truck cannot make the roundtrip coming back every 45 minutes; the time that would be necessary to keep the excavator at a production rate of 25 cubic yards an hour if four trucks are used.

Approximate solution of the interdependent equipment system

The above analysis has successfully recognized the interdependent aspect of the excavator and the haul trucks.

Any one truck takes a minimum of 80 minutes to make a cycle. This is calculated as follows:

Travel to load dump site = (15 miles) times (30 mph)	= 30 minutes
Time to dump at dump site	= 20 minutes
Travel to excavator = (15 miles) times (30 mph)	= 30 minutes
TOTAL	= 80 minutes

It also takes 15 minutes for a truck to be loaded by the excavator. So, at a minimum, it takes a truck 95 minutes to make the cycle. The supervisor has two choices; either have more than two trucks, or plan on having the excavator be idle part of the time, waiting for trucks.

Let us assume only four trucks are in fact available. If this is the case, the trucks, not the excavator, will dictate the hourly production rate.

Accordingly the supervisor calculates the duration, cost and number of trucks as follows:

Duration:

Each truck can make a cycle every 95 minutes or 0.6316 trips per hour

Work for each truck / hour = (0.6316 trips/hr)(6.25 cy/trip = 3.95 cy/hr.

Production per hour for four trucks = (3.95 cy/hr) x (4 trucks) = 15.8 cy

Production per day for four trucks = (15.8 cy/hr) x (8 hrs) = 126.3 cy

Days required = (10,000 cy) / (126.3 cy/day) = 79.2 days

Cost:

Cost per day (see calculations above) = $2,880

Total Cost = ($2,880/day) x (79.2 days) = $228,096

Number of Trucks:

Set as 4

Given the time it takes trucks to make a cycle, the excavator will be idle on occasion. An estimate of the time the excavator will be idle can be calculated by taking the production per hour of 15.8 cy per hour, and dividing by the production rate that the excavator could produce if kept busy (20 cy per hr). This indicates that the excavator will be idle waiting for a truck 21% of the time.

The above calculations represent a more correct analysis of the actual production that will be achieved from the interdependent equipment system. However, it is also flawed. The issue about ignoring the relative cost of the excavator and the trucks is admittedly a moot point given the fact that the supervisor had no choice but to select the four trucks.

However, the analysis has failed to recognize that the trucks will not stay in an exact pattern. The 80-minute truck travel time is an average; sometimes a truck may arrive sooner, sometimes later. In addition, the excavator will not always take exactly 15 minutes; it, too, is an average.

Exact solution to the interdependent equipment system

Equipment production, like labor, is not always the same. The travel time of the trucks (referred to as arrival units) and the loading time of the excavator (referred to as the service unit) will vary from cycle to cycle. Both the service rate of the excavator and the arrival rate of a truck are subject to fluctuation. In mathematical terms the service rate and arrival rates are referred to as being probabilistic.

Given a varying or probabilistic service rate and arrival rates for the trucks, the production system is destined to get out of sync. The location where the excavator and trucks connect to perform work is referred to as the queue. Ideally one truck would be in the queue or waiting to be loaded at all times. However, given a varying service rate and arrival rate, occasionally the line length of trucks in the queue will be longer than one. The end result is that the amount of time the excavator will be idle will be greater than the 21% calculated in the approximate solution shown above.

Mathematically there is an exact solution to the calculation of the production process that has a varying service rate and arrival unit rates.

The equation is as follows:

$$W = (T)(\mu)(L)(1-P(0))$$

Where:

- W = the work performed in the time period t
- T = the time period considered; e.g., 1 hr.
- μ = Service rate expressed in average services per hour
- L = Work performed each service
- P(0) = Probability that no arrival rates are in queue

In our example, the service rate U is 4 services per hour in that the excavator can service 4 trucks in a given hour. The variable L is equal to 6.25 cubic yards per service.

The term 1 minus P(0) in effect calculates the percentage of time an arrival rate is in fact in the queue. As long as there is at least one truck in the queue, the service unit (the excavator) can perform production.

We will not solve or give the equation for P(0) here in that the solution and equation are fairly complex and is doubtful if the supervisor will remember it or use it. However, the value of P(0) and (1 – P(0)); i.e., the probability that an arrival unit is waiting at the queue and available to be loaded, can be approximated using a chart such as that shown in Figure 5-8.

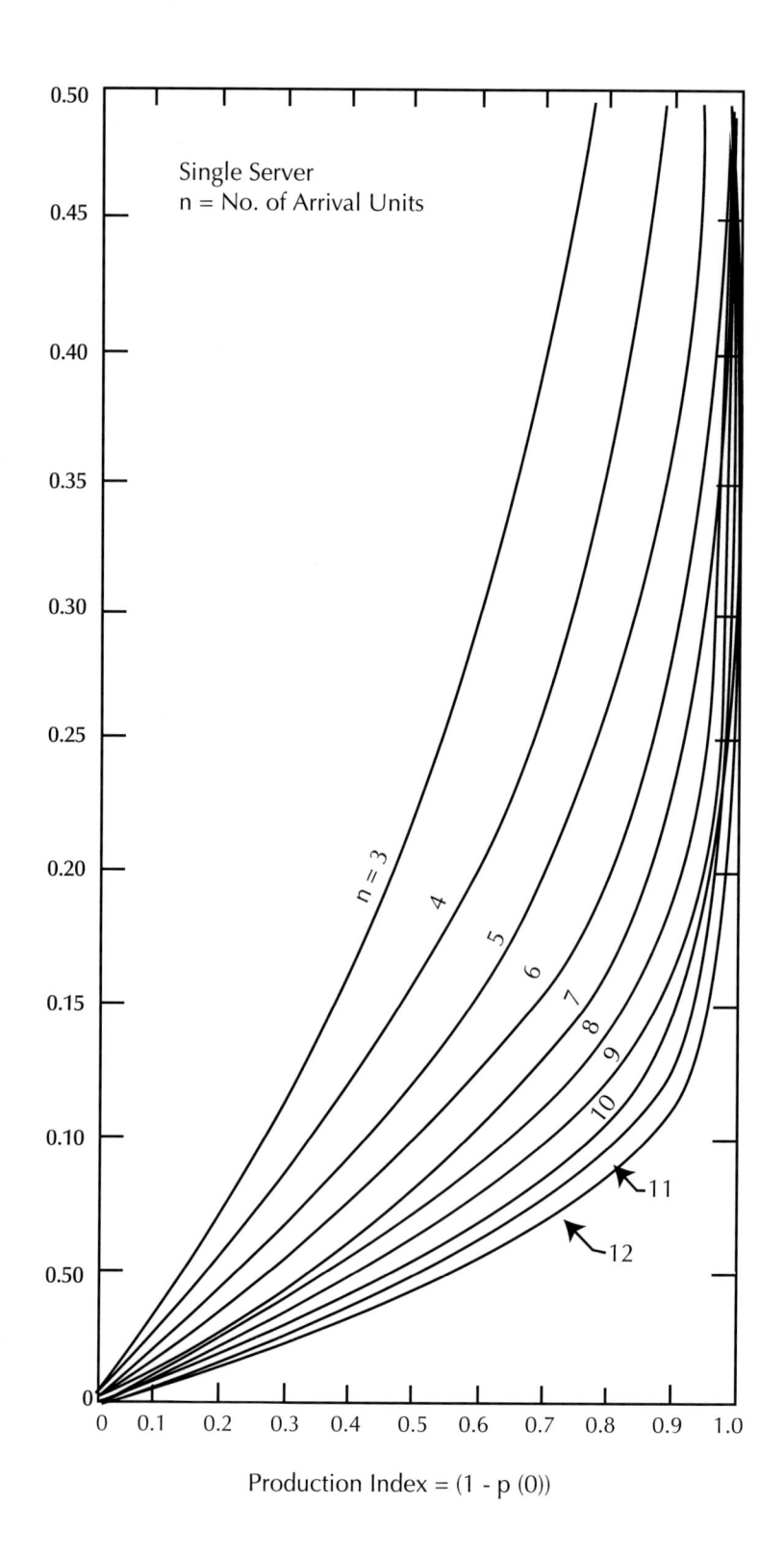

Fig. 5-8

In the example being discussed, given the values for $\lambda = 75$, $\mu = 4$, and $n = 4$; an exact solution will yield the following value for P(0) and (1-P(0))

P(0) = 0.43

1-P(0) = 0.57

The use of the chart shown in Figure 5-8 probably will not enable the user to determine the exact value of P(0) or (1-(P0)); however, it will be close.

Given the value of P(0) shown above, the work (W) that will be produced per hour is calculated as follows:

W = (1 hr) x (4 services/hr) x (6.25 cy/service) (0.57) = 14.25 cy/hr

Whereas the approximate solution yielded a production rate of 15.8 cy per hour, the exact solution is 14.25 cy per hour. This reduced exact production rate reflects the fact that on occasion more than one truck will be in line to be serviced, and at other times no trucks will be at the excavator.

Accordingly the supervisor calculates the duration, cost and number of trucks as follows:

Duration:

Production per hour for the system = 14.25 cy/hour

Production per day for system = (14.25 cy/hr) (8 hrs) = 114 cy/day

Days required = (10,000 cy) / (114 cy/day) = 87.7 days

Cost:

Cost per day (see calculations above) = $2,880

Total Cost = ($2,880/day) x (87.7 days) = $252,576

Number of Trucks:

Set as 4

The difference between the exact solution of 14.25 cubic yards per hour and the 15.8 cubic yards per hour may not seem significant. But consider the ramifications if the project is subject to a liquidated damage clause that assesses the supervisor and the construction firm a $10,000 penalty if the work is completed in a time period greater than 80 days. Having done the approximate solution that yielded a duration of 79+ days, the supervisor might be content to use the four trucks. However, the fact is that the work will take 87+ days if four trucks are used. The result will be that seven days of liquidated damages of $70,000 will be assessed. If the supervisor had known the correct production using the exact solution, the supervisor might have been able to secure more trucks to speed up the operation.

Independent of the above calculations, the supervisor should also recognize the competing objectives of time and cost. If work duration is the only concern, than clearly more trucks should be added to the production process described. Adding more trucks will reduce the time the excavator is idle waiting for a truck.

On the other hand, if the objective is to minimize the cost of doing the work, then the supervisor needs to consider the cost of the excavator relative to the cost of the trucks. For example, if the excavator has a very high hourly rate relative to the hourly rate of trucks, then it may be advantageous to have too many trucks, even if occasionally there is a long line of trucks waiting to be loaded. Given the high cost of the excavator per hour, the emphasis should be on keeping the excavator busy.

Calculating the Lowest Cost Work Method

1. Using the graph from this section that enables you to calculate the probability that no trucks (arrival units) are in the queue to be loaded by the excavator (service unit), approximate the values of the probability that no truck is in the queue [P(0)] for the excavation problem described in this section if five (5) trucks were used. The service rate was 4, and the arrival rate was 0.75.

2. For the excavation problem described in this section, assume the following values for the probability of no trucks in the queue [P(0)] for the following number of trucks:

    3 trucks: P(0) = 0.55
    4 trucks: P(0) = 0.43
    5 trucks: P(0) = 0.31

    Using the excavator and truck costs given in the example, and assuming that there is a $500 per day penalty for completing the project in more than 80 days, calculate the total cost if 3, 4 or 5 trucks are used. Determine the lowest cost method.

Session 5 Review

Look back over Session 5 and review these key points to be sure you understand them.

How to implement a ten-step program of improving equipment productivity.

1. View equipment as money, not just as machinery or metal.
2. Plan the logistics of equipment.
3. Adequately staff equipment with needed labor support.
4. Be attentive to the work capacity of a machine.
5. Be attentive to the percentage of time equipment is working versus being idle or in a "support" state.
6. Be attentive to scheduling work tasks around equipment availability.
7. Be attentive to proper equipment maintenance.
8. Always be attentive to working safely with equipment.
9. Remember that equipment has an ownership cost component and an operating cost component.
10. Be prepared to model or consider the interrelationship of two or more pieces of equipment working together

Using on the Job What You Learned Today

Jobsite Assignment

While on your projects, focus on a few pieces you are using at the project and a few workers. Using random samples of their work states, calculate the amount of time each worker and each machine is in a non-productive work state. If you don't know what the equipment's hourly cost is (ownership and operating), attempt to determine the hourly cost of each piece of equipment by use of a cost estimating book or from information from individuals who know.

To Get Ready for Session 6

Read the Participant's Manual for Session 6.

Session 6

Productivity Improvement and Planning and Scheduling

Learning Goals for Session 6

After this session, you should learn the following:

- The relationship between productivity and planning and scheduling.
- The preparation and use of a master project plan.
- How to update the master project plan
- The productivity benefits of preparing a one- to four-week look-ahead schedule.
- The productivity benefits of preparing a short interval schedule.
- The productivity benefits of using reminder lists.

The above learning goals all have the focus of reducing non-productive time and improving productivity by having the supervisor prepare and use formalized, on-paper project plans and schedules.

Learning Objectives

To accomplish the learning goals, during this session you will:

- Learn the importance of written plans and schedules
- Recognize the relationship between productivity and project planning and scheduling
- Prepare and use an overall project plan and schedule
- Develop a One- to Four-Week Look-Ahead schedule
- Use a Short Interval Production Schedule Form

To Get Ready for Session 6

Reading: Read the pages in this session. Try to think of ideas on how to motivate the construction team to include the craftsperson and foreman.

Major Activities for Session 6

- Discuss the relationship between productivity and planning and scheduling.
- Do an exercise that quantifies "planned non-productive" time.
- Learn how to prepare and use an overall project plan and schedule.
- Do an exercise in which you use a project plan and schedule to make management decisions.
- Learn how to update a project plan and schedule.
- Do an exercise in which you update a work activity.
- Discuss the benefits of using a One- to Four-Week Look-Ahead Schedule Form.
- Discuss the benefits of using a Short Interval Production Scheduling form.
- Do an exercise in which you will prepare a reminder list for a meeting.

A Review of Session 5

In Session 5, you learned the importance of equipment productivity.

Some of the facts that you learned in Session 5 are:

- Equipment, like onsite labor, is either in a productive state, a non-productive state or a support state.

- Many pieces of construction equipment have a higher hourly rate than that of a worker; equipment has an hourly ownership cost component and an hourly operating cost component.

- There are many factors that need to be considered by the supervisor in keeping equipment productive.

- The queuing or waiting line model can be used to model the production of two pieces of equipment working together.

The Benefits of Planning

"Planning" can be defined as the working out of a course of action that will result in the achievement of a goal or objective. Planning is accomplished by three steps:

1. **Setting a goal.**

   In the case of the construction process, the goal of the construction firm and the construction supervisor should be to complete a project on time, on budget, with high quality and no accidents.

2. **Determining what must be done in order to achieve the goal.**

   In the case of the construction process, this entails setting out the work tasks that must be carried out to complete the project; e.g., excavation work, concrete work, etc.

3. **Determining how you are going to do it.**

   This entails determining the labor, material, equipment, supplies and tools needed and when they will be needed to do the work tasks.

Setting out when specific work tasks need to be performed and what resources are needed when is commonly referred to as **scheduling**. Planning is determining what has to be done; scheduling is determining when it has to be done. However, many people use the terms interchangeably.

The failure to do the three steps of planning usually leads to a process of reacting to problems and non-achievement of the goal. In the case of the construction project, this may mean a project time or cost overrun or the failure to meet quality and safety objectives.

Planning is especially critical to the construction process, which is characterized by many uncertain events and requires the joint efforts of many firms and individuals to complete the project objectives. Uncertain weather, the availability and productivity of onsite workers, uncertain material delivery dates and unpredictable equipment breakdowns can all lead to difficulties in carrying out a plan.

Some would argue that, given the many uncertain events that characterize the construction process, it does not pay to plan; i.e., too many events change every day and make a plan outdated. The fact is that if uncertain events did not occur, there would not be as much reason to plan. It is the plan that enables the development of a strategy to counter the uncertain events. What is needed is an updating of the plan. The more uncertain events a process is subjected to, the greater the need to plan, not the less.

> Planning is determining what has to be done. Scheduling entails determining when it has to be done.

Planning is made more complex in the construction process given the many individuals involved in the execution of a construction plan. This includes personnel from the general contractor, personnel from the subcontractors, various vendors and external agencies. If a project is going to be effective, plans must be shared and complied with during the execution of the plan.

The planning function in the construction process can be viewed as shown in Figure 6-1. The process entails three separate steps:

I. Preparing a preliminary project plan as part of and as a basis of the project estimate and bid.

    If the estimate/bid is successful,

II. Preparation of a detailed master project plan and schedule as part of the pre-planning phase of a project. Preparation of weekly, daily or even hourly production plans for onsite work crews.

then, during construction,

III. Preparation and use of one- to four-week look-ahead schedules, short interval schedules and reminder lists. Updating of the master project plan and the schedule for actual events.

While the construction supervisor should be involved in the preliminary project plan that is part of the estimating process, this preliminary plan is usually thought through or prepared by the project estimator. To a certain degree, even knowing when various work tasks have to be performed is an essential part of determining the cost of the event; for example, doing outdoor work in the dead of winter is likely to cost more than if it is done in ideal weather conditions.

The construction supervisor should be involved in the planning process in the pre-construction phase of the project and during the execution of the construction process. The following sections address these planning functions.

SESSION 6

PRODUCTIVITY IMPROVEMENT AND PLANNING AND SCHEDULING

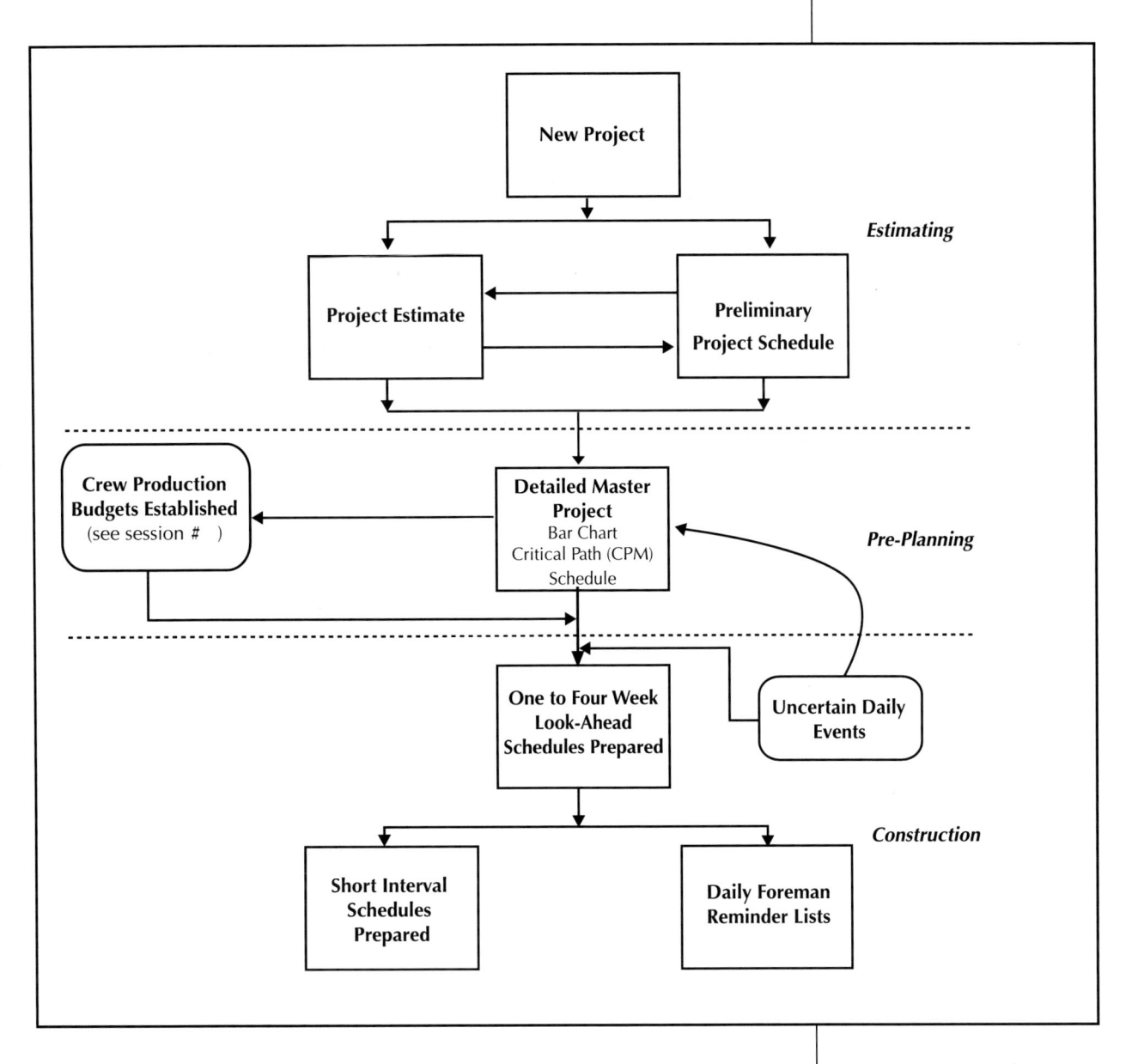

```
                    ┌─────────────┐
                    │ New Project │
                    └──────┬──────┘
              ┌────────────┴────────────┐
              ▼                         ▼                    *Estimating*
      ┌───────────────┐         ┌───────────────┐
      │   Project     │◄────────│  Preliminary  │
      │   Estimate    │────────►│Project Schedule│
      └───────┬───────┘         └───────┬───────┘
              │                         │
─ ─ ─ ─ ─ ─ ─ ┼ ─ ─ ─ ─ ─ ─ ─ ─ ─ ─ ─ ─ ┼ ─ ─ ─ ─ ─ ─ ─ ─ ─
              │                         ▼
  ╭──────────────────╮         ┌──────────────────┐
  │ Crew Production  │         │ Detailed Master  │
  │Budgets Established│◄────── │     Project      │         *Pre-Planning*
  │  (see session # )│         │    Bar Chart     │◄──┐
  ╰──────────┬───────╯         │Critical Path (CPM)│   │
             │                 │     Schedule     │   │
             │                 └────────┬─────────┘   │
─ ─ ─ ─ ─ ─ ─│─ ─ ─ ─ ─ ─ ─ ─ ─ ─ ─ ─ ─ │─ ─ ─ ─ ─ ─ │─ ─
             └────────────────►         ▼             │
                               ┌──────────────────┐   │
                               │  One to Four Week│   │
                               │    Look-Ahead    │◄──┤
                               │Schedules Prepared│  ╭┴──────────╮
                               └────────┬─────────┘  │Uncertain Daily│
                                        │            │   Events     │
                                        │            ╰──────────────╯
                              ┌─────────┴─────────┐                   *Construction*
                              ▼                   ▼
                      ┌───────────────┐   ┌───────────────┐
                      │Short Interval │   │ Daily Foreman │
                      │  Schedules    │   │Reminder Lists │
                      │   Prepared    │   │               │
                      └───────────────┘   └───────────────┘
```

Fig. 6-1

Participant's Manual ■ STP ■ Unit 9   6-5

The Relationship Between Jobsite Productivity and Planning and Scheduling

One of the most important and detrimental reasons for low industry productivity is the lack of project planning and scheduling. Previous sections illustrated the high percentage of jobsite waiting that is characteristic of the construction process. A primary reason for this non-productive time can be traced to the lack of proper project planning. Failure to plan or schedule activities leads to excessive labor and equipment waiting time, delays related to unavailability of materials, lack of subcontractor coordination and management's inability to react to unexpected events such as poor weather, equipment breakdowns or material shortages.

A primary reason for the non-productive time related to waiting can be traced to the lack of proper project planning.

The construction firm would not bid or start a project without first preparing an on-paper, detailed cost estimate and a plan for costs. However, the same firm will often ignore the need to prepare an on-paper plan and schedule. Instead, the firm might argue that a formal plan is subject to too much uncertainty. In reality, the very existence of a plan and schedule can enable a supervisor to effectively react to the many uncertain, unexpected events that characterize the construction process. The more uncertain the production process, the stronger the need to prepare and use a plan and schedule.

The relationship of formal project planning and scheduling and productivity is illustrated in Figures 6-2 and 6-3. Figure 6-2 summarizes the findings of an industrial engineering-based study performed at a project (on a sample day). The figure indicates that direct work was being performed only 42% of the time. Undoubtedly, some projects are much better in regard to this percentage of productive work, but some are worse.

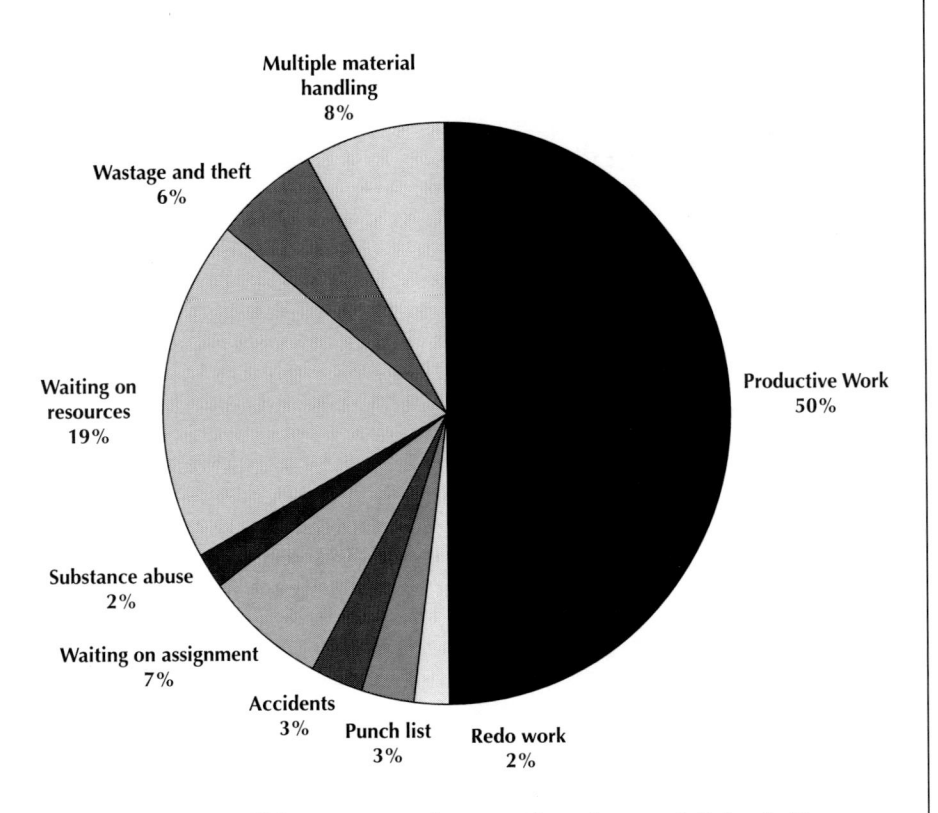

Fig. 6-2. Possible Impact of Poor Planning and Scheduling

- Productive Work 50%
- Waiting on resources 19%
- Multiple material handling 8%
- Waiting on assignment 7%
- Wastage and theft 6%
- Accidents 3%
- Punch list 3%
- Substance abuse 2%
- Redo work 2%

As Figure 6-2 shows, the typical construction project includes a considerable amount of non-productive time waiting; be it waiting for material, waiting for a decision, waiting for another contractor, etc. Formalized planning and scheduling can reduce waiting by setting out materials that need to be ordered and setting out when decisions have to be made so that production can continue, etc.

A plan and schedule that set out material procurement dates will help reduce delays and waiting time associated with material shortages. Similarly, a plan for labor and subcontractor performance can result in a more productive use of available labor crafts and increase subcontractor coordination, attitude and productivity.

Another way of quantifying the relationship of project planning/scheduling and productivity is illustrated in Figure 6-3. This figure plots a bar chart type of schedule for a small project that consists of 10 work activities. Each of these activities requires a finite number of resources if the activity is to be performed effectively. Assume we know optimal crew sizes and have designated the crew size number inside the block beside the activity to which each corresponds, as shown in the figure. We have also plotted the number of laborers needed on any one day; maximum of 13. (The actual number needed on any one day varies significantly from one to the next.)

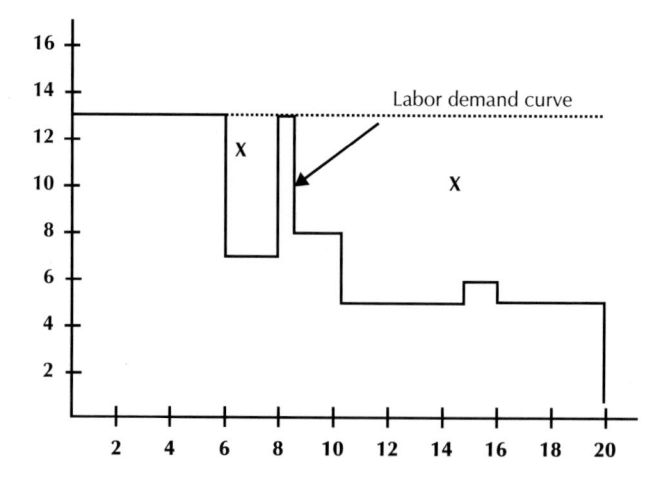

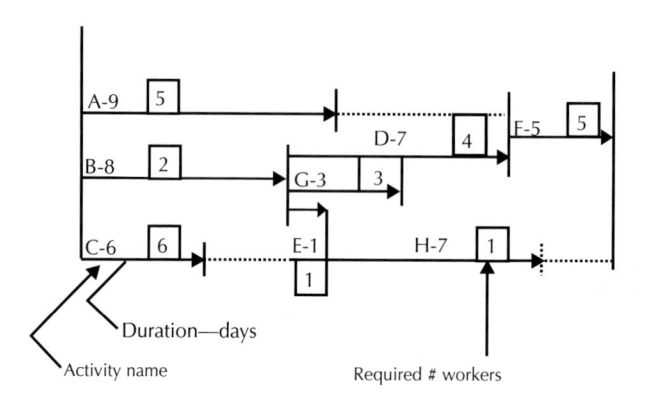

Fig. 6-3

It is unlikely that the supervisor can hire and fire laborers (or any other resource) on a daily basis according to the labor demand curve shown in the figure. Instead, the supervisor probably has a non-optimal number of laborers at the jobsite on any given day. For example, assume that the firm keeps 13 laborers at the site every day for the project's duration. This is illustrated by the horizontal line (solid and dashed) at 13 laborers. The areas marked "X" represent "planned non-productive time" a laborer is actually scheduled to be non-productive.

If a supervisor has 5 person-days of work scheduled on a given day and has 10 workers there to perform the work, the 10 workers will produce 5 person-days of work; that is, they will be 50% productive. The challenge of the planning and scheduling effort thus becomes evident. The supervisor must attempt to schedule workers to match the demand and availability of workers on a daily basis.

Planned Non-Productive Time

Shown below is a project plan and schedule for a small construction project. The graph illustrates the demand curve for labor based on the resource requirements for each work activity. Assume the construction supervisor hires ten workers for the project and keeps them at the project for the duration.

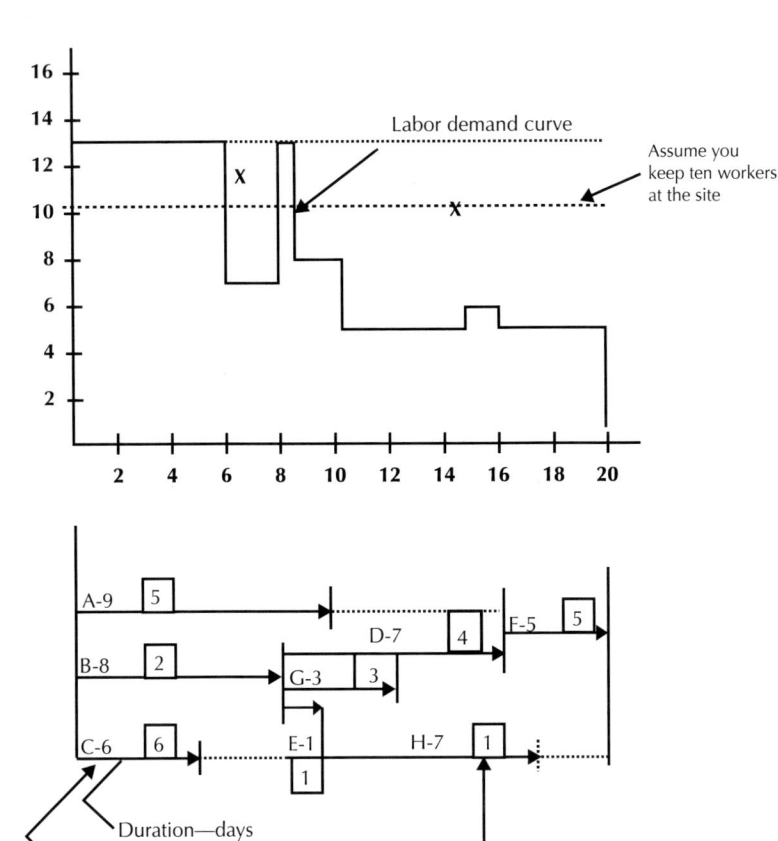

1. Assume that an average worker's wage rate is $25.00 per hour and that he or she works eight hours a day. Calculate the non-productive labor cost scheduled into the project (because on some days more workers are present than are needed).

2. A review of the schedule above indicates that on some days, the supervisor will have fewer workers available than needed. What will be the effect of this understaffing in regard to productivity?

3. The above example illustrates a one-trade project (only laborers required). If more trades are required on the project, will the "planned non-productive time" for workers increase or decrease? Why?

Preparation and Use of the Overall Project Plan and Schedule

The Benefits of a Formalized On-Paper Project Plan and Schedule

Constructing a construction project without a formalized on-paper plan and schedule is comparable to driving a vehicle to a new destination without a road map. If you drive from Illinois to California without a road map, and are persistent, you will eventually get to California. However, there is little question that it will take you more time and money and you will have a more frustrating trip than if you had taken a roadmap. Note that a roadmap by itself will not get you from Illinois to California. You still need to know how to drive the vehicle and how to read and interpret the road map; i.e., you need experience. However, one without the other (experience and using a management tool like a road map) will result in an inefficient process.

The same argument can be set forth for the construction of a project. If you construct a project without using an on-paper plan and schedule, you will eventually complete the project; but it will take more time, incur more cost and result in more frustration and arguments than if you had used an overall project plan and schedule.

> A master project plan and schedule provides the supervisor a management technique for constructing a project more efficiently.

A master project plan and schedule provides the supervisor a management technique for constructing a project more efficiently. In addition, the project plan and schedule should be a means of integrating all the entities of a project for the team: the project manager, superintendent, foremen and subcontractors.

Steps in Preparing and Using a Formalized Project Plan and Schedule

Today several computer software programs are available to help the construction firm and supervisor prepare, print and use a project plan and schedule. Nonetheless, it is still critical that the supervisor understand the process of preparing a plan and schedule, independent of the use of a computer or software program. For one, the computerized schedule is only as good as the data the constructor inputs into the computer. More importantly, to be able to effectively utilize an overall project plan and schedule, the supervisor needs to know the process of preparing a project plan and schedule, using them to manage resources and productivity. He or she should also know how to update the schedule. This process is outlined in Figure 6-4.

> The computerized schedule is only as good as the data the constructor inputs into the computer.

PRODUCTIVITY IMPROVEMENT AND PLANNING AND SCHEDULING

Step 1: Defining Work Activities

⬇

Step 2: Determining Activity Durations

⬇

Step 3: Determining Activity Sequencing or Logic

⬇

Step 4: Adjusting Activity Durations for Contingencies

⬇

Step 5: Obtaining Subcontractor Input

⬇

Step 6: Drawing the Overall Project Schedule

⬇

Step 7: Performing CPM Calculations

⬇

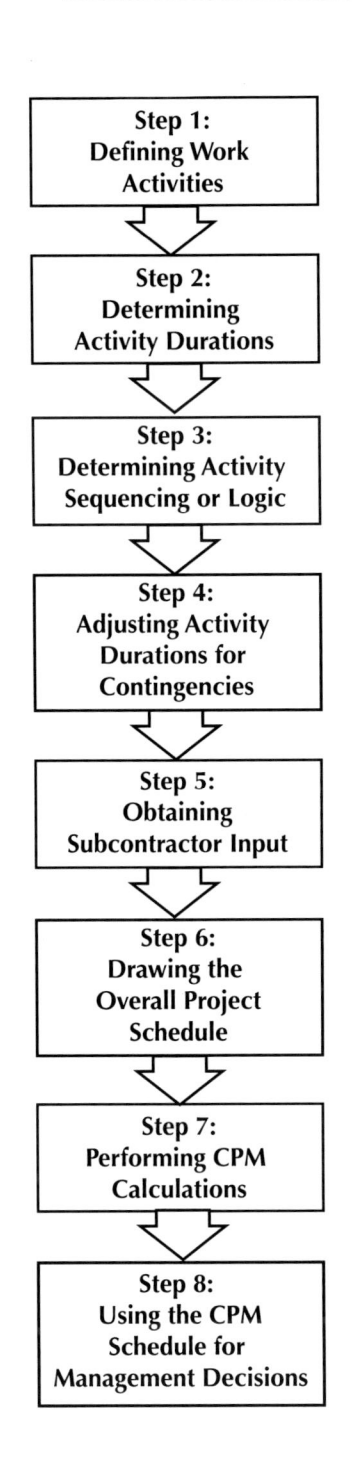

Step 8: Using the CPM Schedule for Management Decisions

Fig. 6-4

Step 1: Defining Work Activities

The first step in preparing a formal master plan for a project is to define the project work pieces or activities. For example, should "form concrete slab," "place rebar in the slab," and "pour concrete in the slab" be defined as three activities, or should one activity, "place slabs," be defined as the activity? At what level of detail should activities be defined? This is a more critical issue than one might at first think. Too detailed a list of activities will frustrate jobsite personnel, whereas too few activities will result in schedules of little benefit as a productivity or control tool. This much can be said: a broader list of activities needs to be defined for a milestone or conceptual schedule than for the detailed schedule that will be used at the jobsite.

While it is impossible to set out a specific "best" list of activities for each project, the following criteria should be considered:

- The activities should be compatible with the intended purpose and use of the schedule.

- To the degree feasible, the activities should be compatible with the estimate breakdown.

- The activities should be compatible with field reporting for cost control.

- The activities should be compatible with the firm's billing system and progress pay requests.

- Any work function that requires a unique set of resources should be defined as a unique work activity.

More often than not, the use of these criteria will result in the constructor defining between thirty and a hundred work activities for the detailed schedule. The actual number will depend on the project size and work complexity, and on the supervisor's ability to revise the schedule periodically.

The first step in preparing the project plan and schedule is to define the list of work activities. The question is how detailed the list of work activities should be.

Step 2: Determining Activity Durations

The duration of every activity should be determined on the basis of the quantity of work, the crew to be assigned to the work activity and the estimate of the crew's productivity. Like cost estimating, determining activity durations is subject to uncertainty and contains a degree of risk.

What follows is one example of determining activity duration. In this instance, the activity is erecting forms.

> Step 1: Determine quantity of work   8,000 sfca
>
> Step 2: Estimate productivity   10 mh/100 sfca
>
> Step 3: Establish crew size   5 workers
>
> Step 4: Calculate duration:
>
> $$\frac{(10mh)(8{,}000\ sfca)}{(100\ sfca)(5\ mh/r)(8\ hr/day)} \quad 20\ days$$

The above calculation needs to be performed for each work activity for the project schedule. If an activity is to be subcontracted, the duration should be estimated or determined from the subcontractor input.

Activity durations should be determined by considering the following information:
- *Quantity of work*
- *Productivity of a worker*
- *Crew size*

Step 3: Determining Activity Sequencing or Logic

Project work activities must be sequenced to reflect the actual planned progress of the project. This sequencing reflects the technology of construction; it is technically impossible to do certain construction operations or activities until certain other tasks are performed. If a project plan and schedule are to be properly prepared, they must reflect three types of logic sequencing.

- Technical logic (based on the technology of construction)
- Resource logic (based on availability of resources)
- Preference logic (which recognizes project economics)

Resource logic addresses the fact that, although it may be possible to perform two work activities at the same time (such as forming the north and east slabs), because of limited resources (say, carpenters) it may not be possible to undertake the two activities together. Preference logic addresses the fact that despite technical ability and the availability of resources, the supervisor may decide for economic reasons to do one activity after another.

Three types of logic should be considered when determining work activity sequencing:
- *Technical logic*
- *Resource logic*
- *Preference logic*

Step 4: Adjusting Activity Durations for Contingencies

In an environment of uncertainty (such as poor weather, material shortages, or equipment breakdowns), it is unrealistic for a contractor to plan for ideal activity durations. Once the activity sequencing is determined and the project plan is sketched, the preparer of the detailed plan and schedule may decide that it is necessary to make some activity duration adjustments. For example, the initial sketch may indicate that certain concrete work will be performed during months when several rainy days are expected. Seeing this, the preparer may want to add a day or two to the duration of the concrete work to reflect the possibility of rain. A plan that does not include such contingencies is unrealistic and misleading, and may prove detrimental to sound management decisions.

Step 5: Obtaining Subcontractor Input

Construction of a project entails the coordination of many interdependent contractors. The construction supervisor must obtain timely and accurate subcontractor information, including input from specialty contractors. On occasion, this becomes a difficult task. The best way to obtain subcontractor schedule input may be to require it contractually. If subcontractors fail to cooperate, they can be penalized: the retainer can be held or they can simply not be rehired.

The construction supervisor should take a positive role in obtaining subcontractor input. Showing subcontractors how their timely and accurate schedule information has prevented problems or increased productivity will help encourage the subcontractors' cooperation. (This approach is taken in Session 7.)

Step 6: Drawing the Project Schedule

Once activities have been defined, durations determined and the sequencing of the activities determined, the project plan can be drawn. This can be done using a bar graph or a CPM diagram. Figure 6-5 is a sample bar graph for a small project.

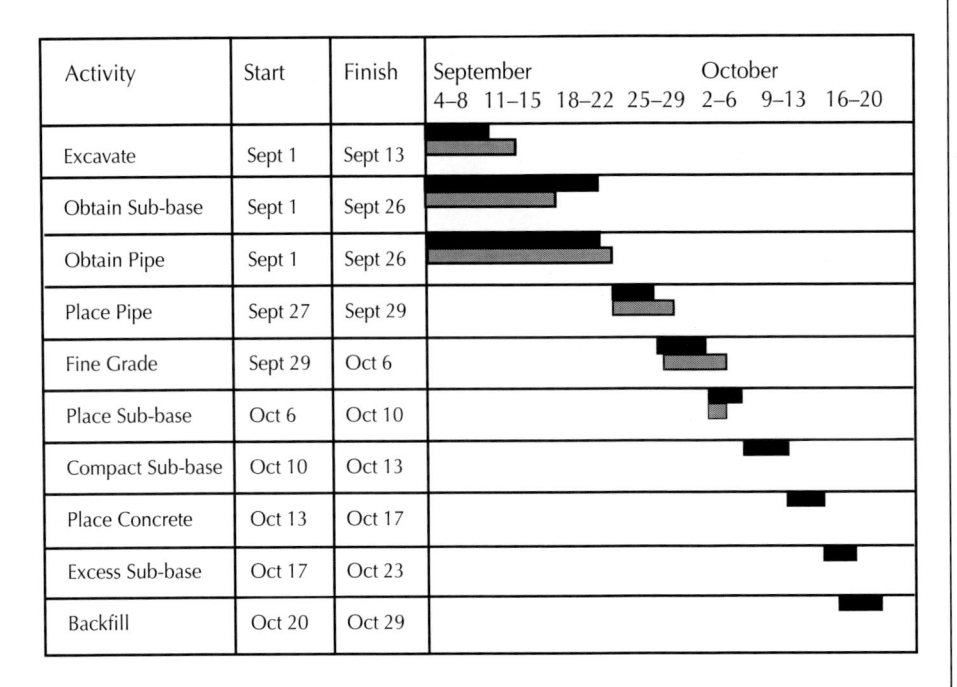

Activity	Start	Finish	September 4–8 11–15 18–22 25–29	October 2–6 9–13 16–20
Excavate	Sept 1	Sept 13	▬▬	
Obtain Sub-base	Sept 1	Sept 26	▬▬▬▬	
Obtain Pipe	Sept 1	Sept 26	▬▬▬▬	
Place Pipe	Sept 27	Sept 29	▬	
Fine Grade	Sept 29	Oct 6	▬▬	
Place Sub-base	Oct 6	Oct 10		▬
Compact Sub-base	Oct 10	Oct 13		▬
Place Concrete	Oct 13	Oct 17		▬
Excess Sub-base	Oct 17	Oct 23		▬
Backfill	Oct 20	Oct 29		▬

Fig. 6-5. Example of a "Simple" Project Plan

The bar chart presents a good visual tool of the breakdown of the work activities and the sequencing between the activities.

The activities are shown as bars; the beginning of the bar designates the start of the activity and the end of the bar shows the planned completion of the activity. The actual progress of the project is often superimposed on the bar chart alongside the planned progress.

A bar chart such as the one illustrated in Figure 6-5 can be an effective tool for communicating the project activity breakdown and illustrating the sequencing of the work activities. However, for more complex projects, the bar chart does not clearly set out the criticality of various work activities and does not set out how much "float" time or available slack time there is for each work activity. This is why more supervisors prefer the use of critical path method (CPM) for managing the overall project plan and schedule.

There are several different formats in which to draw the CPM diagram, three of which are shown in Figures 6-6, 6-7 and 6-8. The first diagram, Figure 6-6, uses arrows to represent work activities. Specific planned milestone dates can be set in the circles at the end of the arrows. These milestone dates can be interim progress dates specified by contract or by the project planner.

CPM diagrams are drawn using either arrow notation diagrams or using circle diagrams, which are commonly referred to as precedence diagrams.

Arrow notation diagram

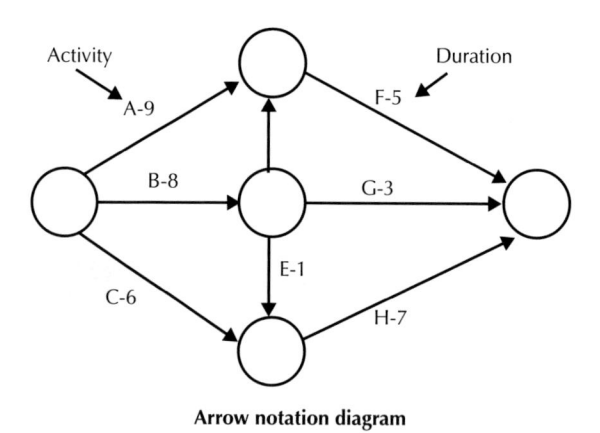

Fig. 6-6. Arrow Notation CPM

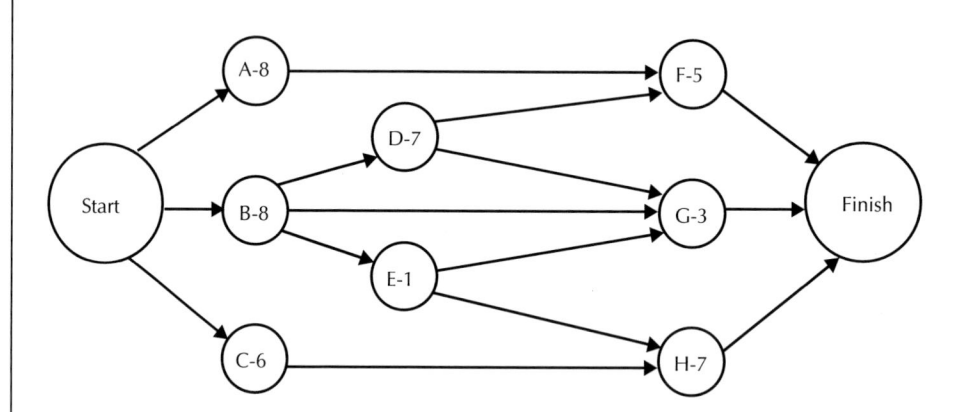

Circle notation diagram–Precedence diagram

Fig. 6-7. Circle Notation CPM

The alternative CPM shown in Figure 6-7 is commonly referred to as a circle notation CPM diagram or a precedence diagram. In Figure 6-7, work activities are represented by individual circles. The arrows between the circles are used to specify the sequencing or logic of the activities.

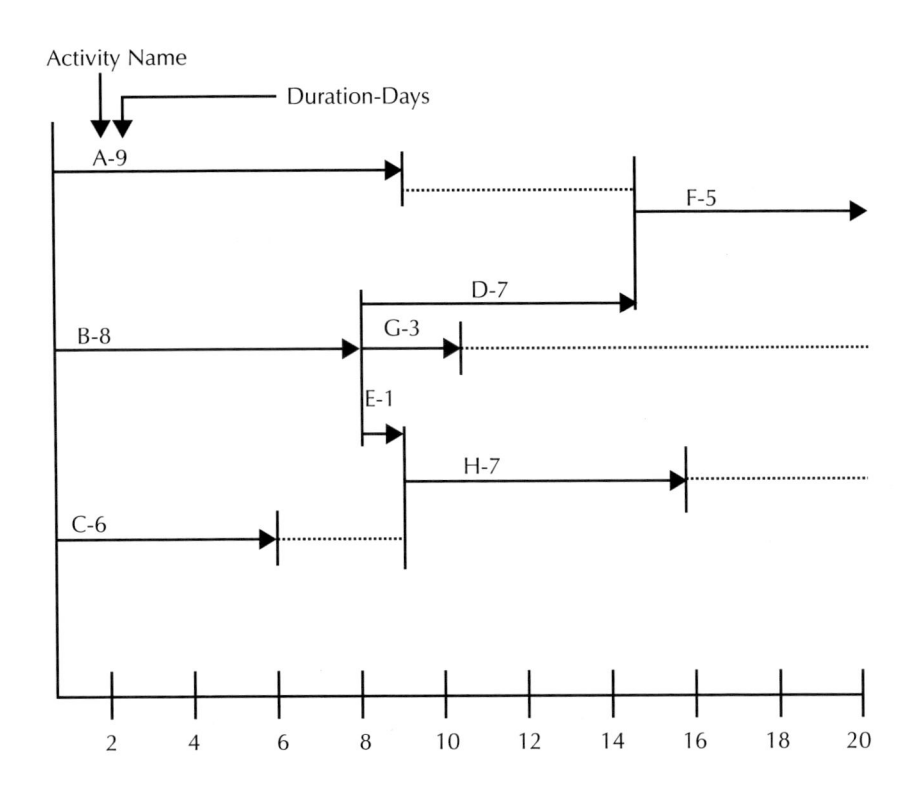

PRODUCTIVITY IMPROVEMENT AND PLANNING AND SCHEDULING

Fig. 6-8. Time Scale CPM

In the third alternative CPM diagram shown in Figure 5-8, the individual activity arrows are proportional in length to the activity durations. This CPM diagram, perhaps the most useful as a visual tool, is commonly referred to as a time scale CPM diagram. The dashed lines following the activity arrows represent activity "float" or slack times during which a manager can react to uncertain events. An explanation of the calculation of activity float or slack time follows.

There are thus several different means by which the supervisor may draw the overall project plan and schedule. Whatever way is chosen, it is important that the plan and schedule be drawn in a manner that is easily understood by field personnel.

Step 7: Performing CPM Calculations

There are several widely used computer programs available that perform CPM calculations. No matter which program is used, the objective of the calculations is to determine the following information for work activity:

- Minimum project duration
- Critical activities and the overall critical path (i.e., this is the list of activities that form a path through the project network that determine the project duration)

CPM calculations yield the following information:
- Minimum project duration
- Critical activities and the overall critical path
- Float or slack time for all the work activities

In addition the CPM calculations yield the following information for each work activity:

- Earliest start time for an activity (EST)
- Earliest finish time for an activity (EFT)
- Latest start time for an activity (LST)
- Latest finish time for an activity (LFT)

The EST for an activity is defined as the earliest possible time at which the activity can start. The EFT of an activity is defined and calculated as an activity's earliest start time plus the activity's duration.

The LFT of an activity is defined as the latest possible time at which an activity can finish without delaying the predetermined project completion date. The LST of an activity is the activity's LFT minus the activity's duration.

The total float for an activity is defined as the activity's latest finish time minus its earliest finish time, or an activity's latest start time minus its earliest start time. In effect, the total float for an activity gives the supervisor a measure of the amount of time an activity can be delayed without extending the minimum project duration.

The EST, EFT, LST, LFT and total float (TF) for each of the activities shown in Figures 6-5, 6-6 and 6-7 are shown in Figure 6-9. The construction supervisor will likely get a computer printout in such a format. The EST, EFT, LST, LFT and TFs may be stated in work days, as shown in Figure 6-9, or may be printed as calendar dates.

Activity	Duration	EST	EFT	LST	LFT	TF
A	9	0	9	6	15	6
B	8	0	8	0	8	0
C	6	0	6	7	13	7
D	7	8	15	8	15	0
E	1	8	9	12	13	4
F	5	15	20	15	20	0
G	3	8	11	17	20	9
H	7	9	16	13	20	4

Fig. 6-9. CPM Calculation

The project duration is equal to the largest EFT in the computer printout shown in Figure 6-9. Similarly, the critical path work activities are the work activities with the least amount of total float; i.e., work activities B, D and F.

Step 8: Using the CPM Schedule for Management Decisions

The CPM process can yield benefits over and above the three basic objectives of establishing the latest project completion date, the critical path and the float or slack times for all activities. Cash management, good billing and pay request procedures and proper allocation of resources are all benefits. Perhaps the most significant benefit relates to using the overall project plan and schedule to make management decisions to improve construction productivity.

Consider the CPM diagram shown in Figure 6-8. It is a time scale schedule for the arrow notation CPM diagram in Figure 6-6 and 6-7. Suppose it rains heavily on days 2 and 3 and that activities A, B and C cannot proceed if it rains. Assume further that in preparing the construction plan and schedule, the construction planner did not anticipate rain. The obvious question is whether the project will take more than 20 days or units of time. At first glance, it may seem so, because activity B, which is on the critical path, has been delayed 2 days. However, activities A and C have total float times of 6 and 4 days, respectively. Therefore, it may be possible to take resources from these two activities on days 4, 5 and 6 if necessary and assign them to activity B to enable it to "catch up" to its original 8-day duration and maintain a 20-day schedule.

This example is a simple but practical application of the CPM technique. Other practical applications of float times include using them to prepare a schedule that better utilizes resources from the point of view of productivity. Figure 6-10 adds a resource requirement (number of laborers required) to each of the activities in Figures 6-6 through 6-8 and also shows the number of laborers needed on any one day to complete the schedule as shown (the earliest-start-time schedule).

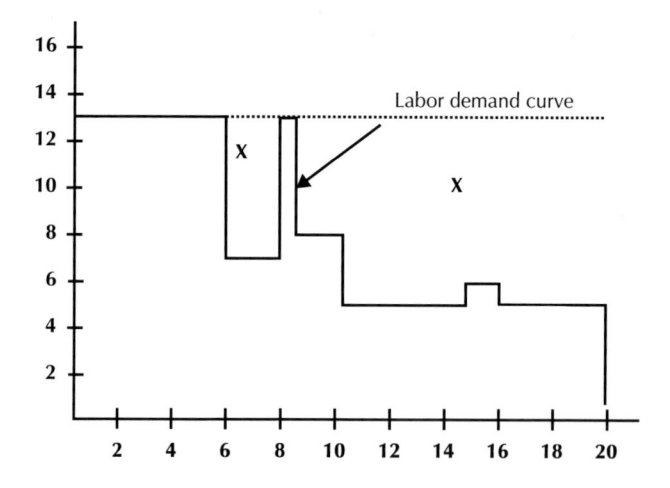

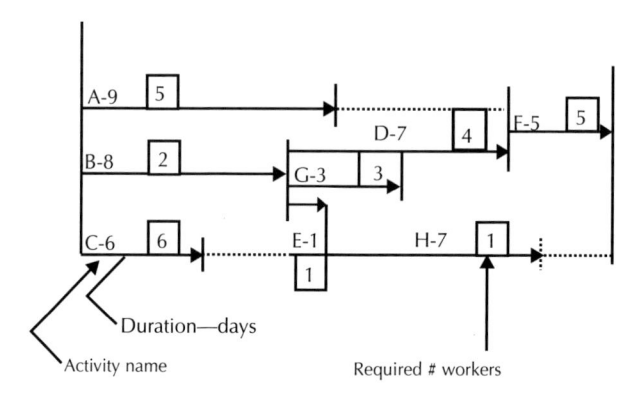

Fig. 6-10. Project Schedule with Resource Requirements

Earlier, we characterized this schedule as one that required the supervisor to hire and fire as needed, or to hire more laborers than needed on several days. Neither alternative is preferred. Can a better schedule be prepared for the 20-day project that satisfies the technical, resource and preference logic and makes more productive use of assigned laborers? The answer is yes. It is possible to shift activities within their float times to yield the schedule illustrated in Figure 6-11. This schedule requires only 10 laborers, not the 13 previously required (a 30% decrease). The schedule makes better use of assigned laborers and results in a better matching of availability and demand for resources, as well as improved productivity.

PRODUCTIVITY IMPROVEMENT AND PLANNING AND SCHEDULING

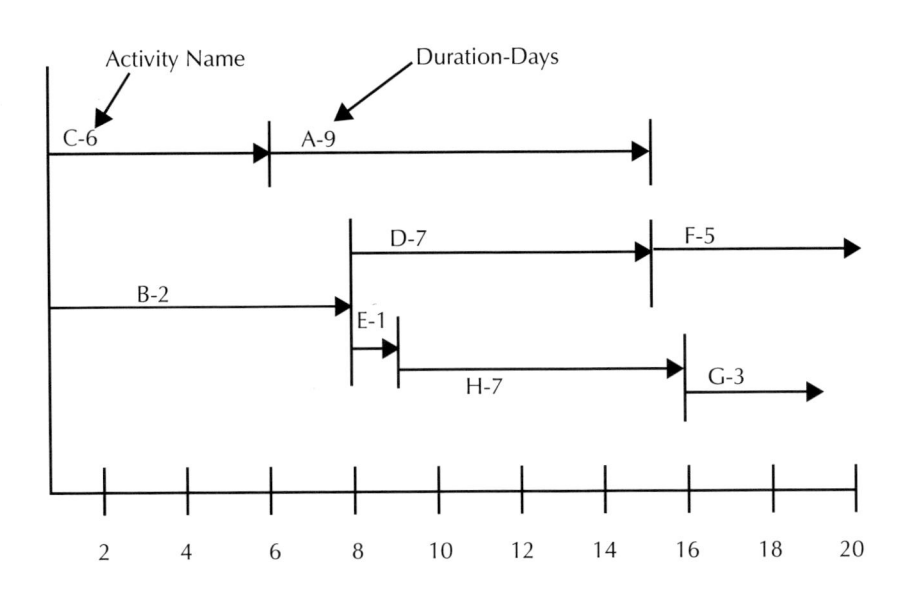

Fig. 6-11. Time Scale CPM

There are many algorithms that can be used to perform resource management.

By using the floats calculated in Figure 6-9, the supervisor can resequence activities to level the number of workers needed on any specific day. This is just one of the many applications of using float to perform resource management. Certain algorithms can be used to schedule resources to meet a specific objective. The floats calculated in Figure 6-9 represent available time with which the supervisor can meet specific objectives; be it leveling resources, recovering lost project time or another defined objective.

The overall project plan and schedule should also let the supervisor see the big picture. For example, focusing on various critical work activities can justify the supervisor's scheduling selected overtime. While the selected overtime might have a slight negative impact on labor productivity and labor cost, it may be more than offset by shortening the overall project schedule and/or eliminating or reducing financial costs associated with finishing a project late. (A late project finish might result in the assessment of liquidated damages.)

Supervisor Decisions Using a Project Plan and Schedule

Exercise

Shown below is the time scale CPM project plan and schedule presented in the previous exercise. Answer the following questions.

- Listed below is the number of laborers required to do each work task. Sketch the number of workers that are required as a function of project time and determine the maximum number of workers needed for the project.

Activity	Duration	Workers Needed
A	6	6
B	4	4
C	5	5
D	6	6
E	10	7
F	8	5
G	6	6
H	4	4
I	2	3

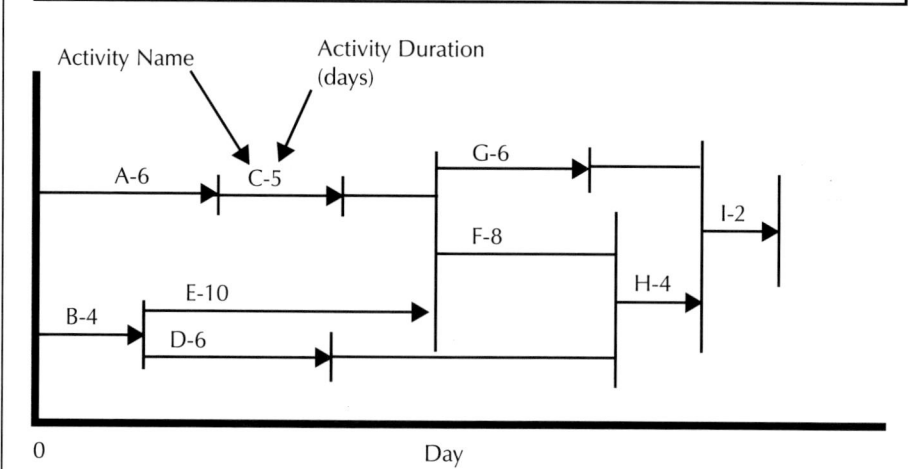

Activity Name → A-6
Activity Duration (days) → C-5

Schedule layout:
- A-6, C-5, G-6, I-2
- F-8, H-4
- B-4, E-10
- D-6

(Day axis starting at 0)

Number of Workers vs. Day

Maximum Number Needed =

Productivity Improvement and Planning and Scheduling

■ How could the maximum number of workers be reduced?

■ If activity A is delayed 2 days, how many days will this extend the project duration?

■ If activity E is delayed 3 days, how many days will this extend the project duration?

■ If activity G and activity F both need a crane and you have only one crane, which activity should the crane be given to first if you want to keep the project duration to a minimum?

How long will this extend the project duration?

Exercise

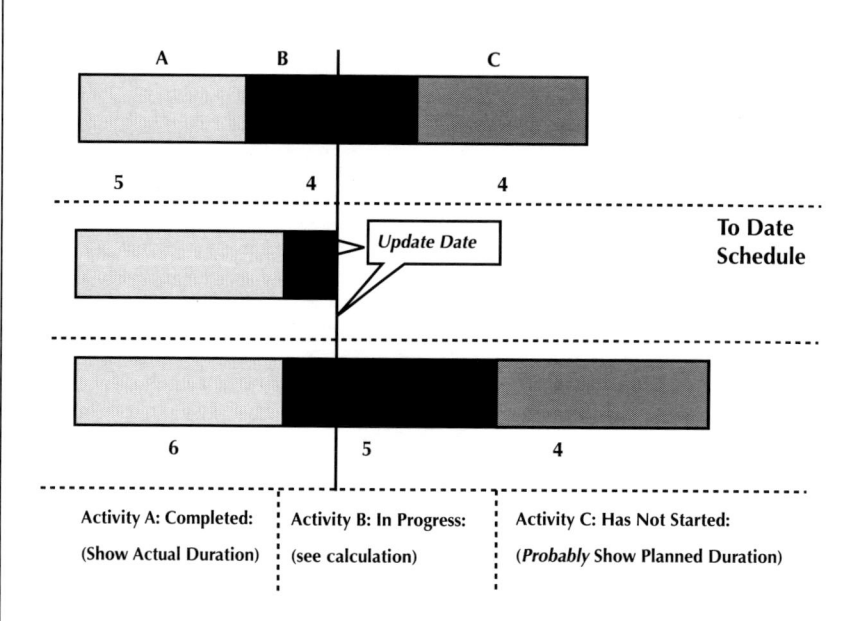

Updating the Project Plan and Schedule

It is critical that the initial project plan and schedule for a project, be it a bar chart or CPM diagram, be updated as the job progresses. If the initial plan and schedule are not updated, they can lead to poor daily management decisions.

Given the many uncertain events that occur during a project, it is important that the overall project plan and schedule be updated on a regular basis.

When a 10-month project is 2 months old, one can argue that there is a new 8-month project to be started. The events that have occurred during the first 2 months of the project should be recognized; this recognition may change the critical path, the project duration, or even require adjustments in the duration or crew sizes needed for remaining activities.

In the process of updating a project in progress, the supervisor must deal with three different types of work activities:

- Work activities completed as of the date of the update
- Work activities not started as of the date of the update
- Work activities in progress as of the date of the update

An example of each of these three possibilities is shown in Figure 6-12.

Update of Schedule

Fig. 6-12. Updating the Project Plan and Schedule

Productivity Improvement and Planning and Scheduling

The first two types of work activities are not difficult to deal with in regard to the project update. For example, consider activity A, illustrated in Figure 6-12. As of the update date, this work activity is complete. In updating the work activity, the supervisor would merely show the actual duration, not the planned duration. The updated schedule would show that work activity took 5 days, not the planned 4 days.

Work activity C in Figure 6-12 has not started as of the update date. Therefore, more likely than not, the supervisor will show the activity as having the originally planned duration of 4 days. However, if the work is similar to a work activity that is complete or in process, and the supervisor has learned that the productivity will be worse (or better) than planned, he or she might consider reflecting this productivity adjustment in a new calculation for the duration for the work activity that has not started. However, when updating a project schedule, the supervisor often will keep the planned durations for work activities that have not started.

More difficult for the supervisor to update are work activities that are in process as of the date of the update. Consider work activity B, illustrated in Figure 6-12. Some supervisors merely update this type of work activity by taking the number of days it has been worked on at the date of the update and subtracting this number from the planned duration. In effect, the supervisor is saying that productivity for the work activity is progressing just as planned. Of course, this is seldom the case. Things happen that result in better or worse productivity than planned.

The proper way for the supervisor to update a work activity in progress is to tie the updating process to the system used for controlling the project labor hours and cost. Consider the job cost report illustrated in Figure 6-13, with work activity B highlighted.

Activity	Quantity	Planned Labor Hrs	Planned Crew Size	Planned Duration	Quantity to Date	Labor Hrs to Date	Projected Total Hrs	Actual Crew Size	Projected Duration	Days Remaining
B	100	160	5	4	20	40	200	5	5	4

Fig. 6-13. Excerpt from Job Cost Report

As noted in Figure 6-13, the plan for activity B was to do the following:

Activity B: PLAN

Planned quantity:	100 units
Planned man-hours:	160 man-hours
Therefore:	0.625 units/man-hour or 1.6 man-hours/unit
Planned crew size:	5 workers
Therefore:	
Planned duration:	(160 man-hours) / [(5 workers) x (8 hours/day)] = 4 days

At the time of the update, the field reports indicate that 20 units are in place. In addition the payroll reports indicate that 40 man-hours have been expended to date. The calculated total days and remaining days for activity B for updating the schedule is as follows:

Activity B: UPDATE

Quantities to date:	20 units
Actual man-hours:	40 man-hours (1 day)
Therefore:	0.50 units/man-hour or 2.0 man-hours/unit
Work to complete:	80 units
Remaining man-hours:	(80 units) times 2 man-hours/unit = 160 man-hours
Therefore:	
Remaining duration:	(160 man-hours) / [(5 workers) x (8 hours/day)] = 4 days
Total duration:	To date + Remaining = 1 + 4 = 5

The 5-day new duration for the in-progress work activity B reflects the fact that productivity that was being planned is not being achieved. Assuming the productivity continues the same as happened to date, and assuming the crew size is kept the same, it follows that the work will take four more days for a total of five. Of course if the supervisor knows information that indicates the productivity will increase (or decrease more than it already has), then this information would have to be reflected in the update calculations.

Actual revisions of the project plan and schedule, including revised CPM calculations, are best achieved with a computer; however, even absent a computer, the need for updating exists, and a project plan and schedule can be updated manually in a simplified form.

Updating the Project Plan and Schedule

Exercise

Shown below is the plan and current status of three work activities as of the date of the project plan and schedule update:

For each of the work activities, update the information to determine:

■ Estimated total days required to do the work activity

Activity	Planned Quantity	Planned Man-hours	Planned Crew Size	Planned Duration (Days)	Quantity To Date	Man-hours To Date	Projected Man-hours	Actual Crew Size	Projected Duration (Days)
A	100	400	5	10	50	150		5	
B	500	1,600	10	20	200	500		10	
C	200	800	20	5	40	200		32	

Activity	Planned Duration	Projected Duration
A	10	
B	20	
C	5	

Using a One- to Four-Week Look-Ahead Schedule

The planning and scheduling discussed so far pertain to the project at large. Using the master schedule as a basis, the supervisor should be focusing on a shorter duration to plan and schedule workers, material, equipment and tools.

The construction process is such that the supervisor may have to take action today if a needed event is to take place a few weeks into the future. For example, for some materials needed two or three weeks from now, it may be necessary to make a telephone, mail, fax or email order today. Similarly, it may take a few weeks advance notice to get needed equipment of specialized labor at the jobsite. It follows that the supervisor should follow a formalized process of breaking down the overall project plan and schedule into more detail for the next few weeks. A planning and scheduling form that can aid the supervisor for this purpose is a One- to Four-Week Look-Ahead Schedule Form, illustrated in Figure 6-14.

The one- to four-week look-ahead schedule shown should be prepared in conjunction with the overall project master plan that is updated on a timely basis. Filling out the form shown in Figure 6-14 serves as a reminder of actions that the supervisor must take to keep the project on schedule and budget.

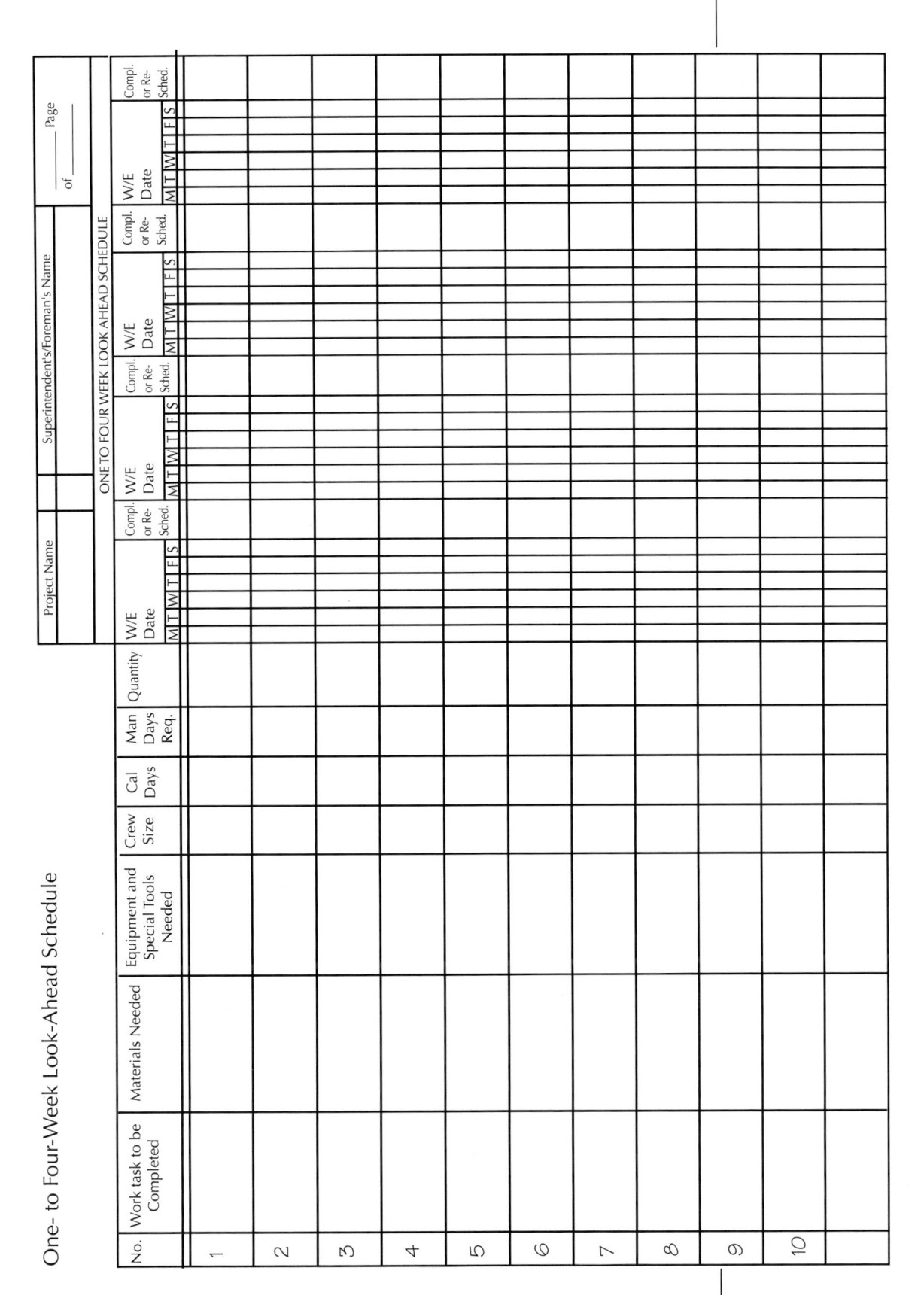

Fig. 6-14. One- to Four-Week Look-Ahead Schedule

Using a Short Interval Look-Ahead Schedule

Not planning tomorrow's work today leads to numerous unnecessary interruptions and delays while you look for or wait for things, people or decisions.

All too often the project superintendent or foreman reacts to problems at the site rather than taking steps earlier to prevent the problems from occurring. A considerable amount of time at a site is non-productive because of the need to look for tools, material or equipment while a craftsperson or entire crew is waiting for them. Not planning tomorrow's work today leads to numerous unnecessary interruptions and delays relating to looking for things and waiting for things, people or decisions.

A simple form such as the one shown in Figure 6-15, if used on a daily basis by the superintendent or foreman, can enable improved productivity. The form is referred to as a Short Interval Look-Ahead Schedule. The objective of the form is two-fold:

- to set goals as to how much work is planned for the next day and
- to set out and line up in advance the resources that will be needed to do the planned work.

The Short Interval Look-Ahead Schedule shown has to be prepared to be consistent with the overall project plan and schedule. In other words, the daily quantity goals have to be such that the work activity durations on the overall project schedule can be met.

The supervisor needs to pay special attention for the next one to four weeks to take necessary immediate actions to reduce the possibility of delays.

The Short Interval Look-Ahead Schedule and the One- to Four-Week Look-Ahead Schedule Form illustrated in Figures 6-14 and 6-15 can be viewed as reminder lists. It might be argued that some supervisors have a knack for looking ahead without the use of a written form. However, the construction process is often complex and it is hard, if not impossible, to remember everything. Secondly, the use of forms makes every supervisor do the same thing. Consistency enhances quality, which in turn aids productivity.

Both the Short Interval Look-Ahead Schedule and the One- to Four-Week Look-Ahead Schedule Form are forms for goal setting. It is critical that the construction supervisor set goals. Goals provide a means of determining required steps and provide ways of measuring performance.

SESSION 6

PRODUCTIVITY IMPROVEMENT AND PLANNING AND SCHEDULING

Project _____
Day _____
Supervisor _____

Work Description	Cost Code	Total Quantity	Quantity Tomorrow	Estimated Productivity	Materials Needed	Tools Needed	Equipment Needed	Labor Needed	Things to do/watch

Fig. 6-15. Short Interval Look-Ahead Schedule

Participant's Manual ■ STP ■ Unit 9

The Benefits of Using Checklists for Planning

Planning and scheduling take many forms. As we'll discuss in an upcoming section, planning and scheduling can entail the preparation of a detailed critical path method schedule for the overall project. On the other hand, planning and scheduling also can mean something as simple as making a daily checklist that reminds the user of actions or things he or she has to do. The preparation and use of checklists not only helps the supervisor organize himself or herself, but also serves as a good reminder list to facilitate productivity and reduce non-productive time.

The construction supervisor is often in a role of having to do more things than he or she has time to do. The hectic pace is compounded by the complexity of the construction process and the fact that uncertain events happen every day. The result is that it is hard for any supervisor to remember everything that needs to be done or lined up to keep a project at peak productivity.

Effective supervisors take the time to prepare reminder lists.

It is easy for the supervisor to forget things, events or decisions that need to be made on a daily basis. Forgetting to order or expedite materials, forgetting to get needed equipment or tools to the project when needed, or not lining up labor or subcontractors when needed, all can lead to expensive, time-consuming delays. Effective supervisors take the time to prepare reminder lists. For example, some supervisors find it advantageous to keep a small notebook such as that shown in Figure 6-16 in their back pocket as a productivity tool.

Fig. 6-16

Similar checklists can be used for other project management tasks such as:

- Organizing and running jobsite meetings
- Organizing the project layout
- Administering change order procedures
- Closing out the jobsite

Exercise

Preparing a Reminder List

Assume you are about to attend a pre-construction job meeting for a project that your firm typically constructs. With the objective of not forgetting to ask an important question, prepare a checklist of issues that you anticipate asking about at the meeting.

Session 6 Review

Look back over Session 6 and review these key points to be sure you understand them:

- The importance of planning and scheduling to achieve productivity.
- The benefits of using a master project schedule.
- The steps required to prepare a master project plan and schedule.
- The importance and use of a One- to Four-Week Look-Ahead Form.
- The importance and use of a Short Interval Look-Ahead Schedule.
- The importance of Daily Reminder Lists.

Using on the Job What You Learned Today

Jobsite Assignment

While at your projects, prepare a written daily plan for the next day's work using a form similar to that shown in Figure 6-15. Use the written plan to set a quantity goal and select the required resources. After each day, write down the quantity of work that was done relative to the goal and try to determine why or why not the quantity goal was achieved.

To Get Ready for Session 7

Read Session 7 in the Participant's Manual.

Session 7
Managing Subcontractors

Learning Goals for Session 7

After this session, you should understand the following:

- The importance of managing subcontractors to attain overall project productivity
- How to use project scheduling so that subcontractors manage their performance
- How to encourage subcontractors to management themselves
- How to implement short interval scheduling for the subcontractors
- How to run effective jobsite meetings
- How to build a team rather than a group of individual subcontractors

The above practices and knowledge help you manage subcontractors without directing them. All the practices are compatible with the premise that the best way to manage subcontractors is to encourage them to manage themselves. If subcontractors are in trouble in regard to project time, budget, quality or safety, then the general contractor is also in trouble.

Learning Objectives

To accomplish the learning goals, during this session you will:

- Learn the importance of managing subcontractors.
- Learn the need to be authoritative.
- Help subcontractors manage themselves.
- Select the right subcontractor.
- Encourage subcontractors to plan and schedule milestone dates and resources.
- Recognize the importance of communication, meetings and team building in subcontractor relationships.

To Get Ready for Session

Reading: Read the pages for this session in your Participant's Manual. Try to think of problems you have had in dealing with subcontractors and how the problems could have been prevented.

Major Activities for Session 7

- Learn the importance of managing subcontractors.
- Do an exercise that discusses major problem areas when dealing with subcontractors and how to minimize the problems.
- Discuss the importance of evaluating subcontractor performance.
- Do an exercise in which you will prepare a post project form or questionnaire for evaluating subcontractor performance.
- Discuss the need to be authoritative.
- Learn how to encourage subcontractors to manage themselves.
- Do an exercise in which you will evaluate the viability of subcontractor plans.
- Discuss proper record keeping in regard to subcontractor performance.
- Do an exercise in which you will develop a checklist of what to monitor when managing a subcontractor.
- Learn the importance of communication, meetings and team building in regard to subcontractor performance.
- Do an exercise that focuses on developing a team approach to the project.

A Review of Session 6

In Session 6, you learned the importance of managing and making construction equipment more productive.

Some of the facts that you learned in Session 6 are:

- Equipment, like labor, is used to transfer material into finished projects including buildings, roads and bridges, and residential units.

- Equipment is often more expensive per hour than labor, and often is in a non-productive state more often than labor.

- Equipment, unlike labor, has an ownership hourly cost (costs that are a function of time) and an operating hourly cost (costs that are a function of use).

- Equipment, like labor, has a quantifiable amount of work capacity during any time period.

- Two pieces of construction equipment often work together. To calculate the production of the machines working together, one must recognize the interdependent nature of the equipment.

The Need to Manage Subcontractors

The Dependence on Subcontractors

In the construction process, the majority of projects are built using several construction firms; typically a general contractor and several subcontractors. While there are several different organizational structures, including the design-build process and the construction management (CM) process, the general contracting process illustrated in Figure 7-1 remains the most common.

> A typical construction project includes a general contractor and several subcontractors.

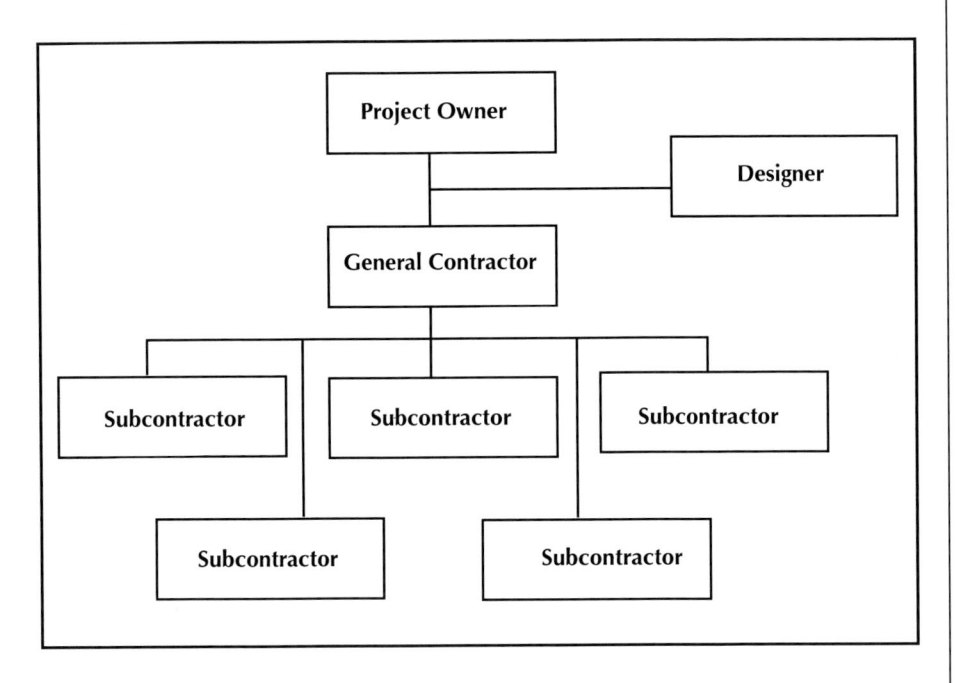

Fig. 7-1. General Contractor/Subcontractor Process

The subcontractors in Figure 7-1 are typically specialty firms and are commonly referred to as trade contractors. For a building project the subcontractors include the electrical, mechanical and plumbing contractors. For a highway project, the subcontractors may include the fencing, painting and stripping, and excavation contractors.

In many cases the general contractor illustrated in Figure 7-1 may do less than 30% of the overall construction work with its own workers. In fact, the general contractor may subcontract all the work.

The Need to Manage Subcontractors Without Directing the Subcontractor

The supervisor working for the general contractor must manage his or her own self-performed work *and also* coordinate and supervise the work of the subcontractors. The project performance (the project time, budget, quality and safety) is only as good as the weakest link.

The role of the general contractor differs when she's managing subcontractors. In the case of self-performed work, the supervisor can "direct" her own workers. She determines how many workers to employ, assigns them work tasks, directs their work efforts and monitors their production efforts.

In the case of the work performed by subcontractors, the role of the general contractor supervisor is less direct. The supervisor does not hire individual craftspeople for the subcontractors, does not estimate their production goals, does not assign individual workers or crews to work tasks and has little ability to reprimand or monitor individual worker or crew performance. In regard to subcontractor performance, the general contractor supervisor is in the delicate role of obtaining performance without having the right to "direct" it. However, the supervisor cannot merely stand by and watch the performance of the subcontractors; such an approach often leads to project difficulties. The supervisor must be proactive in his or her approach to subcontractors; the supervisor has to manage rather than watch their performance.

One might hear a contractor or supervisor say, "We do a good job of project management and managing productivity. However, we cannot get our subcontractors to perform." This approach is one of blaming the other guy. Whether the blame is appropriate or not, the fact remains that any one contractor's performance at a project typically affects the other contractors at the project. If subcontractors are in trouble in regard to their budgeted project time or cost, the general contractor will likely also be in trouble.

The construction project and the firms working on it, including the general contractor and all the subcontractors, should be viewed as a system. In a system it is sometimes important that the needs or objectives of a single individual or firm not be put ahead of the overall team needs or objectives. Put another way, one contractor, be it the general or subcontractor, may occasionally have to sacrifice their own needs or objectives in order to optimize the overall project goals of time, cost, quality and safety.

The supervisor must attempt to manage subcontractors without necessarily having the right to direct the subcontractors.

The dilemma the general contractor supervisor faces is how to get subcontractors to perform without having direct control over their production process. The following practices are recommended:

- Be more selective in hiring subcontractors
- Be authoritative and inform subcontractors what is expected of them and monitor their progress
- Encourage the subcontractors to manage themselves
- Implement performance managing procedures
- Implement accurate and timely accounting and reporting procedures
- Promote a "team" approach to project management
- Serve as an advisor and aid to the subcontractor

Exercise

Addressing Subcontractor Concerns

Your assigned group is to brainstorm issues that cause difficulties between the general contractor and subcontractor — stuff that can affect the time, cost, quality or safety of a project. In addition to listing a difficulty or problem, the group is to make suggestions of how to remedy the problem; either to keep the problem from evolving or to minimize the impact of the problem when it does occur.

Problem Between General Contractor and Subcontractor	Action(s) to be Taken to Keep Problem from Occurring or Minimize Impact
1. One of the two entities promises a completion date or milestone date then fails to staff the project to meet the date.	Each party should make an effort to 1) prepare a realistic and not overly optimistic schedule, 2) set out "how" they are going to meet the date, not just "when" and 3) make every effort to comply with the effort and promised results.
2.	
3.	
4.	
5.	
6.	
7.	
8.	
9.	
10.	

Selection of Subcontractors

The Importance of Hiring the Right Subcontractors

The best way to manage subcontractors is to engage the right subcontractors so that they don't have to be managed as much. Easier said than done!

In construction a premium is given to the low-bid contractor; more often than not the low-bid subcontractor is contracted.

However, a project is only successful if four variables are managed:

- Project time
- Project cost or budget
- Project quality
- Project safety

A subcontractor might be low bidder and be contracted, only to demonstrate a tendency to:

- Understaff the project
- Be uncooperative about attending project meetings
- Be lackadaisical in regard to planning and scheduling work
- Be argumentative with other project contractors
- Do a marginal quality of work
- Ignore project safety requirements

Any one of the above unfavorable characteristics is likely to lead to low productivity and overall project problems for everyone. The general contractor and the supervisor may have contract clauses that enable them to come down on a subcontractor for any of these problems, or even to terminate the subcontractor. But this is not a solution.

Evaluate Subcontractor Performance

The following process for engaging subcontractors is recommended:

- Design a subcontractor evaluation form to be used to evaluate subcontractor project performance.
- During and after project completion, the supervisor should be required to evaluate each subcontractor's performance using the designed form.
- A database should be established that rates subcontractor performance using the completed supervisor evaluation forms.

Subcontractors can affect the overall project time, cost, quality and safety. The best way to ensure subcontractor performance is to hire the right subcontractors.

When a project ends, subcontractors should be evaluated on how they performed on the project.

- The database of past performance should be used to evaluate and select subcontractors for future projects.

Given that the project owner typically engages the general contractor in a low-bid environment, it is obvious that the general contractor also seeks competitive bids from subcontractors. However, if a low-bid subcontractor fails to perform productively, the general contractor and the supervisor may incur problems more severe than losing the bid on the project.

Evaluation of Subcontractor Performance

Exercise

You are to work in a team during this exercise; ideally your team will have participants with diverse industry backgrounds (working for a general contractor and subcontractors or trade contractors).

Your team is to design a form or questionnaire to be used by the general contractor supervisor to rate individual subcontractor performance at the completion of the project. When designing the evaluation form, you should list what factors should be rated and how to rate them so that the firm can establish a database to aid in deciding which subcontractors to contract for future work.

Being Authoritative and Leading by Example

The construction supervisor should view himself or herself as the individual who orchestrates the overall project team to accomplish the project time, cost, quality and safety goals or objectives. As the team leader, the supervisor must be authoritative and lead by example. A good leader typically exhibits the following qualities:

- Thoroughness, steadiness, reliability
- Ability to complete assignments
- Honesty, trustworthiness, conscientiousness
- Good judgment in decision making
- Ability to meet schedules
- Responsibility
- Ability to inspire confidence
- Cooperation
- Consideration of others
- Good personal habits

To effectively orchestrate or manage subcontractors, the supervisor should attempt to earn subcontractor respect. The supervisor should be unbiased and unemotional in his or her dealings with subcontractors and subordinates. The supervisor should show a concern for project goals as well as for individuals. The effective supervisor can show concern for individuals and at the same time be authoritative.

Intelligence is another important attribute of the construction supervisor. In order to be an effective leader of subcontractors, the supervisor's knowledge and intelligence must be respected by the subcontractors. In general, a supervisor's ability to manage increases with his or her level of intelligence. On the other hand, a high level of knowledge or intelligence does not ensure effective leadership or supervision. If the supervisor does not demonstrate the other personal qualities noted above, his or her knowledge or intelligence might in fact be resented by subcontractors and subordinates.

In managing subcontractors, the construction supervisor may be sympathetic to the needs of the subcontractors, but she must also be authoritative. This means setting out responsibilities and tasks for subcontractors and subordinates. The supervisor needs to clearly identify

> The effective supervisor can show concern for individuals and at the same time be authoritative.

[Handwritten margin note: EXPLAIN THE RELATIONSHIP BETWEEN BEING AUTHORITATIVE AND LEADING BY EXAMPLE]

for subcontractors what is expected of them. This includes communicating the following:

- The time and place of various project meetings, and the individuals who must attend.
- Required formalized schedules and updates of schedules.
- Required record keeping.
- Staffing requirements.
- Notification requirements in regard to problems or requests.
- Required progress billing format and detail.

The supervisor should hold the subcontractor accountable for commitments and performance of agreed-upon requirements. The supervisor should be quick, decisive and firm in monitoring the subcontractors' requirements. If the supervisor does not enforce agreed-to requirements, he will lose the respect of subcontractors. This lack of respect and authoritative management will lead to chaos and non-attainment of project goals. If the supervisor accepts excuses for non-attendance at required meetings or excuses for not submitting an updated schedule, these failures will be viewed as acceptable and become commonplace. Leadership includes being attentive to the needs of subordinates but it also involves holding the subordinates accountable for required commitments.

To the extent possible, subcontractor requirements should be set out in the subcontractor contract. The supervisor needs to know these requirements, especially if there are unique requirements for a specific project. Enforcement of contract provisions should be a priority for the supervisor.

The supervisor should hold the subcontractor accountable for commitments and performance of agreed-upon requirements.

Managing Subcontractors by Encouraging Them to Manage Themselves

Helping Subcontractors Help Themselves

The construction supervisor often attempts to manage the subcontractor by taking a results-oriented approach. The supervisor gets the subcontractor to promise results, e.g., a completion date, and then comes down on the subcontractor when the results are not achieved. This approach typically results in finger-pointing, assessing blame, disputes and possibly lawsuits.

A more positive approach, and an approach more likely to achieve results, is to encourage the subcontractor to manage his own construction process using various management practices. This is compatible with the principle that if you fix the process, the results will take care of themselves.

One example of a subcontractor helping himself would be formalized project scheduling. On occasion one hears the general contractor supervisor make the statement; "We do a good job of project scheduling, but we can't get our subcontractors to do it."

Project planning and scheduling was covered in an earlier unit. It was pointed out that formalized on-paper planning and scheduling improves productivity by setting out milestone dates, drawing attention to resources needed to do the work, and by providing a means of measuring and monitoring performance. Formalized planning and scheduling is just as important for an electrical, mechanical or plumbing contractor as it is for the general contractor.

Instead of complaining about the subcontractor that does not do adequate formalized planning and scheduling, the general contractor can require the subcontractor to do formalized planning and scheduling by contract. It can be just as much of a contract requirement as putting in electrical conduit. When the subcontractor agrees in his or her contract to do formalized planning and scheduling, the general contractor supervisor should then enforce it. Letting a subcontractor off the hook when it comes to his or her scheduling commitments is not doing the subcontractor or the general contractor a favor.

While the supervisor cannot "direct" or force the subcontractor to do things that they have not agreed to in the contract, the supervisor does have the right to enforce what the subcontractor has agreed to do. The key is to get the subcontractor to commit to defined management practices in the contract and then enforce the commitments. In effect, the supervisor is encouraging the subcontractor to self-manage.

The best way to manage subcontractors is to encourage them to manage themselves. Require them to do such management functions as planning and scheduling and recordkeeping.

Implementing Performance Management for Subcontractors

One of the problems the supervisor has when it comes to managing subcontractors is having work done when promised; i.e., meeting schedule commitments. This often stems from the fact that the subcontractor has the same problem the general contractor has; more work to do, or more projects to do, than they have resources to do the work.

Having subcontractors commit to a start date and an end date for their work is not enough. Effective subcontractor management entails the following:

- Having the subcontractor break down the work into a detailed list of work activities.

- Having the subcontractor set out various milestone dates as well as the end date.

- Having subcontractors commit to *how* they are going to do work activities as well as when they are going to complete them; getting them to commit to effort, not just results.

Requiring Subcontractors to Break Down Their Schedule into More Detail

When reviewing a formalized on-paper schedule for a project, it is common to observe that the general contractor has broken down his or her work into many individual work activities; often one hundred or more detailed work activities. Then the subcontractor part of the work is often much less detailed. For example, one single work activity might be noted: "Put in plumbing—14 weeks," to represent the total plumbing effort.

Requiring a subcontractor to submit a schedule and then accepting a schedule that does not break down the work in detail is not doing the subcontractor or yourself a favor. If a subcontractor submits a schedule with one work activity, "Put in plumbing—14 weeks," then the first time non-performance can be identified is after the 14 weeks. The schedule becomes a tool for assessing blame rather than a tool for getting things done.

In setting out the subcontractors' scheduling requirements, the following should be considered:

- Specify the minimum number of work activities the subcontractor must set out in the schedule he or she submits.

- Give guidelines on the format of the schedule that is to be submitted; e.g., activities on the first floor are to be separate from activities on the second floor; or activities are to be shown by room location.

> Subcontractors should be required to submit detailed project plans and schedules, and to indicate various work milestone dates.

SESSION 7

MANAGING SUBCONTRACTORS

- Consider requiring that the duration of any one-work activity can be no longer than a defined duration, for example, ten days. This will force the subcontractor to break down the work in more detail.

The principle behind requiring subcontractors to break work into more detail on the schedule is to encourage them to think through the work process. The mere fact that the work is broken down into more detail will make the subcontractor think through potential resource conflicts and construction problems. This in itself should enhance project productivity.

Setting Out Milestone Dates

The last resort in subcontractor management has to be terminating the subcontractor for non-performance. This does not even become a feasible alternative when the supervisor merely gets the subcontractor to promise a completion date. If this is all the subcontractor has promised, the supervisor has a difficult time reprimanding the subcontractor for a lack of effort or staff, until the promised date is missed. This is illustrated in Figure 7-2.

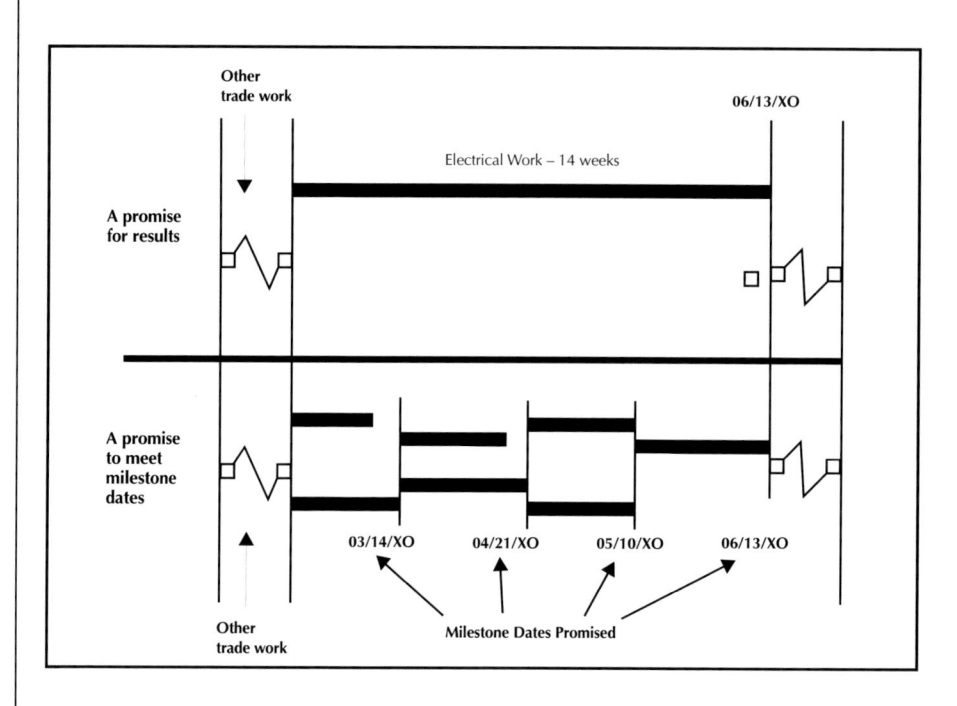

Fig. 7-2. Milestone Scheduling

A more effective means of managing the subcontractor entails having the subcontractor commit to various milestone dates. This at least gives the supervisor the ability to reprimand the subcontractor sooner, so that corrective actions can be taken. Given a desperate situation, the supervisor may even consider terminating the subcontractor; this becomes possible because milestone dates can be set out as contract requirements. The positive purpose of the milestone dates illustrated in Figure 7-2 is that they remind subcontractors to think about how they are going to get work completed to meet milestone dates. Without the milestone date commitments, a subcontractor might procrastinate until it is too late to meet the project completion date.

Commitment for Effort, Not Just Results

Like most businesses, including general contractors, the subcontractor may be over-committed and have limited resources. The supervisor cannot afford to be on the bottom of the totem pole when it comes to getting the subcontractor's attention, effort and resources.

With the dual objective of 1) getting the subcontractor to plan out how he or she is going to get work done and 2) getting a formalized commitment to staff the work, the supervisor can require the subcontractor to submit a resource loaded schedule.

The resource loaded schedule not only sets out work activity durations and milestone dates, but also requires subcontractors to estimate the resources they will use for performing each work activity. For example, if one of the work activities in Figure 7-2 is to put in 20,000 linear feet of ¾-inch electrical conduit, the subcontractor might show this work taking 10 days. To get the work done in 10 days, the subcontractor has had to consider the following three pieces of information:

- Productivity of a worker putting in ¾-inch electrical conduit
- Possible production delays such as weather or disruption
- Number of electricians or crew size that will be used to do the work

For example, using a productivity of 20 linear feet per craft-hour, 1,000 craft–hours will be required. Assuming one day of work disruption (leaving nine), the electrical subcontractor will require the following number of workers doing the work:

Work days available	= 9 days
Craft-hours needed	= 1,000
Craft-hours needed per day	= 111
Work hours per day	= 8
Number of workers needed	= 14

Getting a subcontractor to promise effort and the subsequent monitoring of effort provides improved control. It's better than monitoring only the promised work completion date.

By having the subcontractor work through the above calculations, the supervisor accomplishes the two objectives of 1) getting the subcontractor to plan the work and think through how many workers he or she needs for each work task and 2) committing the subcontractor to having 14 workers present.

Having the subcontractor commit to the 14 workers, the supervisor can now monitor the subcontractor's effort, not just their results. This is not to say that the supervisor should go ballistic every time the subcontractor is short one worker. However, the mere fact that the subcontractor knows that he or she has committed to 14 workers will make him conscious of having the 14 workers doing the work. A promise for effort, not just results, gives the supervisor a much shorter control trigger in regard to recognizing potential project delays.

Getting the Subcontractor to Plan Tomorrow's Work Today

One of the main causes for waiting and non-productive time at projects relates to workers and their supervisors looking for things or waiting for things that should have been lined up the day before. Workers waiting for materials, a crew waiting for a tool that cannot be located, or not having the right equipment at the project when needed are all examples of events that negatively impact overall project productivity.

Employees of the general contractor as well as employees of the subcontractor fall victim to the failure to plan tomorrow's work today. In an earlier session, a short interval scheduling form was presented for use by supervisors to remind them to line up materials, tools, equipment and labor that is going to be needed the following day. The same form requires that supervisors set out a production goal for each work activity they plan to perform the following day.

Recognizing that subcontractor work delays negatively impact the subcontractor's performance as well as the overall project, the supervisor should encourage subcontractors to use the short interval scheduling form. One way to do this would be for the supervisor to provide the subcontractors with a form similar to the one shown in Figure 7-3 and require that the subcontractors submit the completed form to the general contractor supervisor on a daily basis.

Ideally, subcontractors should be required to plan the next workday a day ahead of time. This will help them as well as help you in reducing non-productive delays.

Short Interval Scheduling Form

Project: _____   Foreman: _____
Plan for Day: _____   Supervisor: _____

Work Activity Planned	Quantity Goal	# Workers (Crew) Required	Material Required	Equipment Required	Tools Required	Notes

Fig. 7-3. Form for Subcontractor Daily Planning Input

The intent is to have the subcontractor supervisors to do what they should do anyway; i.e., plan tomorrow's work today. Will the subcontractors submit to the general supervisor? The answer to this depends on how persistent the supervisor is in his or her request. If the subcontractor is advised of this requirement as a basis of his contract, the subcontractor will likely do whatever is required. It is the supervisor's role to enforce the process just as it is his or her role to require the subcontractors to perform work according to the specifications. The alternative is to stand by and watch non-productive waiting time and to point blame at firms for their failure to get things done. A proactive approach focuses on improving the process to get results.

An addition to the form shown in Figure 7-3 could require the subcontractor to report on what they did get done on a given day relative to the budgeted quantities the day before. The intent is to hold the subcontractor accountable for meeting production goals.

Notes:

Evaluating Subcontractor Plans and Schedules

Exercise

With the objective of getting subcontractors to manage themselves, you as a supervisor request that the subcontractors submit schedules of their work activities. Your role as a supervisor is to evaluate whether the submitted schedules are reasonable. Using an estimating manual, reference various reasonable productivities to check the subcontractor schedules.

Included in the schedules submitted, your review indicates the subcontractors have planned the following work activities.

Install electrical wire; #4:

Planned number of workers	4 electricians
Planned duration:	4 days

Install W 10x12 Structural Steel Beams:

Planned number of workers:	5 ironworkers
	1 equipment operator
	1 oiler
Planned duration:	8 days

Each of the subcontractors indicates that he or she plans on working eight-hour days.

In an attempt to validate the subcontractors' estimates, perform a rough estimate of various quantities of work. The information for the above work tasks is as follows:

Install electrical wire; #4

Approximate linear footage of quantity:	8,600 linear feet
Average productivity (per estimating manual)	Crew: 2 electricians 1.5 person-hours/ 100 linear feet

Install W 10 x 12 Structural Beams:

Approximate linear feet of beams:	8,400 linear feet

MANAGING SUBCONTRACTORS

Average productivity
(per estimating manual)

Crew: 5 ironworkers
1 equipment operator
1 oiler
0.1 person-hours per linear foot

Record keeping forces accountability, which in turn should aid overall productivity. Detailed records should be maintained regarding subcontractor performance.

Determine the following:

1. Are the subcontractors' planned durations reasonable given the number of workers planned? State your reasons.

2. Assuming that one or both of the activity durations is not reasonable, what action would you recommend on the part of the supervisor of the general contractor?

Accountability Identifies Responsibility, Which Enhances Productivity

Productivity Through Accountability and Record Keeping

Accountability tends to make people responsible, which in turn makes them more productive. In his or her effort to manage subcontractors and attain favorable jobsite productivity, the supervisor must keep extensive daily records of who did what and when.

It is important that the supervisor keep daily records regarding both 1) subcontractor performance and 2) their own self-performed work. While the types of information recorded on a daily basis may differ, the objective is the same; to be able to "play the project events back like a movie" after the fact.

Record Keeping and Subcontractor Performance

Daily record keeping serves several purposes. It provides a basis of proving right or wrong when a dispute evolves, and input for additional management reports, such as project status reports. However, one of the main purposes of record keeping is to identify who did what and when. Holding individuals and firms responsible enhances the probability that they will perform and own up to their responsibilities. Identifying responsibility and holding individuals and firms responsible for their actions in turn promotes productivity. There is a strong relationship between accountability and productivity.

The form used to record daily subcontractor performance will vary from firm to firm. However, at a minimum, the supervisor needs to record the following information daily regarding subcontractor performance:

Subcontractor Information to be Recorded

- Number of workers
- Supervision present
- Equipment present
- Equipment used
- Type of work performed
- Materials delivered
- Instructions given
- Instructions requested
- Construction method difficulties

SESSION 7
MANAGING SUBCONTRACTORS

> Effective and timely communication with subcontractors can aid problem solving and prevent disputes, resentment and procrastination.

- Productivity difficulties
- Safety issues
- Quality of work issues
- Conformance with contract administration requirements
  — Attendance at meetings
  — Compliance with scheduling requirements

The above list is not meant to be all-inclusive. Given the unique characteristics of each project and the type of work each subcontractor performs, reporting requirements for the supervisor should be reviewed and revised.

It is important that subcontractors know that they are being monitored and evaluated as the project work progresses. The mere fact that they know they will be held accountable will enhance their attention to performance.

New technology is evolving to perform the record keeping requirements of the supervisor monitoring subcontractor performance. This new technology is discussed in an upcoming session.

[Handwritten note: Name: Explain five practices that can be exercised by the CM to increase the effectiveness of communication between the CM & the S/C.]

Communication and Meetings

Positive Communication with Subcontractors

Failure to communicate correctly and in a timely manner is a leading cause of low construction industry productivity. The construction process is characterized by slow or inaccurate jobsite record keeping, different individuals and firms having different objectives and intentionally or unintentionally withholding information, and a job control process that is weekly or monthly. This time frame often means that it is too late to correct productivity problems effectively.

Many of the onsite production problems could be lessened or eliminated if only the problems were identified earlier and communicated to the individuals that could address them. Many of the construction disputes and lawsuits that are part of the construction industry could be avoided if individuals or firms would simply communicate the problem, identify the cause of the problem and remedy the situation. Instead, small problems tend to grow into large dollar problems which eventually negatively impact the project objectives of time, budget, quality and safety.

Effective communication is more a skill or an art than it is a science. As discussed in an earlier session on personnel management, effective communication is an essential component of keeping workers productive. It is equally important that the supervisor be attentive to timely and effective communication with subcontractors. The following practices should be implemented:

- Don't procrastinate; most construction productivity problems become bigger problems if they are not communicated and addressed.

- Try to use positive communication. Spend as much time commending the subcontractors' good efforts as you do blaming them for poor efforts.

- Remember that effective communication entails both talking and listening. Make an effort to listen to subcontractors; ask them for their ideas to solve problems.

- In communicating with subcontractors, try to create ideas and solutions that are a win-win situation for both the subcontractors and the general contractor. If the subcontractors believe everything they are being asked to do only benefits the general contractor or you as the supervisor, they are not likely to adhere to your recommendations or instructions.

> Subcontractors should be required to attend jobsite meetings. Meetings should be prompt, to the point and productive.

- Keep channels of communication open with all subcontractors. Encourage subcontractors to communicate their concerns and problems openly.

- When giving instructions to a subcontractor, always try to explain why you are giving the instructions. Describe the benefits that will be achieved if the instructions are followed.

- Try to act as an advisor to your subcontractors, not just a director.

- Set up a process of communicating success as well as failure.

- Understand your subcontractors. Some need more instruction, some need encouragement, some need reprimanding. Different people and different firms have different needs and knowledge.

- Consider new signage at jobsites that will communicate job status, successes and recognition.

Holding Productive Meetings

Holding formalized jobsite meetings is part of the communication system at construction jobsites. Given the complexity of the construction process and the many different firms and subcontractors that are dependent upon one another in the work process, an essential component of a productivity improvement program entails job meetings.

Meetings can be categorized as one of four types:

- Reporting and information meeting
- Problem solving meeting
- Brainstorming for improvement meeting
- Educational and training meeting

Reporting and information meetings are typically scheduled to occur at a set time and place. Weekly jobsite meetings to discuss project status, project schedules and safety are examples of reporting and information meetings. The meeting has an objective of communicating information to all subcontractors. They should be encouraged to attend.

Problem solving meetings can be viewed more as emergency meetings. The meeting should be scheduled as soon as a significant problem arises. A construction failure, an accident or the recognition of a significant cost overrun should initiate a meeting with all entities that caused the problem, can solve the problem or are affected by the problem. The supervisor should use problem-solving techniques and data analysis to facilitate these meetings.

Brainstorming for improvement meetings can be combined with one of the above two types of meetings or held independently of them. The purpose is to challenge current practices, to think "out of the box," to find a better way to do things. The construction process is such that the supervisor seldom holds this type of meeting with project subcontractors. Holding these meetings on a random or scheduled basis may reduce the need for problem solving meetings. The mood and productivity at a project will be more positive if new improvement ideas can be uncovered at a brainstorming meeting (as opposed to possibly spending the majority of the time pointing fingers at a problem solving meeting).

The resistance to holding brainstorming meetings probably stems from the fact that there is no guarantee that the meeting will yield results or benefits. However, given the potential that exists in the construction process, there often is a favorable benefit cost ratio associated with the brainstorming meeting. In addition, such a meeting has the potential to draw out subcontractor creativity and improvement.

Educational or training meetings have the objective of providing information to enable workers and firms to be more productive. Training entails giving individuals information that is likely to yield benefits or improvement quickly. Education is giving individuals information that will benefit them over a longer time frame.

Training and education historically have not been major priorities of construction firms. On occasion, construction firms hold in-house training or educational sessions or seminars. Usually, however, they are offered or given on a project basis. When one considers the fact that a project fails at the weakest link, the supervisor should consider offering training or education on a project basis; especially if the project is complex and requires the cooperation and knowledge of all entities. For example, instead of complaining about subcontractors not knowing or using formalized scheduling, the supervisor might weigh the benefits of providing them scheduling training or education.

Independent of the type of meeting held, the purpose is communication. The meeting(s) should be productive. The meeting agenda should be well defined and communicated to all subcontractors prior to the meeting. The meeting should be structured so that all parties have an opportunity to contribute input. However, the meeting should not be allowed to drift to non-productive chit chat or turn into a name-calling and negative environment. Meetings can be an effective tool of integrating subcontractors into a team if the supervisor promotes a positive atmosphere.

Jobsite performance fails at the weakest link. It is important to build a team approach to overall project objectives and problem solving. The team approach is much preferred to a finger-pointing environment.

Building a Team Approach to the Project

Team Building with the Subcontractors

The very nature of the construction industry results in firms, supervisors and craftspersons working for "jobs" as opposed to a "firm" concept. The average construction project takes only a year or two to construct, if not less. Individuals and firms go from job to job and may only work with one another on a single project. As a result individuals and firms may take a shortsighted view and think, "What's in it for me?"

The fact that subcontractors may be working with a general contractor supervisor on only one or a few projects, makes it even more important that the supervisor be attentive to taking a team approach to the project. There are too many ways that one contractor on a project can negatively impact another contractor if they are not working toward a common goal. On the majority of construction projects, if one contractor, be it the general contractor or a subcontractor, is in trouble, then the others are probably in trouble. Time, cost, quality and safety problems on a project tend to ripple to everyone.

Developing a "team" approach to the project and subcontractor management is easier said than done when there is such a large emphasis on low cost and profits. The supervisor needs to be creative in coming up with ideas and procedures to have all contractors and individuals work as a team. Team building ideas include the following:

- Recognition and awards for all team accomplishments rather than individual accomplishments

- Developing a win-win environment where one firm's success is not at the expense of another's loss.

- Implementing a quick problem-resolution system so that problems cannot grow to such a point that they prove divisive.

- Forward approach to problem solving by identifying potential problems and agreeing to methods and means of problem resolution ahead of time.

Partnering and dispute resolution boards are processes that the construction industry is using to develop more of a team approach to construction. Partnering focuses on a win-win situation for everyone. Included in a partnering agreement between contractors for a project are the following:

- Developing a trust relationship between all parties.
- Developing a "give and take" relationship between all parties.
- Putting team goals ahead of individual goals.
- Identifying potential problems ahead of time so that a game plan can be established for their resolution.
- Development of a "we" approach to project performance as opposed to a "they" approach.

Productivity improvement can best be achieved when everyone is pulling in the same direction!

Team Building by Focusing on Common Goals

Listed below are the four project variables of project time, cost, quality and safety. With the objective of getting all project contractors pulling in the same direction, your group should write down potential conflicts or "bumps in the road" that may disrupt a project team effort for each of the goals, and define positive actions that can be taken to reduce or eliminate various firms from becoming divisive in regard to actions they take that may curtail achieving the goal.

Goal: Build the project for the least amount of cost that will enable contractor profits

Potential conflicts or "bumps in the road"	Positive action to build "team approach"

Exercise

Exercise

Goal: Build the project on schedule so that the project owner is content

Potential conflicts or "bumps in the road"	Positive action to build "team approach"

Goal: Build a high quality project that exceeds project specifications

Potential conflicts or "bumps in the road"	Positive action to build "team approach"

Goal: Construct a safe project with the goal of zero worker accidents

Potential conflicts or "bumps in the road"	Positive action to build "team approach"

Session 7 Review

Look over Session 7 and review these key points to be sure you understand them.

- The supervisor working for the general contractor must manage his or her own self-performed work and also coordinate and supervise the work of the subcontractors.
- The best way to manage subcontractors is to engage the right subcontractors so that they don't need to be managed much.
- The effective supervisor can show a concern for individuals and at the same time be authoritative.
- An effective approach to subcontractor management is to encourage them to manage themselves.
- It is important that the supervisor keep daily records regarding subcontractor performance.
- The supervisor needs to be creative in coming up with ideas and procedures to have all contractors and individuals work as a team.

Using on the Job What You Learned Today

Jobsite Assignment

At your projects, take note of the management practices of supervisors of subcontractors. Compare these to your own. The objective is to learn from their actions and improve your own so that you can help subcontractor supervisors improve.

Session 8

Quantifying Lost Labor Productivity

Learning Goals for Session 8

After this session, you should understand the following:

- How change orders, project changes and external events can negatively impact labor productivity
- Six different categories of factors that can negatively impact labor productivity
- Quantitative measures of lost labor productivity owing to impact factors
- Methods of quantifying lost productivity for disputes and claims

The above knowledge will enable you to identify and quantify lost labor productivity due to project change orders, project changes and external events.

Learning Objectives

To accomplish the learning goals, during this session you will:

- Identify six different categories of factors that negatively impact labor productivity
- Quantify lost productivity for working overtime
- Quantify lost productivity due to worker learning
- Quantity lost labor productivity because of weather changes
- Quantity lost labor productivity due to changes in project logistics
- Quantity lost labor productivity due to change and change orders

To Get Ready for Session

Reading: Begin reading this session in your Participant's Manual. Try to think of reasons it is important to quantify lost labor productivity.

Major Activities for Session 8

- Review important points from Session 7.
- Study various external factors that negatively impact on-site labor productivity.
- Do a group exercise in which you will calculate lost labor overruns and cost owing to overtime.
- Do a group exercise in which you will measure productivity as a function of worker learning.
- Do an exercise to quantify lost labor productivity owing to unexpected weather conditions.
- Do an exercise to quantify lost productivity owing to a change in project logistics and access.
- Study various methods used to quantify and present lost labor productivity (optional).

A Review of Session 7

In Session 7, you learned the importance of managing subcontractors to enable a productive jobsite. You learned that you cannot attain overall productivity if you ignore the performance of subcontractors; the project fails at the weakest link.

You learned in Session 7 to take a proactive role in managing subcontractors:

- The importance of hiring subcontractors attentive to productivity and a team approach to projects.

- How to help subcontractors help themselves by encouraging them to manage and practice sound productivity practices. Practices include performance management, project planning and scheduling, and short interval scheduling.

- Proper record keeping for managing subcontractors.

- How to communicate with subcontractors and hold productive meetings.

- The importance of team building.

Loss of Labor Productivity (Impact) Owing to Changes and External Events

Project changes and events often occur that result in a negative impact to labor (and equipment) productivity. Changes might be direct, whereby the project owner adds more work to the construction firm's base bid work. These may be of such a large dollar value that it upsets the work flow and sequencing of the base bid work. The result is a "negative impact" on the labor productivity for the base bid work.

Construction changes occur when the base bid work is done under conditions that the construction firm and the supervisor did not anticipate when putting together the project estimate, and which were not agreed to in the signed contract. Examples of construction changes include the following:

- Schedule changed and work shifted into colder temperatures

- Contractor required to work overtime due to owner or designer delays

- Contractor required to add workers to project to accelerate schedule

- Contractor required to do work in an unexpectedly crowded or tight working area

- Contractor required to store materials farther from project than planned, due to unavailability of lay-down areas

- Contractor required to start-stop, start-stop work process because design documents or design decisions are unavailable.

Construction labor productivity is a complex process.

The productivity or units of output produced per person-hour of effort or input is very sensitive to many input factors: the amount and quality of labor, equipment, materials, weather, and expected working conditions; the quality and completeness of the drawings and specifications; and the expected actions of the project owner. The contractor's labor productivity estimate is predicated upon a reasonable estimate of each of these factors. This is illustrated in Figure 8-1.

> Project changes occur when the base bid work is done under conditions that the construction firm and the supervisor did not anticipate when putting together the project estimate and that were not agreed to in the signed contract.

SESSION 8

QUANTIFYING LOST LABOR PRODUCTIVITY

Project Definition	The Plan	Unexpected Events	Negative Impact on Labor Productivity	Result: Loss of Labor Productivity

A. Worker Ability to do Work
(A.1) Difficulty of Work/Fatigue
(A.2.) Overtime

B. Sequencing
(B.1.) Concurrent Operations
(B.2.) Learning Curve
(B.3.) Crew Size
(B.4.) Dilution of Supervision
(B.5.) Stacking of Trades

C. Environmental Factors
(C.1.) Temperature, Wind, Humidity
(C.2.) Noise
(C.3.) Lighting

PROJECT CONTRACT DOCUMENTS — Drawings, Specifications, PROJECT SITE CONDITIONS

The Plan:
- Planned Labor
- Planned Equipment
- Planned Material
- Expected Weather
- Expected Working Conditions
- Expected Drawings and Specifications
- Expected Owner and Designer Actions

Unexpected Events:
- Added Work Change Orders
- Changed job conditions
- Incomplete Drawings Specs
- Late Owner Designer Decisions

PLANNED PRODUCTIVITY

$$\frac{\text{UNITS}}{\text{PERSON HOUR}}$$

PRODUCTIVITY IMPACT

IMPACTED PRODUCTIVITY

$$\frac{\text{UNITS}}{\text{PERSON HOUR}}$$

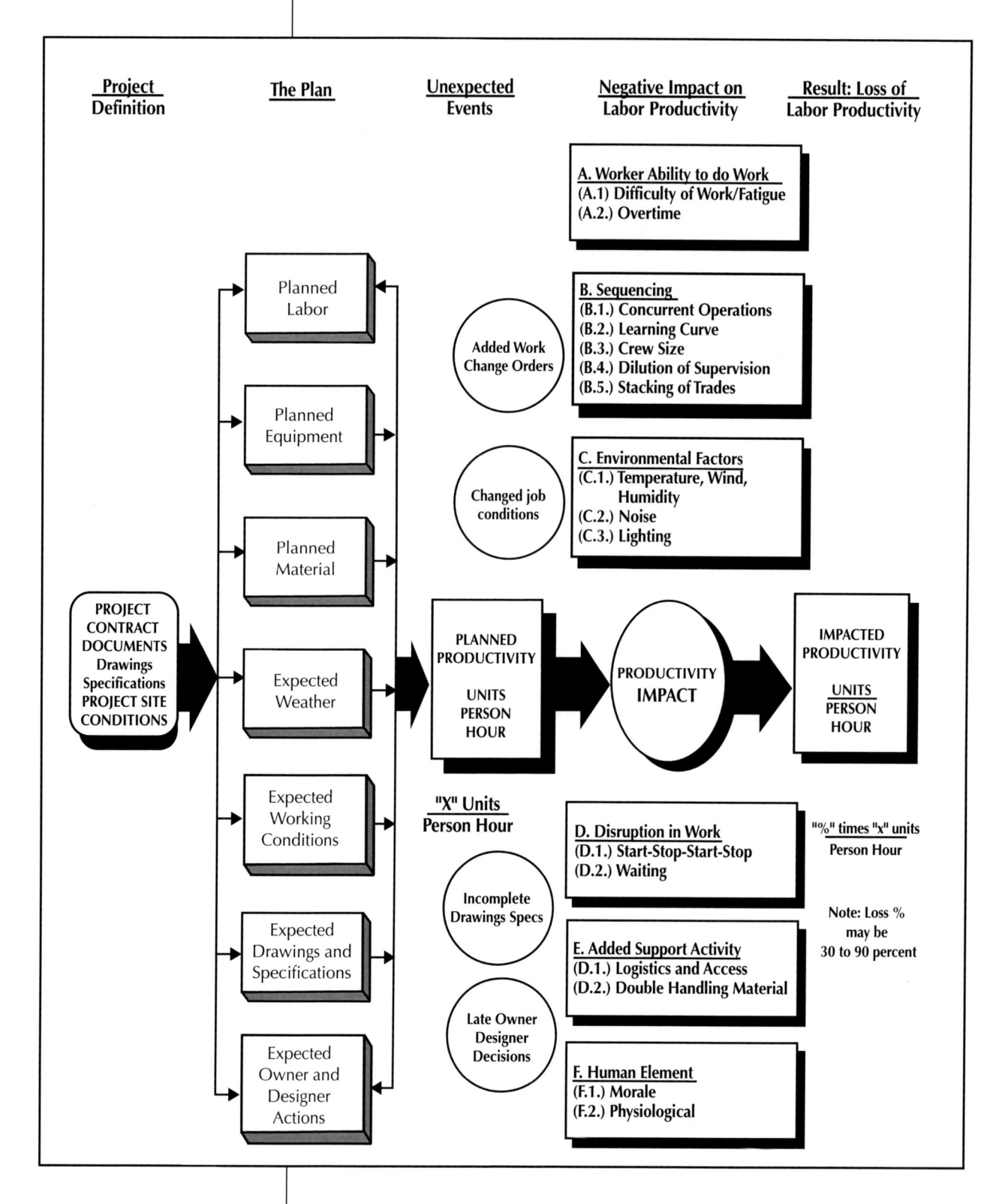

"X" Units Person Hour

D. Disruption in Work
(D.1.) Start-Stop-Start-Stop
(D.2.) Waiting

E. Added Support Activity
(D.1.) Logistics and Access
(D.2.) Double Handling Material

F. Human Element
(F.1.) Morale
(F.2.) Physiological

"%" times "x" units Person Hour

Note: Loss % may be 30 to 90 percent

Fig. 8-1. Loss of Construction Productivity Owing to Impact

Unexpected events outside the control of the construction supervisor may negatively impact on-site labor productivity. Examples are the following:

- Added work due to change orders
- Changed job conditions; e.g., different weather, soil conditions, material lay-down areas
- Incomplete drawings or specifications
- Late project owner and designer decisions

These are also shown in Figure 8-1. These factors often result in work under one or more of the following adverse work conditions:

- Overtime
- Learning curve
- Temperature, wind, humidity
- Start-stop-start-stop
- Double handling of material
- Morale problems

These and other negative productivity impact factors are also shown in Figure 8-1.

So that the supervisor can quantify the financial impact these external negative factors have on his or her project, it is important that the supervisor understand these factors (referred to as "Negative Impact Factors") shown in Figure 8-1.

In recent years, there has been considerable funded research conducted to aid in quantifying productivity losses as a function of various impact factors. Many of these studies have been performed by Dr. Adrian, both as part of his Ph.D. thesis and through consulting engagements. Other major construction entities that conduct productivity studies are the Corp of Engineers, the Business Roundtable and large firms such as Exxon Mobil. The negative impact factors shown in Figure 8-1 can be classified into six categories as shown:

- Worker ability to do work
- Continuity of work process
- Environmental factors
- Disruption of work process
- Added support activities
- Human element

In recent years, there has been considerable funded research conducted to aid in quantifying productivity losses as a function of various impact factors.

Negative productivity impact factors can be classified into six categories:

- Worker ability to do work
- Continuity of work process
- Environmental factors
- Disruption of work process
- Added support activities
- Human element

Loss of Productivity

(A) Worker Ability to Do Work

(A.1.) More Difficult Work Process; (A.2.) Fatigue

A worker's ability to perform work can be expressed in scientific terms. Although physical characteristics, including height, weight and muscles, all relate to work potential, an individual is capable of only a finite amount of work because of the physical limitations of the human body. The study of the human body's ability to do work is referred to as human factor engineering.

The normal body can be thought of as a mechanism that takes on, stores and expends energy as shown in Figure 8-2. Obviously, a worker can only expend energy to the level he or she can restore it or has it in reserve.

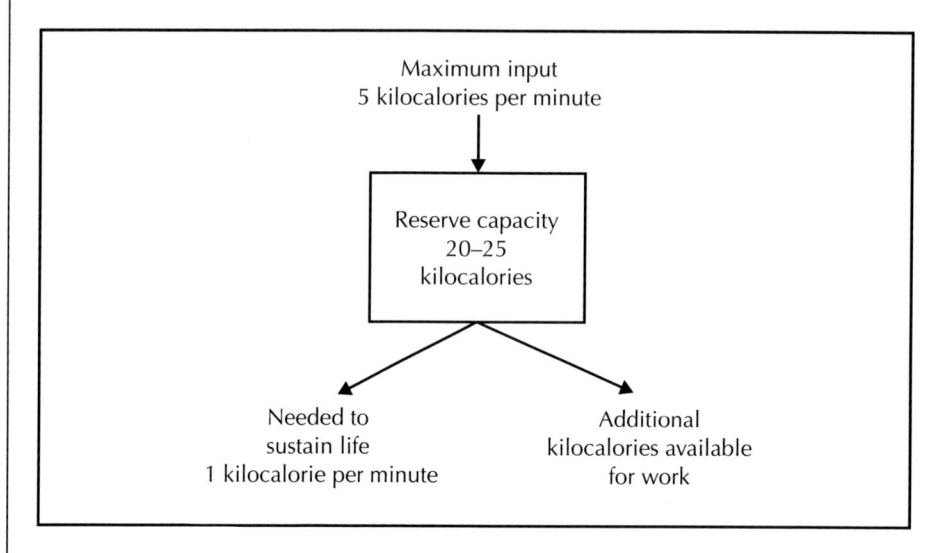

```
           Maximum input
        5 kilocalories per minute
                  |
                  v
         ┌─────────────────┐
         │ Reserve capacity │
         │      20–25       │
         │   kilocalories   │
         └─────────────────┘
           /              \
          v                v
   Needed to            Additional
   sustain life       kilocalories available
  1 kilocalorie per minute     for work
```

Fig. 8-2

A kilocalorie may be expressed as follows:

1 kilocalorie	= 3.97 British thermal units (BTUs)
	= 3,086 foot-pounds
	= 1.162 watt-hours

As shown in Figure 8-3, a worker moving 10 pounds for ten feet in effect produces 100 foot-pounds of work.

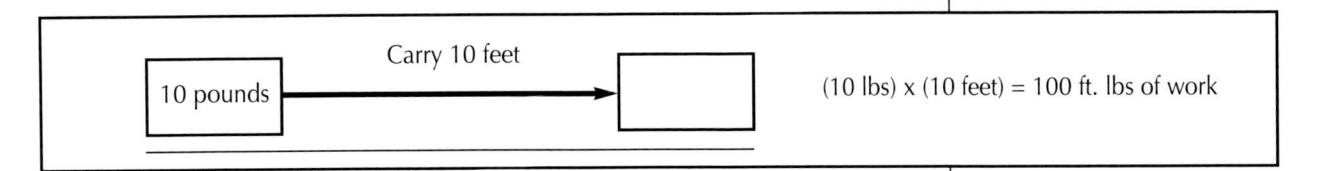

```
┌─────────────────────────────────────────────────────────────────────────┐
│                        Carry 10 feet                                     │
│   ┌──────────┐                      ┌──────┐                             │
│   │10 pounds │─────────────────────▶│      │   (10 lbs) x (10 feet) = 100 ft. lbs of work │
│   └──────────┘                      └──────┘                             │
└─────────────────────────────────────────────────────────────────────────┘
```

Fig. 8-3

Workers do many activities during a day. Therefore, it is rather complex to measure precisely the energy expended by an individual during an entire day. However, there is no question that the different activities require different amounts of work effort. This is illustrated in Figure 8-4.

Activity (Office Worker)	Time (min)	Energy kcal/min	Total kilocal's	Activity (Construction worker)	Time (min)	Energy kcal/min	Total kilocal's
Sleeping and lying in bed	460	1.3	598	Sleeping and lying in bed	460	1.3	598
Sitting	620	1.6	993	Construction work	560	6.6	3,696
Standing	120	2.25	270	Standing, rest, instructions	200	2.4	480
Washing and dressing	40	2.9	116	Washing and dressing	30	2.9	87
Walking	70	5.6	392	Walking	80	5.6	448
Sporting/leisure activities	60	4.8	288	Sporting/leisure activities	40	4.8	192
Domestic work	70	3.0	210	Domestic work	70	3.0	210
TOTAL	1,440		2,867	TOTAL	1,440		5,711

Fig. 8-4

The construction supervisor may find that there are project changes that require more difficult work or the use of methods that require more worker energy. The following are examples:

- Concrete design changed such that each forming panel weighs 84 pounds instead of the planned 64 pounds.

- Design changed such that workers are required to carry materials 100 feet to work location instead of the planned 60 feet.

- Logistics of the project changed such that workers have to lie on their backs and use pulleys to secure material and put it in place rather than have the material lifted to them by a machine.

In each of the above situations, the completed work may be the same. However, the construction supervisor would likely want to take a position that more labor effort, time and cost was required to perform the work given the added work effort and kilocalories required to do

> The construction supervisor may experience project changes that require more difficult work or the use of methods that require more worker energy.

the work. Using human factor engineering data such as that shown in Figure 8-4, the supervisor could quantify his or her presentation of the issues.

(A.3.) Impact of Overtime

The supervisor may be required to work onsite craftworkers overtime in an attempt to accelerate the work process. Often a wage premium such as time and a half needs to be paid to workers for time over 8 hours in a given day. In addition to the wage premium, the supervisor should recognize that, owing to the human body's ability to perform only limited work as an energy-producing mechanism, there also is a probable loss in productivity for each hour of overtime. Construction is hard, physically demanding work. When required to work overtime, the onsite craft worker is likely to become fatigued and do less than his or her normal hourly output.

There has been considerable research conducted on the negative impact of overtime on construction worker productivity. Studies have been conducted by the Business Roundtable, the National Electrical Contractors Association (NECA) and various contractor associations and contractor groups. A summary of select studies is shown in Figure 8-5.

> Because there is a limit to the body's energy-producing capabilities, the onsite craft worker required to work overtime is likely to become fatigued and do less than his or her normal hourly output.

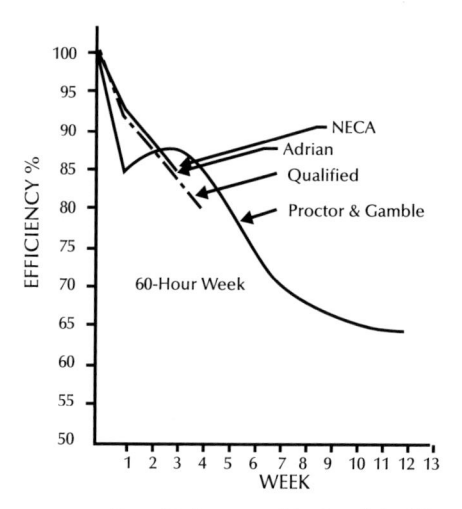

Figure 3.2 Summary of the Cumulative Effect of Overtime on Productivity. 60-Hour Workweek.

Fig. 8-5

In a study for concrete-related work during ideal weather conditions (60 to 80 degrees Fahrenheit), the impact of overtime was studied and is quantified in Figure 8-6.

Days	Daily hours	Total weekly hours	Inefficiency % 7 days of overtime	Inefficiency % 21 days of overtime
5	9	45	2-4	6-8
5	10	50	5-7	11-13
5	11	55	9-11	16-18
6	9	54	3-5	7-11
6	10	60	6-8	13-17
6	11	66	11-13	20-22
7	8	56	8-10	18-20
7	9	63	10-12	21-23
7	10	70	13-15	26-29
7	11	77	19-21	38-41

Fig. 8-6

It should be pointed out that the loss of productivity stated in the two right columns applies for every hour worked, not just the overtime hours. The above findings would have to be modified if different work were considered (for example, less strenuous work) or the work were performed in an adverse temperature (for example, hot-humid conditions would increase the negative impact of overtime).

SESSION 8

QUANTIFYING LOST LABOR PRODUCTIVITY

Exercise

Calculating the Loss of Productivity Due to Overtime

On a construction project, 10,000 units of a work task have to be performed. Assume that the contractor doing the work planned on using a crew of five onsite craftspersons working five days a week and eight hours per day. No overtime was planned. A productivity of 10 units per person hour was estimated. The average wage rate for standard time for a worker was correctly estimated at $15.00 per hour.

Further assume that, for reasons outside the control or responsibility of the contractor, the construction supervisor has been asked to work the five workers six days a week and 10 hours a day for the duration of the work. The owner has agreed to pay for the wage premium increase of time and a half for the overtime hours. As the supervisor, calculate the additional money you should request for the impact of the overtime on the labor productivity. Use the overtime loss productivity data shown in Figure 8-6.

Loss of Productivity

(B) Continuity of the Work Process

(B.1.) Concurrent Operations

The construction firm and supervisor plan the work process so that there is natural sequence of work activities. For example, in working on a roadway, the supervisor likely follows a linear progression from one end of the planned new road to the other. Similarly, a supervisor placing concrete wall forming follows a natural progression around the building perimeter.

Some work tasks required for the construction process are planned as sequential (one after the other), while other work tasks are planned as concurrent (happening at the same time). For example, assume three work processes were planned as shown in Figure 8-7.

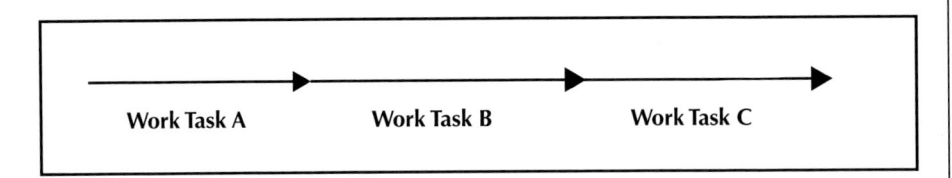

Fig. 8-7

Further assume that for whatever reason (perhaps because the project owner wants the supervisor to accelerate the work process) the supervisor had to perform the three work activities concurrently as shown in Figure 8-8.

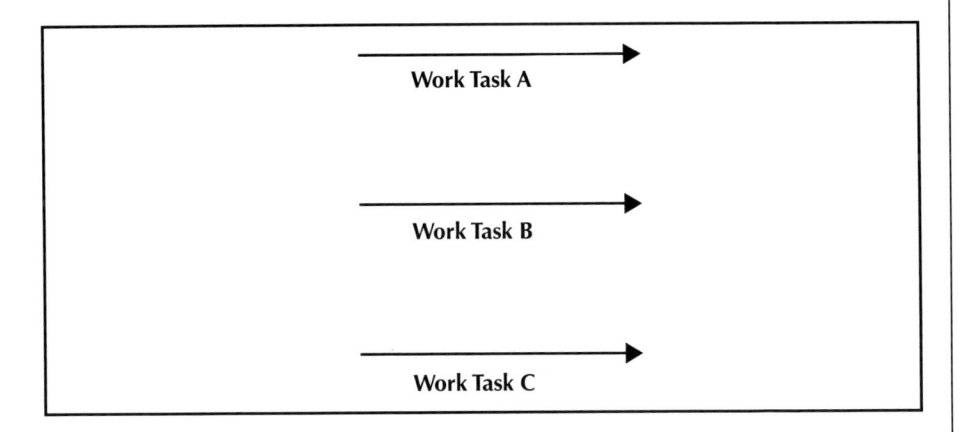

Fig. 8-8

Further assume that one crew of on-site workers was scheduled to work on task A, then work on task B, and then work on task C as shown in Figure 8-7.

The concurrent work sequence shown in Figure 8-8 would likely have a negative impact on labor productivity for at least three possible reasons: 1) the learning curve of the additional workers needed, 2) the non-optimal crew size and/or 3) the dilution of the supervisor is energy to manage the three work activities performed concurrently.

(B.2.) Learning Curve of Workers

If the three work tasks shown have to be performed concurrently, the supervisor will have to employ added workers. Depending on the complexity of the task and the worker's familiarity with the work process, new workers are likely to experience lower initial productivity owing to a "learning" process. Scientific studies have been conducted that have modeled a worker's ability to produce as a function of how many times he or she has done a work process. An example is illustrated in Figure 8-9.

Scientific studies have been conducted which model a worker's ability to produce as a function of how many times he or she has done a work process.

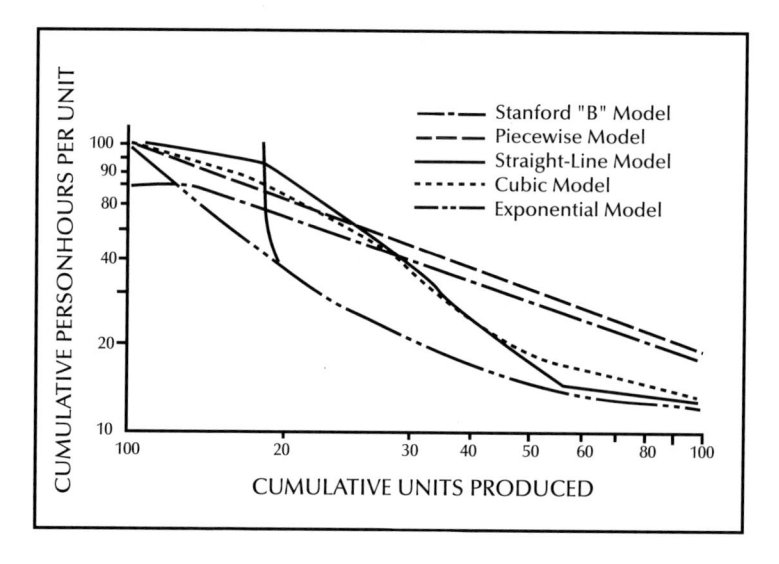

Fig. 8-9

Given the need to accelerate the work process, the supervisor could use such "learning data" to quantify extra labor hours to accomplish the tasks.

(B.3.) Crew Size

The construction work process is such that there normally is an ideal crew size and mix for every work task. Assume six workers is an ideal number of craftspersons for a specific work task. If a seventh worker is added to the work crew, the total work duration might decrease, but the total person hours required to do the work will likely increase (i.e., the productivity per worker is less). Similarly, if five workers are used on the crew, the total person hours required (and the work duration) will probably increase.

In the example of the three work tasks shown in Figure 8-7 and 8-8, instead of hiring additional workers to do the three tasks concurrently, assume the supervisor assigns two of the six workers to each of the concurrent work tasks, A, B and C. Given an ideal crew size of six workers for each task, the assigning of only two workers to each task will probably result in lower labor productivity and increased labor costs.

Published data is not readily available regarding the decreased work productivity one would expect when "ideal" crew sizes are changed. However, the construction firm and supervisor can collect such data from past performances of work tasks so that the lost productivity can be estimated.

(B.3) Dilution of Supervision

Supervision is a critical component of craftsperson productivity. While it would be ideal if workers managed themselves and did not need supervision, typically the work crew needs direction and assistance from the supervisor. Studies have indicated a 15% to 20% possible decrease in worker productivity if needed supervision is absent. It follows that, if each of the three work tasks shown in Figure 8-9 needs supervision, the supervisor's inability to be in three places at one time will result in lower worker productivity for the unsupervised work tasks.

(B.4.) Stacking – Available Work Space

When the work process is knocked out of sequence, the supervisor often has on-site workers in situations not conducive to optimal labor productivity. Workers may get "stacked up" against another trade, or have to work in an area too small to support the ideal crew size to do the work. While the addition of more workers is likely to shorten a work process, the lack of working space may result in more worker hours being required to do a work task; i.e., lower productivity. For example, workers may not have adequate room for their tools or for areas to move their arms, etc. In effect, workers will get in the way of one another.

The construction work process is such that there normally is an ideal crew size and mix for every work task.

SESSION 8
QUANTIFYING LOST LABOR PRODUCTIVITY

Research studies have been conducted to study the ideal workspace required for workers to be most productive. Figure 8-10 illustrates summary data from select studies, named in parentheses.

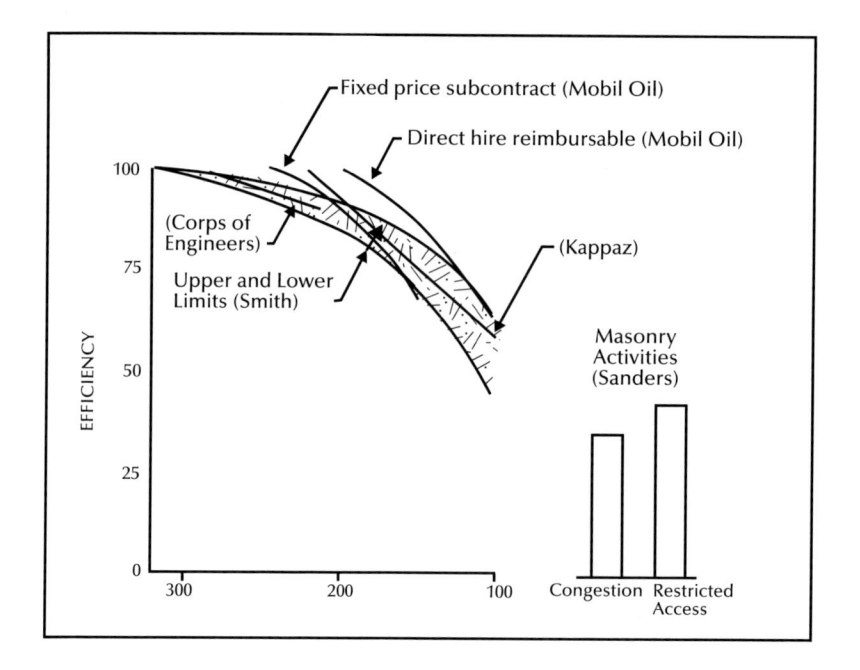

Fig. 8-10

For example, the data illustrated in Figure 8-10 indicates that a worker needs an area approximately 17 feet by 17 feet (approximately 300 square feet) to be most productive. If the same worker was put into an area of approximately 14 feet by 14 feet (approximately 200 square feet), the chart infers a loss of productivity of approximately 12% to 15%.

Obviously the data shown in Figure 8-10 needs adjustment depending on the type of work involved. However, the fact remains that if a worker or a crew of workers is "stacked" into a corner or not given adequate work space, there will be a lowering of productivity.

The Learning Curve and Pricing a Contract

A contractor has been engaged to fabricate five steel storage tanks. All five tanks are the same. The project owner will provide the material and the contractor will provide the labor for fabricating the tanks.

Owing to the unique design and shape of the tanks, the contractor is unwilling to give a fixed price for all five tanks. Instead the contractor and the owner have agreed that the contractor will fabricate the first two tanks on a cost-plus basis. Based on the experience of fabricating the first two tanks, the contractor is required to give a fixed price contract for the remaining three tank fabrications.

The construction supervisor has judged that the work process is such that the workers fabricating the tanks will "learn" the process and increase productivity as each tank is fabricated.

The following equation has been proposed for the learning rate for the workers fabricating the tanks:

$Y = (A) \times (X)^{-n}$

Where: y = the person-hours required to produce the Xth unit of work
A = the measured value of the hours required to produce the first unit of work
X = the number of work units produced
N = the derived exponent that describes work output variation

The contractor is using a crew of three workers, each of whom has a wage rate of $24.00 per hour. The three workers fabricated the first unit in 360 minutes, and the second unit in 320 minutes. Based on the learning rate equation, calculate the expected labor cost of fabricating the first two tanks and the labor cost for fabricating the remaining three tanks.

Exercise

Loss of Productivity

(C) Environmental Factors

Often the construction supervisor may be required to work in environmental conditions that he or she did not expect, and which are adverse to labor (and perhaps equipment) productivity. Examples include the following:

- Adverse temperature (hot and/or cold)
- Humidity / Wind
- Precipitation
- Noise
- Poor lighting

Because the project is not constructed in a factory where it is possible to control the above factors, the supervisor can expect some variation in the factors from day to day. However, if one of the above factors varies significantly from what one would expect or what was assumed in the estimate, the supervisor should attempt to quantify the impact of the condition on the productivity of his or her on-site workers.

(C.1.) Adverse Temperatures, Humidity and Wind

Common sense indicates that a worker's productivity is adversely affected by extreme temperature changes, be they hot or cold temperatures. If the human body is exposed to high temperatures over an extended period of time, heat stress will occur. In addition to causing slowdowns in work produced, the hot temperatures will result in frequent worker breaks to cool off and consume water. These breaks also distract from the productivity objectives.

Extreme cold also negatively affects worker productivity, especially in activities referred to as "wet" construction. This includes masonry and concrete work.

Humidity is defined as the amount of water vapor or moisture in the air.

High concentrations of moisture in the air, or humidity combined with hot temperatures proves very adverse to labor productivity. Humidity affects the evaporation of perspiration from a person's skin. Thus in warm weather, the ease of stabilizing one's internal temperature depends not only on temperature, but also on the humidity level.

QUANTIFYING LOST LABOR PRODUCTIVITY

Considerable research has been conducted on the impact of high temperatures and high humidity on the productivity of the construction worker.

Wind is yet another factor that affects the productivity of the construction worker. Winds greater than 10 to 20 mph not only affect a worker's productivity, but may cause a safety concern. Roof work or work entailing the carrying of objects such as concrete are such that high winds jeopardize the safety of the worker. Another adverse effect of wind is the nuisance of airborne foreign matter. This material can impact productivity and safety by impairing the vision of the worker.

High winds combined with cold air can cause extremely cold conditions referred to as the "wind-chill" factor. In effect the high winds make cold temperatures feel even colder. Figure 8-11 gives the effective temperature as a function of the wind speed and the temperature, measured in degrees Fahrenheit.

Wind Speed (MPH)	50°F	40°F	30°F	20°F	10°F	0°F	-10°F	-20°F	-30°F
Calm	50	40	30	20	10	0	-10	-20	-30
5	48	37	27	16	6	-5	-15	-26	-36
10	40	28	16	4	-9	-21	-33	-46	-58
15	36	22	10	-5	-18	-36	-45	-58	-72
20	32	18	4	-10	-25	-39	-53	-67	-82
25	30	16	0	-15	-29	-44	-58	-74	-88
30	28	13	-2	-18	-33	-48	-63	-79	-94
35	27	11	-4	-20	-35	-49	-67	-82	-98

Fig. 8-11

Whether or not the construction supervisor has a right to request additional money owing to unexpected weather conditions depends on contract language and how extreme the weather change is. Independent of this issue, the construction supervisor should be able to quantify the impact of the weather on productivity.

> Considerable amounts of rain often influence jobsite productivity many days after the rain has stopped.

(C.2.) Precipitation

Precipitation in the form of rain and snow have a significant impact on construction productivity. Precipitation may even stop a construction process. When it is raining lightly, construction workers can proceed with the work; however, because of the discomfort created by even a light rain, productivity is negatively affected. Considerable amounts of rain often influence jobsite productivity many days after the rain has stopped, as muddy working conditions affect both labor and equipment.

Unlike temperature, humidity and wind (to varying degrees always present), precipitation does not always occur. Therefore, its effect on productivity is more difficult to predict and quantify.

It helps for the supervisor to know the expected number of days and the amount of rain at the jobsite location as a function of the time of the year. Such historical data is available from the weather bureau for specific geographic locations. For example, historical data indicate that in Illinois one can expect annual precipitation in the range of 32 to 48 inches of rain in a year. Data also is available that sets out expected monthly rainfall for specific geographic locations.

Knowledge of soil conditions is also critical when quantifying the impact of precipitation at a jobsite. Some soils absorb or hold water more than others. Thus the impact of precipitation on the site and productivity as a function of time is dependent on the type of soil at the site.

(C.3.) Noise

While not as obvious a factor as temperature and precipitation in its possible detrimental impact on construction productivity, noise can be a health hazard and can have an adverse effect on the amount and quality of work performed.

One dimension of noise is its frequency, which is a measurement of the vibration of noise-producing bodies and is measured in a standard unit called a Hertz. Changes in degrees of frequency are referred to as changes in pitch. Another characteristic of noise is amplitude, or loudness. The speed at which a sound source vibrates does not directly determine the strength of the sound; the strength depends on the energy behind a sound wave; the force (loudness) with which it strikes one's hearing system. Amplitude is measured on a decibel scale. Decibels (dB) measure sound pressure or power in a given environment. One decibel is used to express relative difference in power between two sounds, equal to 10 times the common logarithm of the ratio of the two levels.

Besides the annoyance factor, noise can negatively impact effective communication at the jobsite. Noise levels greater than 90 decibels are often related to possible hearing damage and decreased work performance. Examples of various noise levels for various types of construction as measured in dBs are illustrated in Figure 8-12.

Type of Work	Domestic Housing	Building Construction	Public works (incl. housing)
Ground clearing	83 dB	84 dB	87 dB
Excavation	85 dB	87 dB	89 dB
Foundations	81 dB	83 dB	88 dB
Erection	75 dB	82 dB	83 dB
Finishing	74 dB	78 dB	83 dB

Fig. 8-12

These should be viewed as examples only. Depending on the work activity, the noise level may be higher or lower than shown.

While research has been conducted on how noise affects a person's ability to think and do a particular kind of work (e.g., mistakes made while typing); less is known about the impact of noise on the construction worker's productivity.

Perhaps what is most relevant about noise level and construction worker productivity is laws or restrictions on when and where the construction work can proceed, given noise ordinances. For example, while working on an addition to a hospital, a construction supervisor is not to do work louder than 70 dB while the existing operating room is being used. The hospital may impose this regulation because the loud noise would jeopardize procedures in the operating room. In this case, the construction supervisor would need to be attentive to scheduling construction operations that keep the noise to an acceptable limit.

(C.4.) Lighting

Proper lighting is required so that an onsite worker can perform work tasks productively. If the construction worker is required to work at night, lighting is the single most important element in regard to productivity. The objective of lighting design is to provide the proper quantity and quality of light for a particular task. Given the recent increase in nighttime construction by highway departments on public works projects, there has been considerable attention drawn to the issue of lighting and construction productivity.

Lighting standards are typically given in foot-candles (fc). A foot-candle is defined as the amount of direct light thrown by one international candle on a surface one foot away.

Owing to the limited lighting research in construction, few standards exist. However, the construction supervisor can learn from the standards set by other industries. Examples of recommended illumination standards for various non-construction operations are listed in Figure 8-13.

> A foot-candle is defined as the amount of direct light thrown by one international candle on a surface one foot away.

Industry	Name of Activity	Recommended lighting (fcs)
Automobile Industry	Welding activities	50
	Machining operations	75
	Outdoor vehicle entrance	5
Pulp & Paper Industry	Cutting and sorting	70
	Log unloading	5
Industrial Outdoors	Excavation	4
	General construction	15

Fig. 8-13

Construction workers who do more detailed work and work with tighter tolerances need more light to be productive than do those in excavation or concrete related work.

Limited research has been conducted as to the decrease in productivity when there are fewer fcs of light available than recommended. In addition to concerns about decreased productivity when light is not adequate, the safety concerns increase. It follows that if project conditions are changed so that workers have to work in less than suitable lighting conditions, the supervisor should expect decreased productivity.

Exercise

Temperature and Lost Labor Productivity

A construction firm is scheduled to place 10,000 linear feet of electrical conduit for a new project it has estimated. A crew size of 3 electricians is planned. The average wage rate for a worker on the crew is $20 per hour. The work is planned for the months of August through October when the weather is expected to be ideal. Productivity is estimated at 15 feet of conduit per person-hour. A contract is signed based on these assumptions.

After signing the contract, the project owner delays the start of the project. The result is that the work starts later and is completed during more adverse weather conditions. The building is not totally enclosed when the electrical work is performed and the average environmental conditions are as follows:

Temperature	30°F
Wind	15 mph
Humidity	60%

Further assume that following data has been collected regarding the loss of productivity for electrical work.

Relative Humidity	Effective Productivity (%)	Effective Productivity (%)	Effective Productivity (%)	Effective Productivity (%)	Effective Productivity (%)	Effective Productivity (%)
90	57	71	82	89	93	96
80	58	73	84	91	95	98
70	59	75	86	93	97	99
60	60	76	87	94	98	100
50	61	77	88	94	98	100
40	62	78	88	94	98	100
30	63	78	88	94	98	100
Effective Temperature (°F)	-10	0	10	20	30	40

Fig. 8-14

Calculate the expected lost labor hours and added labor costs related to doing the work in the adverse weather conditions relative to the planned labor hours and labor cost. Use the table shown in Figure 8-14 to determine the effective temperature.

Loss of Productivity

(D) Disruption of Work Process

Two frequent negative factors that affect on-site labor productivity are start-stop-start-stop work processes and waiting. These events commonly occur due to owner or designer indecision or changes. Start-stop-start-stop work or waiting may relate to one of the following:

- Contract drawings and/or specifications may lack detail. The workers wait while the supervisor seeks clarification from the project owner/designer.

- The project owner or designer may impose a change order that requires the contractor to stop and do the change order work, then come back to the original work.

- Another trade may be in the way of the contractor, causing the contractor to stop work and return to it later.

Each of the above events will probably slow momentum, cause non-productive worker waiting time, add more time for support activities such as walking to and from the work area, and ultimately result in a negative impact on the morale of the worker. The worker may be required to re-mobilize and re-learn the work process or task.

(D.1.) Start-stop-start-stop

The construction firm plans the work process to develop a certain rhythm. As noted in an earlier session, the worker can be viewed as being in one of three work states:

- Productive (putting in finished work; e.g., sheet metal, concrete, asphalt, etc.)

- Non-productive (waiting, unnecessary walking, etc.)

- Support (carrying material, reading drawings, etc.)

Every project and every task will have some of each work state. However, the contractor and the construction supervisor strive to increase the percentage of time the workers are in a productive state. In effect, the construction firm only makes money and achieves schedule progress when workers are in a productive state.

SESSION 8

QUANTIFYING LOST LABOR PRODUCTIVITY

When subjected to a start-stop-start-stop work process, the construction supervisor finds that workers are in a productive state less of the time. Workers have to leave an area, mobilize to do a different task, or start the new task — only to have to return to the original task later, remobilize again and complete the work process.

To some degree each start-stop-start-stop situation is unique. The amount of lost "productive" time and increase in "non-productive" or "support" time is unique to the work being performed (which in part dictates the time to remobilize), the distance to the secondary task, etc. The number of interruptions is also relevant to the issue. One research study on interruptions or start-stop-start-stop work processes concluded as shown in Figure 8-15.

Efficiency by number of interruptions:
- No Interruptions: 100
- 1 Interruption: 90
- 2 Interruptions: 60
- 3 or more Interruptions: 30

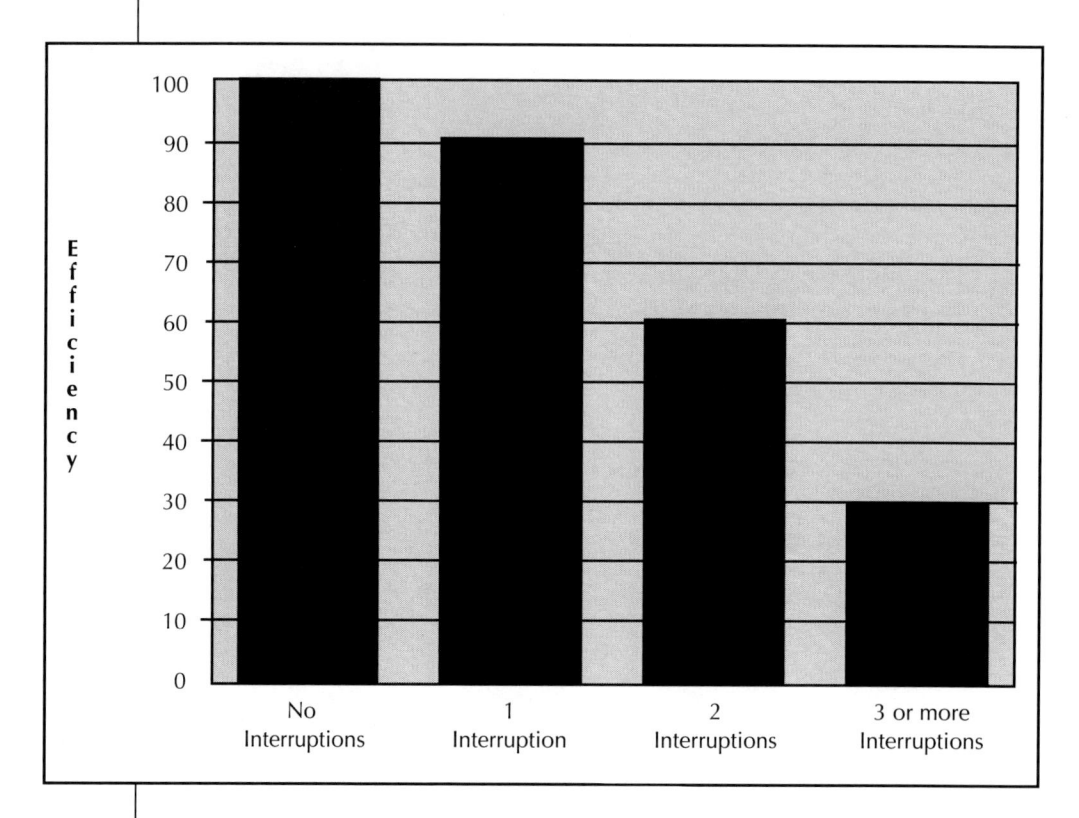

Fig. 8-15

Given the uniqueness of each project and each start-stop-start-stop situation, the best way of illustrating the impact on productivity is to do a job-specific analysis of the work process. Figure 8-16 illustrates a non-impacted day versus a day with a start-stop-start-stop work process. Design issues led to requests for information (RFIs).

Unimpacted Work Day

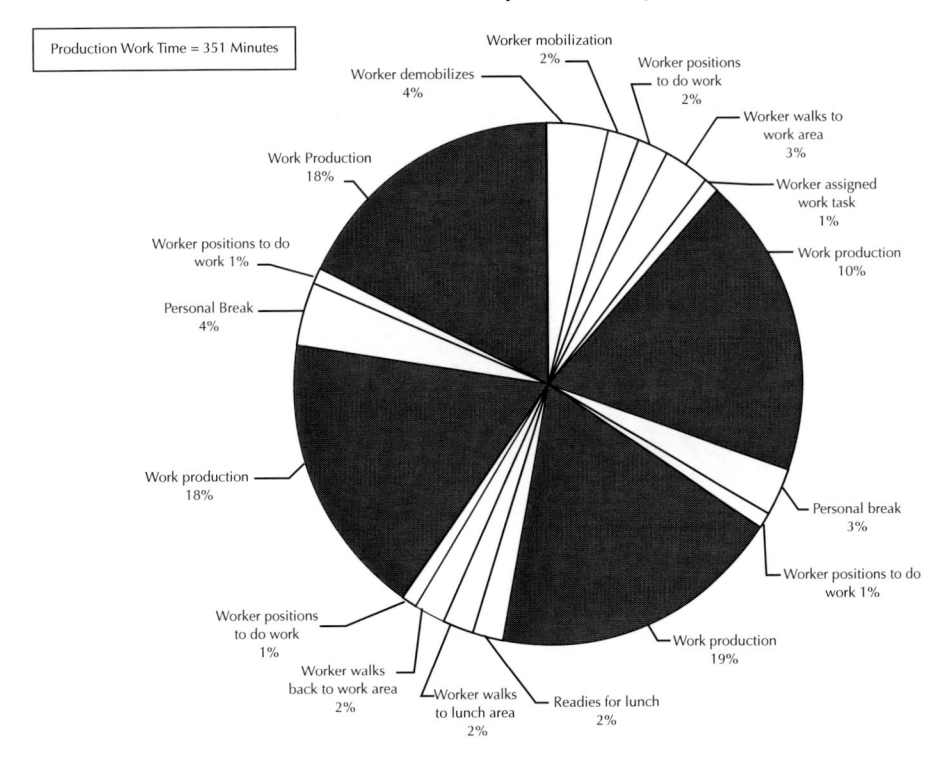

Production Work Time = 351 Minutes

- Worker mobilization 2%
- Worker positions to do work 2%
- Worker walks to work area 3%
- Worker assigned work task 1%
- Work production 10%
- Personal break 3%
- Worker positions to do work 1%
- Work production 19%
- Readies for lunch 2%
- Worker walks to lunch area 2%
- Worker walks back to work area 2%
- Worker positions to do work 1%
- Work production 18%
- Personal Break 4%
- Worker positions to do work 1%
- Work Production 18%
- Worker demobilizes 4%

Fig. 8-16a. Unimpacted Work Day

Impacted Day Owing to RFI's

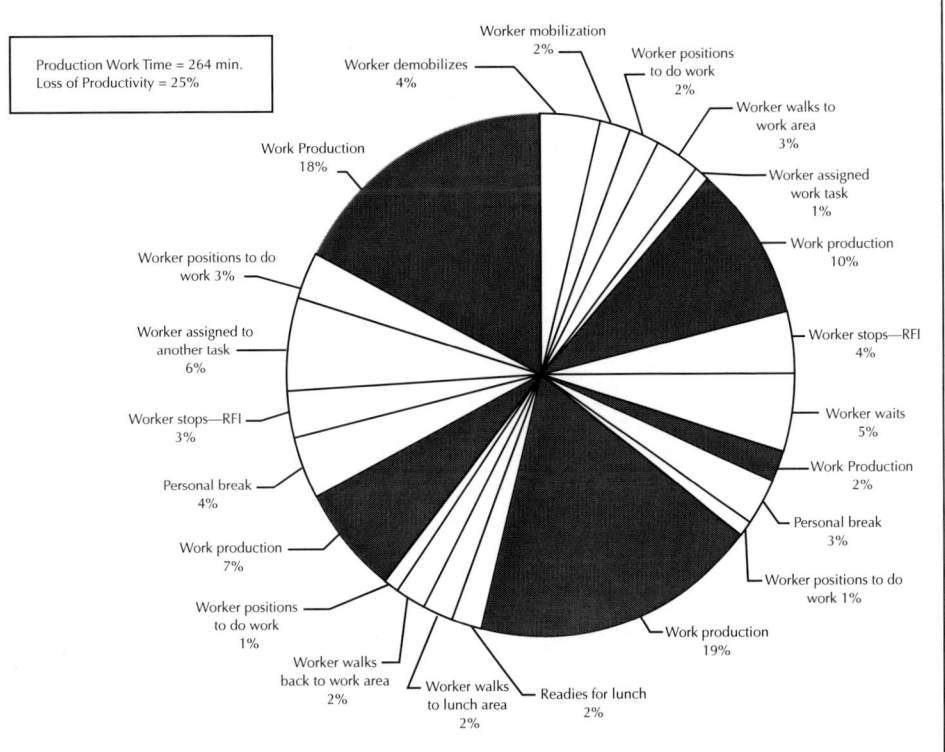

Production Work Time = 264 min.
Loss of Productivity = 25%

- Worker mobilization 2%
- Worker positions to do work 2%
- Worker walks to work area 3%
- Worker assigned work task 1%
- Work production 10%
- Worker stops—RFI 4%
- Worker waits 5%
- Work Production 2%
- Personal break 3%
- Worker positions to do work 1%
- Work production 19%
- Readies for lunch 2%
- Worker walks to lunch area 2%
- Worker walks back to work area 2%
- Worker positions to do work 1%
- Work production 7%
- Personal break 4%
- Worker stops—RFI 3%
- Worker assigned to another task 6%
- Worker positions to do work 3%
- Work Production 18%
- Worker demobilizes 4%

Fig. 8-16b. Impacted Day Owing to RFIs

The result of the analysis indicated a loss of productivity owing to the unexpected start-stop-start-stop nature of the work. Knowing of the existence of an unexpected non-productive event, the supervisor should quantify the non-productive impact via a measurement process.

(D.2.) Waiting

The impact of having workers waiting for information or decisions is similar to the situation of a start-stop, start-stop work process. In both situations, the percentage of time the worker(s) are able to perform productive work decreases and the percentage of time doing non-productive activities increases. The only difference is that in the "waiting" issue, the worker does not go off to another work task, he or she merely waits for information or a decision. If the supervisor does not know how long it will take to get the needed information or decision, and in fact thinks it will be provided quickly, the supervisor may choose to simply have the workers wait. The lost productivity in this situation is easier to quantify than in a start-stop-start-stop.

However, when subjected to an obvious "wait" situation such as having a work crew wait for a project owner or designer to interrupt the drawings, the supervisor should be attentive to recording the "wait" time in a time reporting or daily report. In effect, the supervisor should create a new cost code called "waiting." There is no better way to request added money owing to lost productivity than to record the actual lost productivity as it is incurred. The time lost will of course will depend on how long it takes to get the information or decision that allows the workers to get back to doing productive work.

> There is no better way to request added money owing to lost productivity than to record the actual lost productivity as it is incurred.

Loss of Productivity

(E) Added Support Activities

Events may occur in the construction process that require the construction supervisor to increase the percentage of time workers spend doing what might be referred to as "support" activities. These support activities may include walking longer distances to get materials, obstructions that require workers or machines to perform additional activities, or extra material handling.

(E.1.) Logistics and Access

A construction firm may prepare its estimate/bid based on site conditions observed and specified by the project owner, only to find out later that the site conditions were changed when the firm performed its contracted work. Examples include the following:

- A piping contractor was informed that the firm could store its pipe on the north side of a new hospital they were helping construct. However, notified to be at the jobsite, the contractor found that the planned laydown area was not available. The firm had no choice but to store the pipe in a vacant lot two blocks from the hospital site. The result was that the construction supervisor had to have onsite workers transport the material from the storage lot to the place of installation when it was needed.

- A mechanical contractor, in estimating the construction of a large industrial plant, was informed that it would be able to bring material into the plant through an access door, then use elevators to bring the material to the floor on which it was to be placed. However, when the work started, the construction supervisor was informed that the access door was off-limits owing to other operations. The result was that the supervisor had to rent a lift that allowed workers to attach material, lift it vertically and then use portable horizontal platforms to move the material to where it was needed.

- The bid documents for the construction of a new terminal at an airport indicated that the excavation crew would be able to enter the site with their scrapers from a specific highway entrance. Once on the job, the contractor was required to access the site with the loaded scrapers from a congested entrance on the other side of the airport. This added considerable travel distance and time was lost in traffic.

In each of these examples, the support time related to additional moving materials, a different method of moving the materials, or increased distance traveled leads to added "support" time and takes away from the percentage of time the onsite workers are actually putting in or placing the materials. Even if the same work was completed as planned, the cost would be higher. The supervisor should attempt to track or measure the added time for the non-productive or support activities.

(E.2.) Double (+) Handling of Materials

In the ideal construction process workers handle material once. For example, if a steel erector can arrange for a truck to arrive with the steel when needed, then the supervisor can have equipment pick it right off the truck and swing it in place for final placement by the ironworkers. However, if the material has to be unloaded from the truck, placed on the ground and lifted again to be installed, added "support" labor hours are required.

There are many reasons for onsite workers to handle material multiple times. The work process may require a double handling of the material.

However, it may be that the workers are unnecessarily handling multiple materials, for reasons outside of their control and the construction firm's responsibility. Let's say various subcontractors' work got out of sequence. The supervisor of a sheet metal crew may have to move his or her stored sheet metal material from room to room before it can be installed. The stored material may in turn get in the way of various other out-of-sequence trade contractors.

Excessive material handling was one of the defects of the construction process called out in an earlier session. While the workers appear to be working, the fact is that unnecessary carrying of materials is not productive. Working hard does not necessarily mean working smart.

Perhaps the best way to document lost labor time related to excessive material handling is to create a cost code on which a worker's time handling material is reported. Lacking such a recording process, the supervisor might be limited to quantifying the added cost by comparing actual cost to estimated cost. However, such a "total cost" approach may be flawed — there may be reasons (other than the excessive material handling) for the cost overrun.

> While the workers appear to be working, the fact is that unnecessary carrying of materials is not productive.

Logistic Changes and Productivity Loss

Assume that a construction supervisor is responsible for placing concrete blocks for interior walls in a structure. The contractor has to place 6,000 concrete blocks. The blocks were delivered and stored on the west side of the project being constructed. It was agreed that the firm would be able to bring the blocks through open access overhang door area on the west side of the building, near the block storage area.

After four days of work, the supervisor was informed that for the next four days, the contractor would not have access to the door on the west side of the building and would have to bring the blocks into the building from the east side. The supervisor had to have some of the crew members occasionally bring the blocks around the building to enter the structure on the east side. The supervisor kept the following records regarding blocks put in place on a daily basis.

Day	Crew Size	Access	Blocks placed per day
1	3 masons, 2 laborers	East	650
2	4 masons, 2 laborers	East	760
3	3 masons, 2 laborers	East	620
4	3 masons, 2 laborers	East	640
5	4 masons, 2 laborers	West	580
6	3 masons, 2 laborers	West	520
7	3 masons, 2 laborers	West	470
8	3 masons, 1 laborers	West	400
9	4 masons, 2 laborers	East	720
10	3 masons, 2 laborers	East	640

A mason's wage rate is $24.00 per hour and a laborer's wage rate is $22.00. By comparing the productivity when using the west side access versus the east side entrance, calculate the labor hours lost and the related cost damage that should be quantified.

Exercise

Loss of Productivity

(F) Human Element

Unlike machines, human beings have free will, can be motivated or unmotivated and can make choices. These human labor characteristics can be favorable attributes for productivity but can also prove detrimental to productivity improvement.

(F.1) Morale

Most research studies indicate that the onsite construction worker is frustrated by many of the same things that frustrate the supervisor in his or her attempt to improve productivity and construct on time, on-budget, a high-quality and safe project. Distractions like waiting, redoing work owing to changes, and frustration with someone being in the way, lower the overall morale of the worker.

Imagine the frustration of a worker who must construct the same wall three or four times owing to changes in the design during or after the construction process. If the worker believes that it may have to be torn down and rebuilt again, how can he or she have a positive attitude and be motivated to give his or her best work effort?

Every worker is different in regard to their attitude and what motivates them. However, a job in chaos because of changes that complicate the work, breaks in its continuity, adverse weather conditions, disruptions in the work process and the need to do added support activities (e.g., double-handling of material), all lead to lower project morale. In other words, each of the previously discussed negative productivity impact categories leads to another negative productivity impact factor — lower morale.

Limited research studies have measured construction productivity and the morale of the worker. However, what studies have been conducted indicate that one can expect a decreased construction productivity in the range of 10% to 20% if worker morale is low.

Lower morale of the construction worker is of particular concern because the onsite construction worker is often not attended or supervised. As was discussed in Session 4, the ratio of onsite supervisors to the number of onsite workers is such that the only person who can effectively monitor or supervise the onsite worker is the worker himself. Given decreased morale owing to project changes, interruptions, etc., the productivity of the worker can decrease or stay at a low level for several days before it is detected and corrected by the supervisor.

Distractions like waiting, redoing work owing to changes, and frustration with someone being in the way lower the overall morale of the worker.

(F.2.) Physiological Effects

For reasons within or outside the construction supervisor's control, she may require onsite workers to work overtime or a second shift. On many highway projects, state transportation departments have reverted to the use of nighttime construction. This may be a way to limit traffic congestion or it may be the result of the need to accelerate the construction schedule.

While there may be many good reasons for working a second shift or night shift, the supervisor should understand that such a change has a physiological impact that deters productivity. The typical worker develops patterns of sleeping, eating, working and leisure time. If the pattern changes, the worker's mental and physical system is upset; perhaps so much that some of the functions may be negatively affected. While difficult to quantify, it is not unusual to detect a difference in nighttime and daytime productivity of 5% to 15%. Admittedly, some of the decrease stems from factors such as lighting and wetness (as was previously discussed). However, even given proper lighting and dry conditions, there will likely be a small decrease in productivity on the order of 5% or more.

> **Note:** This section is optional.

> Given the need to submit a formal change order or prepare a claim, the supervisor is likely to consult the construction firm's main office staff, including the project manager.

Methods of Quantifying Lost Labor Productivity for a Construction Claim

The construction firm and the project owner may not always agree as to whether or how much labor productivity was lost when an unexpected situation occurs. If that is the case, a representative from the construction firm will need to quantify the lost productivity for presentation to the project owner, an arbitrator or even for possible litigation. The project supervisor probably would not be in charge of such an effort, but he will have a better feel for why he is asked to keep track of information if he understands how the lost productivity will be presented.

The intent here is not to make the supervisor an expert in the use of these methods or approaches, but to let the supervisor be familiar with them. Given the need to submit a formal change order or prepare a claim, the supervisor is likely to consult the construction firm's main office staff, including the project manager.

Discrete Method

In the discrete method, the construction jobsite personnel attempt to record the alleged productivity inefficiencies directly on the daily time card or daily report. "Impact" codes are created and lost time is recorded right on the timecard or on the daily report as shown in Figure 8-17.

DAILY TIMECARD	
Description	Hours
Erect slab forms	2.0
Place rebar	2.5
Place concrete in slab	2.5
Waiting for materials	0.5
Waiting for drawings	0.5
Total	8.0

Fig. 8-17. Sample Timecard

This approach is often viewed as the best because the lost hours are identified and segmented on the time card. In reality, this method is seldom used. First, experience has shown that many supervisors don't get serious about a problem until it is nearly gone, or over. This prevents them from recognizing the hours on the timecard as they occur. Second, timecards are traditionally used to record labor hours against the budgeted hours. Because defects or time delays are not part of the budget, they are not normally recorded on the timecard.

Measured-Mile Approach

In this method, the productivity achieved during the alleged troublesome period is compared to the productivity achieved when there was no trouble or impact. This approach is illustrated in Figure 8-18.

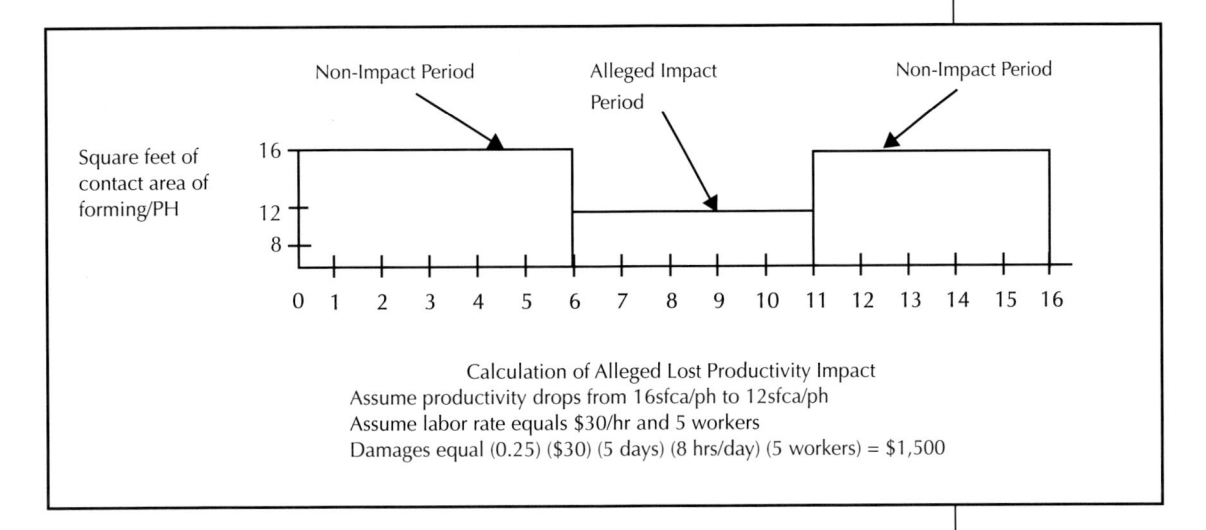

Calculation of Alleged Lost Productivity Impact
Assume productivity drops from 16sfca/ph to 12sfca/ph
Assume labor rate equals $30/hr and 5 workers
Damages equal (0.25) ($30) (5 days) (8 hrs/day) (5 workers) = $1,500

Fig. 8-18. Measured-Mile Approach

The measured mile presents a graphical or mathematical means of illustrating alleged lost labor productivity. The method assumes that the work performed in the non-impact periods and the work performed in the alleged impact periods was similar.

The measured-mile exhibit can be prepared as the claim issue evolves or can be prepared from past records. Therefore, this math can be prepared after the fact.

Total Cost Method

In this method, the alleged labor productivity cost damage is calculated as the difference between the actual project labor cost and the estimated labor cost or hours. An example is illustrated in Figure 8-19.

> The total cost method compares the actual labor cost or actual labor hours to the estimated or budgeted labor cost or hours.

Example:

Actual Project Labor Hours to Place 1,000 units of work
= 650.0 ph

Estimated Project Labor Hours to Place 1,000 units of work
= 480.0 ph

Difference	170.0 ph
times Project Labor Rate	$30.00/hr
equals Total Claim Damage	$5,100.00

Fig. 8-19. Total Cost Method Example

Industrial Engineering Approach

In this approach, industrial engineering models such as time study and work sampling are used to measure productivity impact as it occurs. While this approach represents the most scientific method, it is seldom used. First, the approach requires the contractor to be knowledgeable about various industrial engineering models. Second, the method or approach assumes that the contractor documents the problem as it happens.

Earned Value Method

In the earned value approach, the calculation of added labor hours is determined by comparing (for select time periods), the hours it took to do a group of activities versus the budgeted (or earned) hours for the activities.

Activity	Planned Duration	Planned Work Days	Planned Person-hours	Planned PH/Day & Crew	Actual Duration	Actual Work Days	Actual Person-hours	Actual PH/Day
A	4	1-4	128	32-4	4	10-13	148	37-4.6
B	6	1-6	288	48-6	6	1-6	192	32-4
C	2	1-2	64	32-4	2	5-6	60	30-3.75
D	6	5-10	240	40-5	6	14-16,18-20	290	48.3-6+
E	12	7-18	384	32-4	13	7-19	424	32.6-4+
F	12	3-14	288	24-3	12	7-18	328	27.3-3.4
G	4	19-23	160	40-5	4	20-23	154	38.5-4.8
H	4	23-26	192	48-6	3	24-26	180	60-7.5
I	2	23-24	128	64-8	2	25-26	118	59-7.4
J	8	23-26	256	32-4	7	20-26	280	40-5
Total			2,128				2,174	

Fig. 8-20. Sample Project Data for Earned Value Method Example

Assume the planned schedule per the contractor's submitted "as planned schedule" was as follows:

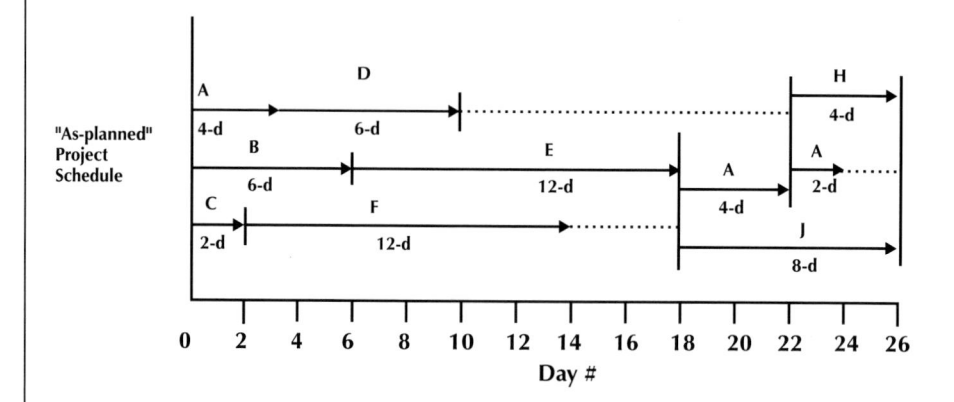

Fig. 8-21. As-Planned Project Schedule

Let us further assume that, for reasons outside the control and responsibility of the contractor, labor productivity impact occurred during days 11 through 20. Let us further assume that for whatever reason, project activities are delayed and shifted and the "as-built" project schedule for the above project is as illustrated below:

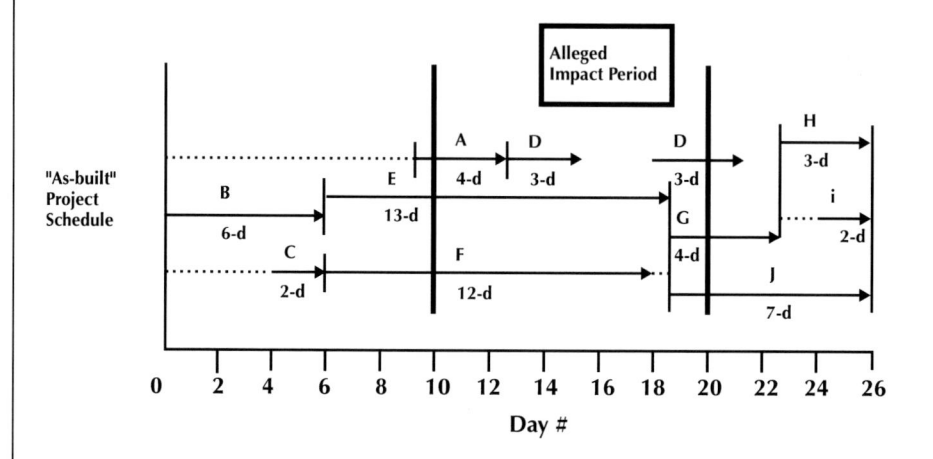

Fig. 8-22. As-Built Project Schedule

Assuming the contractor has kept track of the actual person-hours expended every day (from the timecards), the lost productivity or person-hours calculated using the Earned Value Method are as follows:

Day	Actual Hours	Earned Hours	Lost (Prod.) Hours
1	32	48	(16)
2	32	48	(16)
3	32	48	(16)
4	32	48	(16)
5	62	80	(18)
6	62	80	(18)
7	60	53.5	6.5
8	60	53.5	6.5
9	60	53.5	6.5
10	93	85.5	7.5
11	93	85.5	7.5
12	93	85.5	7.5
13	93	85.5	7.5
14	108.2	93.5	14.7
15	108.2	93.5	14.7
16	108.2	93.5	14.7
17	60	53.5	6.5
18	60	53.5	6.5
19	81	69.5	11.5
20	126.8	116.6	10.2
21	126.8	116.6	10.2
22	78.5	76.6	1.9
23	78.5	76.6	1.9
24	100	100.6	(0.6)
25	159	164.6	(5.6)
26	159	164.6	(5.6)
Total	2158	2128	

The earned value method (EVM) compares the actual labor hours expended each day to the hours earned on that day.

Fig. 8-23. Earned Value Calculations

The "earned person-hours" for each time period are calculated through a linear interpolation of the time in the impact period. For example, for activity B, the planned or estimated person-hours were 288. The actual duration for activity B was six days. Therefore, each day that B was performed or worked, 48 hours were earned (i.e., 288/6). The "actual person-hours" for each time period would come from the timecards.

Expert Approach

In this approach, a productivity expert(s) reviews the project conditions, project correspondence and project documentation, and applies industry productivity knowledge and data to the alleged issues at hand to determine a reasonable lost labor productivity damage. For example, the expert might reference some of the research studies and illustrations presented in this session.

Session 8 Review

Look back over Session 8 and review these key points to be sure you understand them.

- There are six different categories of factors that negatively impact labor productivity

- There is a loss of productivity when a worker is subjected to conditions that were not expected.

- There has been a considerable amount of research conducted on measuring lost productivity as a function of various impact factors.

- Change orders can negatively impact overall project productivity.

Using on the Job What You Learned Today

Jobsite Assignment

While at your project, identify situations or events that may have a negative impact on overall labor productivity. This doesn't mean they are a changed condition or a basis for a change order or claim. However, the objective is to make the supervisor more aware of unexpected project conditions that can indirectly impact labor productivity.

To Get Ready for Session 9

Read the Participant's Manual for Session 9.

Session 9

Record Keeping, Control, Change Orders and Defect Analysis

Learning Goals for Session 9

After this session, you should know the following:

- The importance of timely and accurate jobsite record keeping to the monitoring and improvement of productivity.

- The importance of the project control report for monitoring project performance, identifying problems and reducing or eliminating the problems with the objective of improving productivity.

- The importance of record keeping for change orders.

- What jobsite data is needed to support a new approach to productivity improvement — defect analysis.

- The above practices emphasize the importance of record keeping to control and improvement of job productivity and time.

Learning Objectives

To accomplish the learning goals, during this session you will:

- Develop an effective job record keeping system.

- Develop job control reports to improve productivity.

- Manage and control the change order process.

- Brainstorm and develop a list of procedures to collect productivity defect data.

- Use data in a defect analysis model to improve productivity.

To Get Ready for Session 9

Reading: Read the pages in this session before the class. Try to think of various defects or factors that cause non-productive time at construction jobsites.

Major Activities for Session 9

- Learn the importance of timely and accurate jobsite record keeping and learn three rules to enhance record keeping.

- Do an exercise that requires you to set out ideas and solutions for common jobsite reporting problems.

- Discuss the importance of the job control report and how it can be used to monitor, control and improve productivity.

- Do an exercise in which you will identify new uses of the job control data for productivity improvement.

- Learn the importance of change orders and how the supervisor needs to be proactive in identifying the occurrence of a change order.

- Do an exercise in which the participants will share ideas of recommended do's and don'ts in regard to change orders.

- Learn a new more proactive approach to jobsite data collection that focuses on reducing a productivity defect.

- Do an exercise in which you will identify procedures to collect new jobsite data regarding various productivity defects.

A Review of Session 8

In Session 8, you learned the importance of identifying and quantifying the effect of various negative productivity impact factors.

Some of the facts that you learned in Session 8 were:

- There are many events or factors that cause actual jobsite productivity to be less than planned; events or factors that may be outside the control and responsibility of the supervisor. The various events or factors can be categorized as:

    A. Worker ability to do work

    B. Continuity of work process

    C. Environmental factors

    D. Disruption of work process

    E. Added support activities

    F. Unique nature of construction

- Each of the above categories of impact factors comprises several issues or causes. For example temperature, precipitation, noise and lighting are all environmental factors.

- The supervisor needs to be able to identify productivity impact factors and quantify the impact in order to substantiate money related to a change order or a dispute. Independent of a change order or dispute, the supervisor will need the information to make proper management decisions.

The Importance of Good Jobsite Record Keeping

The construction industry has been characterized as an industry with inaccurate or untimely written record keeping at jobsites. Inaccurate timecards, late reports, failure to give the worker or supervisor adequate feedback and lost or misplaced documents can occur at the construction jobsite. Part of the reason for these inadequacies relates to the decentralized nature of the work process. Most industries create and monitor their written communication system at the same location that they make their product. But in the construction industry written jobsite records are created at the job and transferred to the company's main office. Follow-up information then is communicated back to the jobsite. This decentralized process creates problems with accuracy and timeliness.

Jobsite record keeping serves several purposes:

- Controls and monitors company assets (e.g., minimizes theft)
- Internal reporting (e.g., payroll accounting)
- External reporting (e.g., supports various reports for surety company)
- Job control (e.g., reports on status of in-progress job)
- Productivity improvement (e.g., identifies problem so that it can be addressed)

Inaccurate or untimely record keeping can be promoted by the various designs of the forms that are used to collect data. The use of a weekly timecard may result in an on-site foreman doing time reporting, filling it out at the end of the week instead of daily. It is unlikely that the foreman can remember at the end of a week what workers did during the week.

The construction firm and supervisor should remember the following three rules for obtaining timely and accurate jobsite record keeping (note: the rules are good rules for any type of required reporting):

- An individual required to fill out a form should be showed where the data goes and how it is used.
- An individual required to fill out a form should be shown by example that the data was in fact used.
- Any individual who fills out a form or inputs information or data should be given subsequent feedback.

These three rules for obtaining accurate and timely information hold true for the many types of jobsite record keeping, including timecard reporting, daily reporting and meeting minutes.

Sidebar:

Jobsite record keeping serves the following purposes:
- Controls company assets
- Internal reporting
- External reporting
- Job control
- Productivity improvement

Three rules for data collection are:
- Explain how the information will be used.
- Show by example that the data is used.
- Give feedback.

Exercise

Common Jobsite Record Keeping Problems

Listed below are some of the typical jobsite reporting problems that occur in the construction firm. With your fellow group members, identify procedures that can lessen or eliminate the problem or issue. In addressing solutions to the problems identified, assume that the construction firm and supervisor are using a manual reporting process.

- Timecards for self-performed work by craftspeople are illegible, incorrect in regard to time adding up to eight hours, inconsistent (some foremen fill out work time to cost codes to the nearest ½ hour, others to the nearest 1 hour, and still others to the nearest 2 hours), or may be miscoded (i.e., time charged to the wrong code).

- Daily report forms that the construction supervisor is to fill out are not completed.

- Vendor invoices that come to the main office from suppliers cannot be identified by job and by work task due to failure to collect information from the jobsites.

- Tools and materials that cannot be substantiated and costed to the job report are being purchased at jobsites.

- Monthly projects are being underbilled because of inadequate input from the jobsite supervisor.

Project Control and Record Keeping

Controlling project time and cost is key to the construction supervisor's ability to complete a project on time and within budget. While the project estimate and the project schedule set out the potential for profits and an on-time project, it is the control system that enables the contractor to achieve them.

A control system has five key elements:

- In a *timely* manner,
- it compares *actual*,
- to *plan*,
- with the objective of *detecting a problem*,
- and a *follow-up action* is taken to attempt to correct the problem.

If any one of these five elements is absent or is done improperly, the control process fails.

Job Control Report

The objective of the job control report is to enable the construction supervisor to "see" the status of an in-progress project from the report. It is the timely job control report that provides the supervisor the potential to identify productivity problems and address the problems for productivity improvement.

The largest risk factor, and potentially the largest profit center, for the supervisor is the on-site self-performed labor cost. Two key jobsite reports support the preparation of the job cost report; the daily report that summarizes quantities in place, and the timecard that summarizes craft hours worked. This process is shown in Figure 9-1.

Project control has the following elements:
- Timely
- Compare actual
- To Plan
- Detect a Problem
- React to the Problem

The largest risk factor, and potentially the largest profit center, for the supervisor is the onsite self-performed labor cost.

SESSION 9

RECORD KEEPING, CONTROL, CHANGES AND DEFECT ANALYSIS

Items taken off from drawings	Quantities taken off by estimator	Budgeted hours based on historical data	Quanitites to date from daily report at job	Craft hours to date from daily time cards	Calculated from previous 4 columns
Work Item	Budgeted Quantity	Budgeted Hours	Actual Quantity	Actual Hours	Project Over or Under Hours

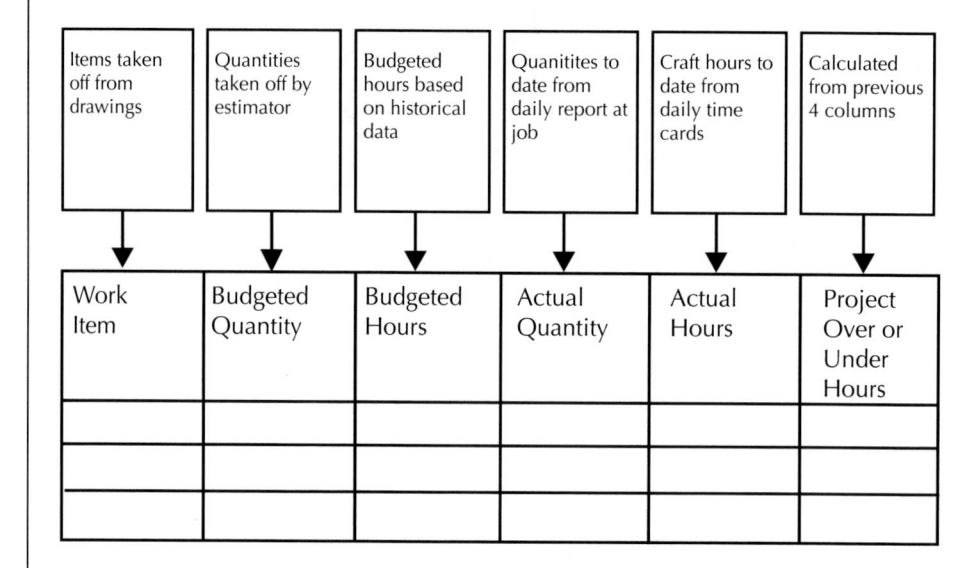

Fig. 9-1. Example Columns for a Project Control Report

In order to be effective, the budgeted quantities and craft hours have to be accurate. Equally important, the field reporting system must be timely and accurate. The source documents for the quantities of work put in place to date and the craft hours expended are the daily reports and the timecards filled out at the jobsite.

Various supervisors use various formats of the job cost report. One format is shown in Figure 9-2. This format can hardly be viewed as being effective. It merely measures the labor hours expended to date against the budget. This enables the supervisor to detect a problem when the labor hours exceed the budgeted hours; much too late to take corrective actions. For example, the report shown in Figure 9-2 would enable the firm to know they have a productivity (and cost over-run) problem with forming slabs only when the actual craft hours exceeded the budgeted 500 craft hours.

Name of Work Item	Budgeted Quantity	Budgeted Craft Hours	Actual Craft Hours
Form Slabs	500	500	350
Rough Carpentry	200	300	150
Roofing	100	200	80

Fig. 9-2. Comparing Actual Hours to Date Versus Budgeted Hours

RECORD KEEPING, CONTROL, CHANGES AND DEFECT ANALYSIS

A more effective control report that monitors percentage of effort or labor hours expended versus the percentage of work put in place is illustrated in Figure 9-3. In Figure 9-3, 500 units of work (forming is usually measured in square feet of contact area) and 500 craft hours are budgeted. At the time of the job control shown, 250 units of work are in place. This represents 50% of the budgeted quantity. However, the firm has already expended 350 craft hours to do the work; this represents 70% of the budgeted craft hours.

Looked at another way, it has taken 350 craft hours to place 50% of the quantity of work. If this productivity (person-hours per unit) trend continues, it follows that it will take a total of 700 craft hours to complete all the work. This is 200 more than budgeted. This 200-overrun variance is projected in the last column of Figure 9-3.

An effective control report compares percentage of work in place to the percentage of effort expended.

A similar analysis comparing the percent of quantity in place and hours expected to date indicates that the carpentry work item is right on budget. The roofing item is projected to come under budget by 40 craft hours.

Using the control system report shown in Figure 9-3, the supervisor can detect a potential problem as soon as the percentage of labor hours expended is greater than the percentage of work put in place. This potential problem may occur as soon as the work is started. Early detection of a productivity problem is critical to the firm's ability to correct a problem.

Name of Work Item	Budgeted Quantity	Budgeted Hours	Actual Quantity to Date	Percent of Quantity in Place	Actual Hours to Date	Percent of Hours to Date	Forecast Variance @ Completion
Form Slabs	500	500	250	50	350	70	+200 hrs
Carpentry Framing	200	300	100	50	150	50	—
Roofing	100	200	50	50	80	40	–40 hrs

Fig. 9-3. Job Control by Comparing Percent of Hours to Percent of Work in Place

This comparison of the percentage of work put in place versus the percentage of effort expended to date can be made by comparing hours, labor costs or unit costs. A report illustrating labor dollars instead of labor hours is illustrated in Figure 9-4. An hourly rate of $20 per hour is assumed in Figure 9-4. The variances in the last column are calculated the same way as they were in Figure 9-3. For example, it has taken $7,000 of labor cost to do 50% of the work item "Form Slabs." If the productivity stays the same, it will take $14,000 to complete the work — an overrun of $4,000.

Name of Work Item	Budgeted Quantity	Budgeted Labor Dollars	Actual Quantity to Date	Percent of Quantity in Place	Actual Labor Dollars	Percent of Dollars to Date	Forecast Variance @ Completion
Form Slabs	500	$10,000	250	50	$7,000	70	+$4,000
Carpentry Framing	200	$6,000	100	50	$3,000	50	—
Roofing	100	$4,000	50	50	$1,600	40	−$800

Fig. 9-4. Job Control by Comparing Percent of $s Expended to Percent of Work in Place

A similar report using unit costs is illustrated in Figure 9-5. The $20 unit cost for the work item "Form Slabs" is determined in the estimating process by dividing the $10,000 budget (i.e., 500 craft hours at $20 per hour), by the budgeted 500 units of work to do. The actual unit cost of $28 for the "Form Slabs" work item is determined by dividing the $7,000 cost to date by the 250 units of work put in place to date. Using this report, any time the actual unit cost gets larger than the budgeted unit cost, a "flag" goes up that an apparent problem exists.

Name of Work Item	Budgeted Quantity	Budgeted Unit Cost	Actual Quantity to Date	Actual Unit Cost to Date	Forecast Variance @ Completion
Form Slabs	500	$20.00	250	$28.00	+$4,000
Carpentry Framing	200	$30.00	100	$30.00	—
Roofing	100	$40.00	50	$32.00	−$800

Fig. 9-5. Job Control by Comparing Unit Costs

The job cost report formats illustrated in Figures 9-3, 9-4 and 9-5 satisfy the first four elements of an effective control system. These control elements are:

- A *timely*
- comparison of *actual*
- vs. *plan* (or budget)
- to detect a *potential problem.*

When the percentage of effort for a work activity is greater than the percentage of work completed, there are at least six explanations or reasons. If the control system is to be effective, it is critical that the supervisor investigate the reasons for the overrun. Each of the reasons listed below should result in a follow-up action.

- **Productivity problem**

    It may be that there is one of many productivity problems occurring; for example, inadequate supervision, understaffing of the work, poor worker attitudes, etc. If this is the reason, the project control report identifies or "flags" this and the supervisor should attempt to immediately correct the productivity problem. Some problems, like inadequate or improper supervision, can be addressed. Other problems, like inclement weather, may be more difficult to address.

- **Estimating problem**

    It may be that there is no onsite problem; the problem may be that there was too optimistic an estimate of labor productivity. If this is the case, the supervisor should recognize this fact and incorporate this information into future estimates.

- **Inadequate record keeping**

    The fact that the report indicates more hours expended for the Form Slabs than should have occurred to date may be the result of intentional or unintentional inaccurate jobsite record keeping. For example, it may be that the foreman has filled out daily timecards inaccurately by charging craft hours to the wrong work code. If this is the case, the record keeping process needs to be improved.

- **Improper method of handling change orders**

    The contractor is often required to do additional work via a change order process. For example, additional concrete work may have been assigned to the firm. In doing this work, the supervisor would update the actual labor hours and work quantities performed.

It is critical that the supervisor react to apparent problems detected on the control report.

However, they may not have updated the estimate and therefore the percentages illustrated for the labor hours expended and quantity of work placed are in error. If this is the reason for the apparent lack of matching of the percentages, the change order process should be corrected; the budget and the actual quantities and hours must be updated for change orders.

- **Improper or bad list of work item codes**

    The job control report should be set up so that if the supervisor is 50% done with a work item and everything is going as planned, then 50% of the labor hours should have been expended. It may be that the reason for the apparent problem with the Form Slab work item is that the firm has a bad list of work items. Maybe the work codes are defined too broadly. If this is the case, the firm should redefine the work codes in the cost system.

- **Changed work conditions or a claim**

    It may be that the supervisor is being required to do the concrete wall work under changed or unexpected work conditions (for example; the work is impacted by an obstruction). The supervisor may be entitled to extra payment for the changed condition or may initiate a claim. If this is the case, this should be documented so that the claim can be negotiated. The job control report can support this with documentation.

The job control report is effective only if overruns are investigated and attempts are made to correct them. One way the construction firm can force the "reaction" to the job cost report would be to require the onsite supervisor to formally respond (with a short written report) as soon as the variance is projected.

Focusing on Under-budget Work Items and Variation

It is important for the supervisor to investigate underruns as well as overruns. It is fairly common for a firm to place considerable emphasis on investigating problems, identifying the blame and reprimanding the guilty individual. However, it is also important to spend time identifying the reasons various work items on the job control report are under budget.

For example, for the work item in Figure 9-3, the item is projected to come under budget by 40 person-hours. Just as there are reasons a work item is over budget, there have to be reasons the work item is under budget. By spending time with the supervisor who beats the budget for various work items, the cause can be identified and

The job control report is only effective if overruns are investigated and attempts are made to correct overruns.

attempts made to duplicate the success. The job control report can be useful in meeting these objectives.

An addition to the typical job control report can also aid the supervisor by measuring the risk of the work. Risk can be defined as variation from the average. A column can be added to the job control report shown in Figure 9-3 that reports the productivity achieved this week relative to last week or the average achieved to date. The reader of the report will soon be able to sense the productivity risk for individual work items. The productivity variation from one week to another will likely be much higher for work such as forming concrete than for work such as placing rebar or concrete. It is important for supervisors to be aware of productivity and/or cost risks so that they can apply the appropriate degree of supervision to the work task.

Exercise

Using the Job Control Report as a Productivity Improvement Tool

It was suggested that the job control report shown in Figures 9-3, 9-4 and 9-5 can be improved and used as a productivity improvement report by adding a column that measures the variation in productivity for a work task from one week to the next.

1. Explain how information regarding the variation in productivity from one week to the next could be used by the supervisor to improve jobsite productivity.

2. Explain other uses of the job control reports shown in Figures 9-3, 9-4 and 9-5 in regard to the productivity improvement objective. In other words, using the information shown in these reports and assuming that these reports are accurate and are available on a timely basis (weekly or monthly), how can the information be used by the supervisor to improve jobsite productivity?

Change Order Work Versus Base Bid Work

Change Order Work

Construction work performed by the contractor can be classified as one of two types; base bid work and change order work. Base bid work is the work that should have been anticipated by the contractor when the firm prepared its estimate and signed a contract. Change order work is extra work; work that was not anticipated.

When a project owner or their designer representative recognizes a need for a change order and directs the contractor to do the work, the change order is referred to as a *directed* change. However, sometimes conditions change that result in what is referred to as a constructive change. For example, if the project owner causes the project schedule to change so that the firm has to do the work in a colder work environment that in turn impacts the firm's productivity, it can be argued that the firm has been subjected to a *constructive* change.

The Change Order Process

In theory, when a project change occurs, the contractor should be issued a change order. Independent of the cause of blame for a project change, when a change order occurs it is typically accompanied by three different forms. The typical process is illustrated in Figure 9-6.

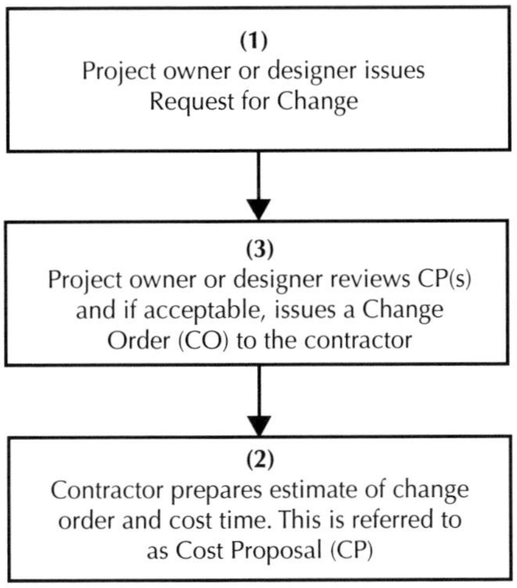

> A directed change order occurs when the contractor is instructed by the project owner or designer to do additional work. A constructive change can occur when the contractor does base bid work under conditions that were not anticipated and are outside the control of the contractor or supervisor.

```
(1)
Project owner or designer issues
Request for Change
          |
          v
(3)
Project owner or designer reviews CP(s)
and if acceptable, issues a Change
Order (CO) to the contractor
          |
          v
(2)
Contractor prepares estimate of change
order and cost time. This is referred to
as Cost Proposal (CP)
```

Fig. 9-6. The Change Order Paper Flow

Exercise

Change Order Do's and Don'ts

Change orders are often troublesome in negatively affecting overall project cost and project time. With the objective of aiding all participants, your group should list specific change order ideas, practices and procedures that you or your firm have observed as beneficial or detrimental to the project time and cost.

Beneficial Practices:

Detrimental Practices:

Defect Analysis Versus the Accounting Approach

There is definitely a need to implement an effective job control system such as that described in the previous section. Obviously knowing the status of projects relative to the budget is important. However, it is also important to remember that the typical construction project includes considerable non-productive time that can be traced to what one might refer to as productivity defects.

Shown in Figure 9-7 is a sample breakdown of work states for a worker during an eight-hour day at a construction project. Obviously the percentage of time of each of the work states shown varies from project to project. However, the illustration is fairly typical of the construction process; it might be referred to as the four-hour construction workday.

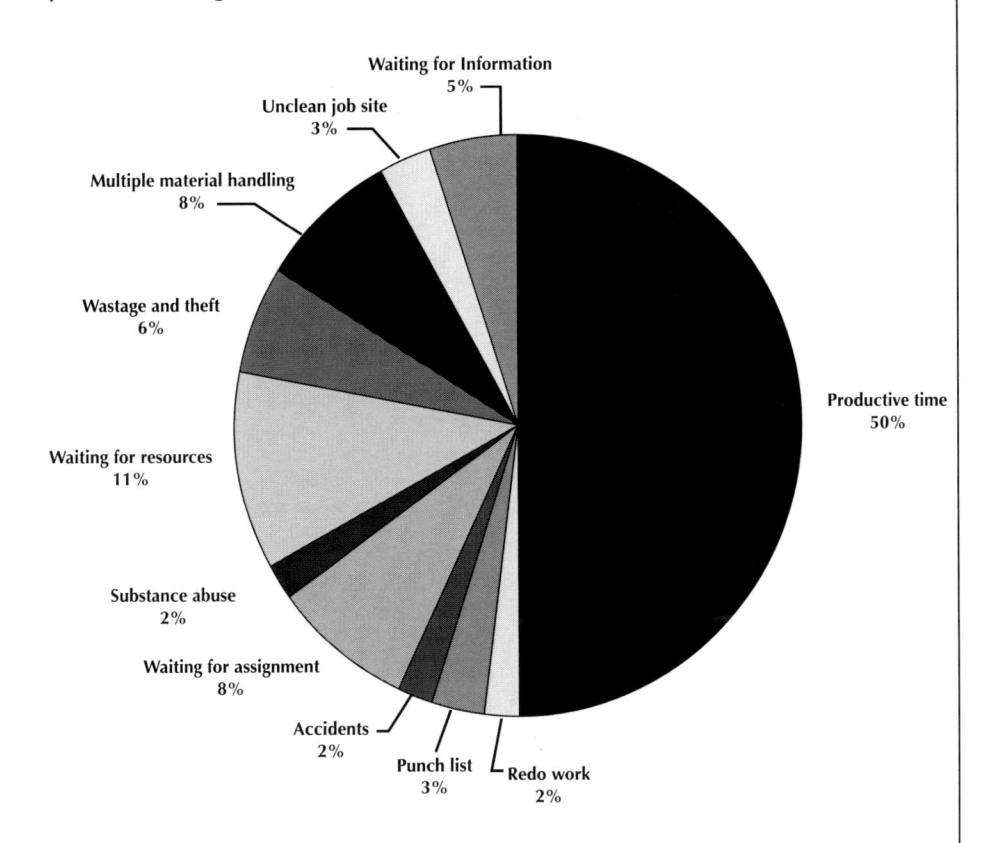

Fig. 9-7. Defects of the Construction Process

> Productive work can be defined as work that is absolutely necessary to completing the project.

This is not to say that workers want to be non-productive. The fault may be traced to the onsite supervisor. For example, the large percentage of non-productive waiting time illustrated might be traced to the supervisor's failure to plan and schedule. The benefits of planning and scheduling were discussed earlier.

It should be noted that the worker illustrated in Figure 9-8 is only in a productive state approximately 50% of the workday. Productive work can be inferred to mean, "doing work that is absolutely necessary to completing the project"; for example, putting in a concrete block, properly performing carpentry framing work, etc. The rest of the time the worker is in a non-productive state doing redo work, doing punch list work, waiting for a supervisor to tell him or her what to do, handling material unnecessarily, waiting for resources, looking for a tool or material he or she cannot find, etc. It is interesting to note that most workers normally do not like to be in many of the non-productive work states any more than the contractor likes to pay for the time. Most workers have a dislike for redo work, punch list work, double handling of material, waiting, etc.

The "defects" tend to become commonplace on construction projects. In effect they are budgeted or estimated. The result is that when the supervisor observes that he beat the budget for a work item in Figure 9-8 by five hours relative to the 1,000-labor hour budget, he should not feel good about it; in effect he or she just came close to duplicating the four-hour workday.

A Proactive Program for Improvement of a Defect

What is needed is a proactive program to improve jobsite productivity through the measurement of defects. It is proposed that one cannot improve or eliminate a defect unless one measures the defect and investigates its causes. The process of continuous improvement is illustrated in Figure 9-8.

Step 1: Select a Defect to Improve

It is unlikely that the supervisor will be able to initially or simultaneously measure or attack each of the defects shown in Figure 9-8. Instead it is being proposed that the supervisor initially focus on one defect. By focusing on measuring, identifying and eliminating the causes for a single defect for a given time period (say a year or two), the supervisor can focus everyone's attention on the need to reduce or eliminate the defect.

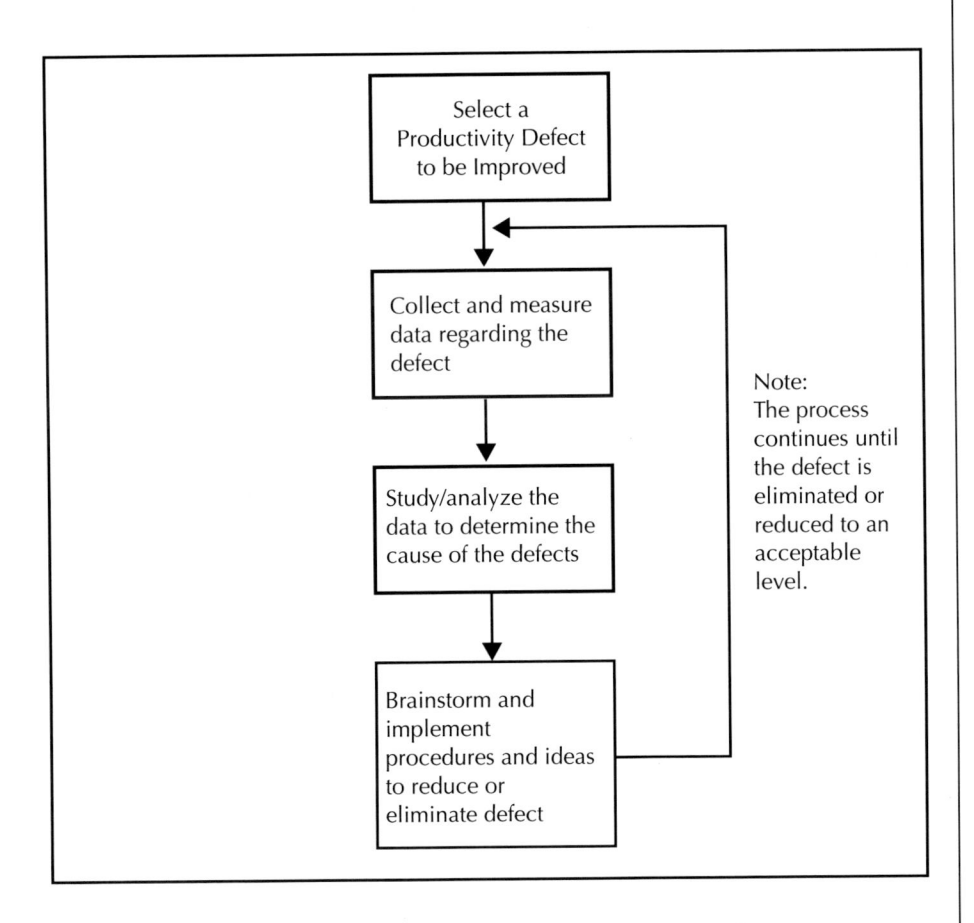

RECORD KEEPING, CONTROL, CHANGES AND DEFECT ANALYSIS

```
┌─────────────────────────┐
│  Select a               │
│  Productivity Defect    │
│  to be Improved         │
└─────────────────────────┘
            │
            ▼
┌─────────────────────────┐         Note:
│  Collect and measure    │         The process
│  data regarding the     │         continues until
│  defect                 │         the defect is
└─────────────────────────┘         eliminated or
            │                        reduced to an
            ▼                        acceptable
┌─────────────────────────┐         level.
│  Study/analyze the      │
│  data to determine the  │
│  cause of the defects   │
└─────────────────────────┘
            │
            ▼
┌─────────────────────────┐
│  Brainstorm and         │
│  implement              │
│  procedures and ideas   │
│  to reduce or           │
│  eliminate defect       │
└─────────────────────────┘
```

Fig. 9-8. Continuous Improvement Cycle

In selecting the defect to measure, analyze and reduce, and ultimately eliminate, the supervisor should consider the following:

■ Which defect is causing the most non-productive time for your firm's typical project?

■ How easy is it to gather data regarding the incidence and cause of the defect?

■ How easy is it to improve the productivity defect? (i.e., which defect can the firm expect to improve and measure the improvement on soonest?)

Step 2: Collect and Measure Data Regarding the Defect

Once the defect is selected, the supervisor should develop a form or procedure for measuring it at the project site. In some cases this may mean simply adding a new cost code for redo work or material handling. In other cases it may mean creating a new procedure or form for random testing/measurement of the defect (for example, of waiting).

Data can be collected in many ways. Creativity should be used in collecting the data. It can be collected continually or by using a random data collection process.

Various data collection models can be used:

- Time study techniques
- Work sampling techniques
- Productivity rating models
- Crew balance models
- Method productivity delay model

These and other industrial engineering models are described in many textbooks. If used properly, they do not intimidate workers. Just because they have not been used extensively by construction supervisors in the past does not mean they cannot be used.

It is important that the supervisor retain the right to manage. He or she should use data collection models with the philosophy that the data is being collected to identify improvement, not to blame people. If workers feel they are being measured to be blamed, they will frown on the approach. However, if the approach is one of improvement; i.e., working smarter, not harder, the measurement process will be accepted.

Flowcharting work methods is another way of analyzing the work process and identifying productivity defects. Using simple flowchart symbols enables the supervisor to identify improvement potential.

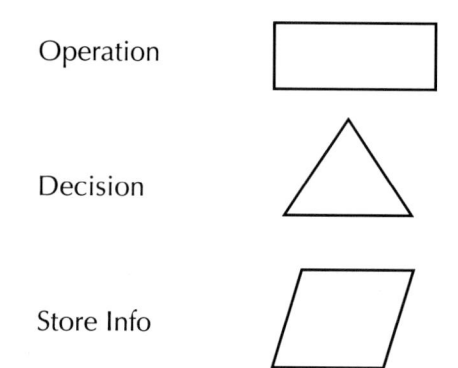

Operation ▭

Decision △

Store Info ▱

The supervisor might even consider the use of a second timecard for collecting data; a "defect timecard" such as that shown in Figure 9-9. Instead of focusing only on measuring labor hours against the budget or estimate, the supervisor may want to measure project defect time. By measuring defect time, identifying the causes and addressing the causes, the firm will be able to reduce, if not eliminate, the defect.

RECORD KEEPING, CONTROL, CHANGES AND DEFECT ANALYSIS

Timecard for Defect Time							
Project _____ Supervisor _____ Date _____							

Cost Code	Worker ___	Worker ___	Worker ___	Worker ___	Worker ___	Worker ___	Total Hours
Productive Time							
Redo Work							
Punch Work							
Accidents							
Waiting for Assignments							
Substance Abuse							
Waiting for Resources							
Wastage and theft							
Multiple matl. handling							
Unclean job site							
Waiting for information							
TOTALS FOR DAY							

Fig. 9-9. Timecard for Recording Defect Time

Admittedly the use of a timecard such as that shown in Figure 9-10 or the use of one or more of the data collection models noted above is not the "norm" for the construction supervisor. However, just because it has not been the norm doesn't mean it cannot be useful. All she has to do is look at the high percentage of non-productive time illustrated in Figure 9-8 and she can argue that new techniques, procedures and ideas need to be tried.

Step 3: Studying the Cause of the Defect

As noted above, data regarding a defect is not collected merely to "blame" individuals or to "point the finger" at individuals. The data is collected to focus on causes and to identify means of improvement.

When an incidence of a defect occurs, the cause of the defect must also be identified. For example, in the case of redo work, the cause may be one of the following:

- Worker not given proper instructions
- Worker did not have proper skills
- Worker did not have proper tools

Documenting defects should not be done to blame people but to investigate opportunities for improvement.

- Worker did not have proper materials
- Another worker or the owner/designer caused the damage, requiring redo work
- Work not properly inspected

The collected data regarding a defect should be charted and analyzed. A histogram as shown in Figure 9-10 might be used to chart the collected data.

INCIDENCE OF REDO WORK PER WEEK

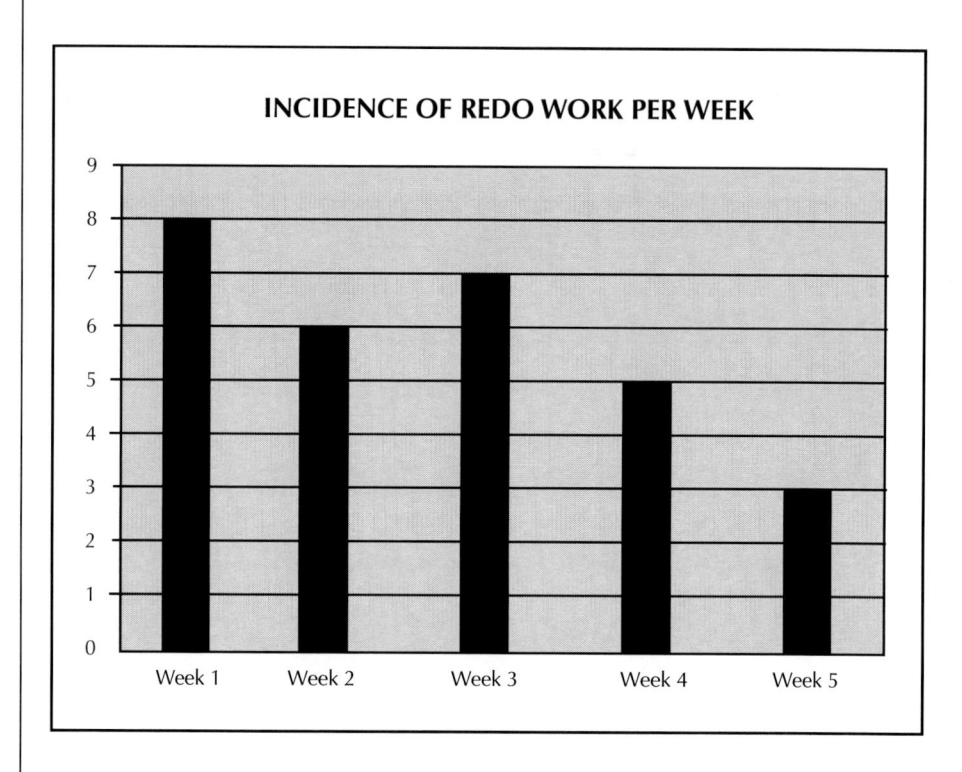

Week	Incidents
Week 1	8
Week 2	6
Week 3	7
Week 4	5
Week 5	3

Fig. 9-10

Brainstorm by getting several different individuals together and having them study the collected data. This may stimulate creative thinking for improvement as workers go on to the next step.

Having collected the information regarding the frequency of the defect and its causes, the supervisor can hold brainstorming meetings to address improvement ideas. Brainstorm by getting several different individuals together and having them study the collected data. This may stimulate creative thinking for improvement. Individuals should be encouraged to consider new ideas, i.e., to think out of the box. For example, perhaps a sign displaying the information in Figure 9-11 can be posted at jobsites to bring attention to the firm's objective of reducing the defect. Just because such a sign is not common at jobsites does not mean it cannot contribute to productivity. Sometimes the strangest idea is the best idea.

RECORD KEEPING, CONTROL, CHANGES AND DEFECT ANALYSIS

INCIDENCE OF REDO WORK PER WEEK
Give us your suggestions

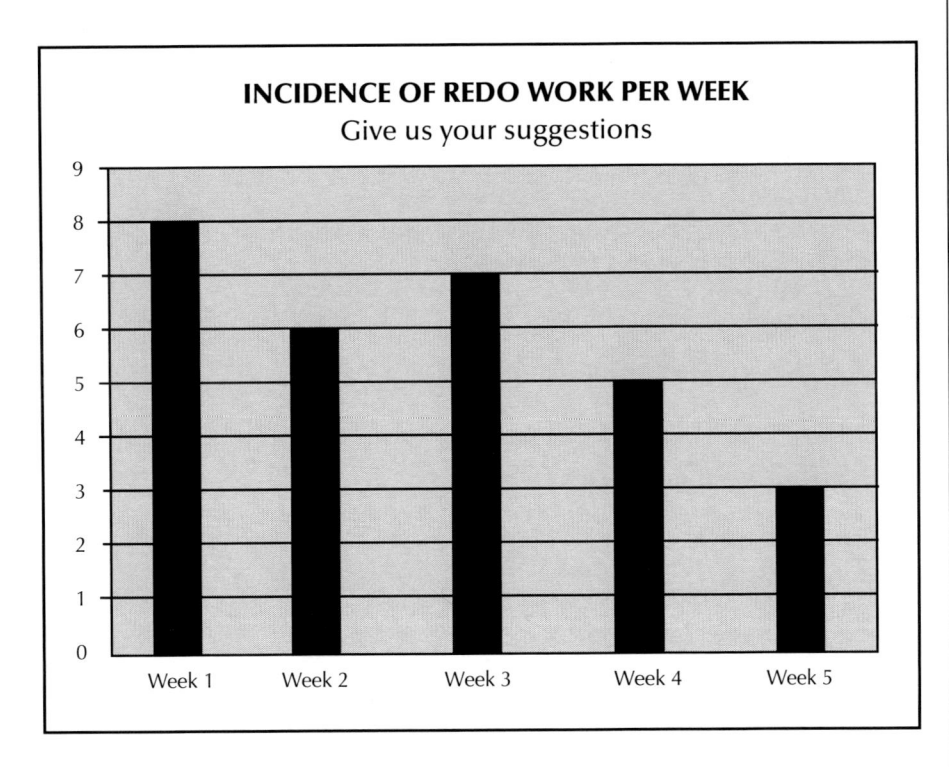

Week	Incidents
Week 1	8
Week 2	6
Week 3	7
Week 4	5
Week 5	3

Fig. 9-11. Sign at Jobsite Measuring Incidence of Redo Work

Once new ideas and procedures are decided upon for implementation, they should be implemented to determine if in fact they work. Not all new ideas or procedures will yield results. The point is that the supervisor cannot tell unless the new ideas are tried. Once the new idea or procedure is implemented, the measurement process should continue, and the cycle repeats itself as illustrated in Figure 9-8. Hence the term "continuous improvement."

It should again be emphasized that the increased focus on measurement is not to place blame on individuals. Instead, the focus should be on team problem solving. The emphasis should be on proactive management to reduce defects rather than just a reaction to problems; i.e., a fire drill.

As the supervisor achieves a commitment to the reduction of a selected defect and reduces the defect to zero or an acceptable number, the firm can select another defect as its focus. The defects become standards unless they are measured, analyzed and corrected. The concept of zero defects is not merely theory. The supervisor probably has constructed a project with zero defects; for example, zero hours of redo work, or zero hours of doubling handling of material. Given that they have done it, zero defects should be the goal on all the projects!

Exercise

Data Collection for Project Productivity Defects

For each of the following productivity defects, you should identify specific ideas for collecting data at jobsites to measure the frequency and number of defects and their cause.

- Redo work
- Punch list work
- Accidents
- Waiting for assignment
- Substance abuse
- Waiting for resources
- Wastage and/or theft
- Multiple material handling
- Unclean jobsite
- Waiting for information

Session 9 Review

Look back over Session 9 and review these key points to be sure you understand them.

- The importance of timely and accurate jobsite record keeping.
- The importance and use of the job control report.
- Proper record keeping for change order administration.
- Defect analysis, which includes the collection of productivity defect information for productivity improvement.

Using on the Job What You Learned Today

Jobsite Assignment

Try to identify what defect or factor causes the most non-productive time at your jobsites. Collect data regarding the number of times the defect occurred and also attempt to identify the cause of the defect.

To Get Ready for Session 10

Read the Participant's Manual for Session 10, *Increasing Productivity with New Technology.*

Session 9

Record Keeping, Control, Changes and Defect Analysis

Session 10

Improving Productivity with New Technology, Review

Learning Goals for Session 10

After this session, you should understand the following:

- The importance of new technology in improving the efficiency of jobsite record keeping and improving jobsite productivity.

- Specific applications to jobsite record keeping, including labor time reporting, materials and tools management, equipment management and daily reports and jobsite records.

- The importance of improving jobsite communication using new technology

The above learning goals all have the focus of aiding the supervisor to understand new technology and how it can improve construction productivity.

Learning Objectives

To accomplish the learning goals, during this session you will:

- Use new technology to improve jobsite record keeping and data management

- Apply new technologies to labor time reporting, material and tool control and equipment management

- Improve communication and record keeping through computers, PDAs and computer portals

- Develop a plan for technology implementation

To Get Ready for Session

Reading: Pages 10-1 through 10-22. **Jobsite Assignment:** Be prepared to discuss the jobsite assignment given at the end of Session 9.

Major Activities for Session 10

- Discuss the importance of jobsite record keeping and difficulties in achieving it.
- Do an exercise that focuses on new types of data that can be gathered using new technology.
- Discuss the process of recording onsite labor time and how bar code technology can be used to eliminate paperwork.
- Do an exercise that quantifies the benefit of using new technology for time reporting.
- Discuss the importance of managing materials, tools and supplies and how new technology can be used to improve this function.
- Do an exercise that addresses effective tool management and demonstrates methods of managing materials.
- Discuss how new GPS technology can be used to improve equipment productivity.
- Discuss the importance of daily reports and jobsite record keeping and how new technology can be used for these functions.
- Do an exercise that addresses the difficulties of implementing new technology and developing a strategy for implementation.

A Review of Session 9

In Session 9, you learned the importance of new supervisory skills:

- The importance of change orders and change order administration.

- The importance of quantifying lost labor productivity when a construction change, dispute or claim evolves.

- The negative productivity impact of various factors (overtime, weather, re-sequencing of work and change orders) on productivity.

- Methods of quantifying lost labor productivity.

The Importance of Information to the Construction Firm

There are many reasons why the construction industry has struggled in its attempt to increase productivity. One of the reasons relates to the industry's lack of accurate and timely jobsite information and record keeping. The dependence on information and record keeping is illustrated by the type and amount of information illustrated in Figure 10-1. To gather all the information illustrated requires a commitment on the part of many individuals in the construction firm.

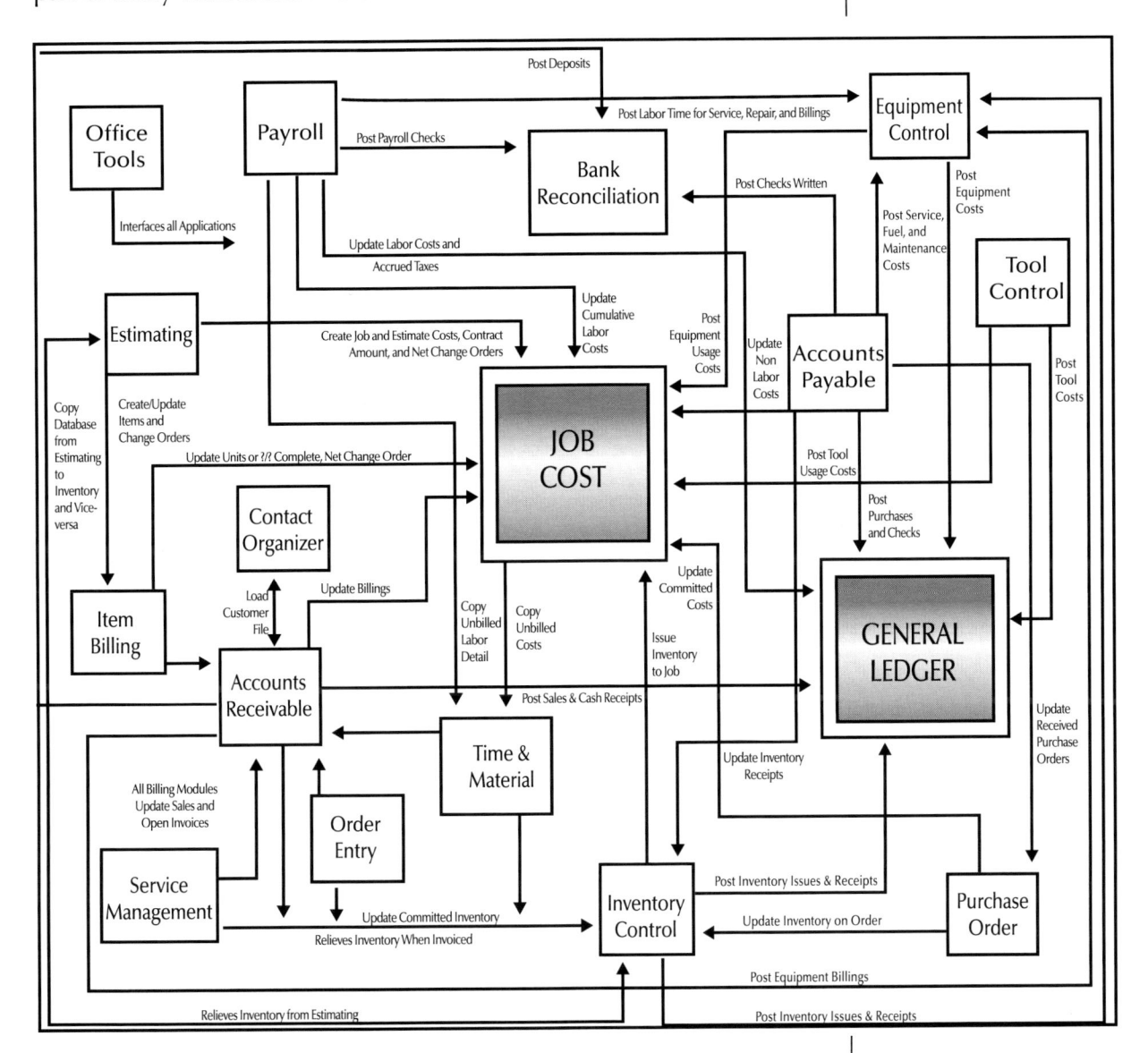

Fig. 10-1

Not only do jobsite personnel get bogged down doing paperwork, but inaccurate and untimely data collection and reports result in the construction firm not recognizing a problem in a timely manner. You can't fix a problem if you don't know you have one!

The difficulty of obtaining accurate and timely jobsite reporting is compounded by the decentralized nature of the construction process. A construction firm has its main office and accounting department at one office site and has projects scattered throughout many locations. The paperwork is typically gathered at the jobsite and transferred and processed at the main office. Resulting reports are transferred back to the jobsite for use by supervisors. This creates problems with timeliness and accuracy. Another difficulty relates to the fact that source data (e.g., timecards and daily reports) are initiated by production personnel, not accountants. Individuals such as foremen and superintendents typically place a higher priority on performing construction work than they do on paperwork.

Record keeping, while time consuming, is critical to a successful construction project.

No one should deny the importance of job cost record keeping and reporting. Record keeping and the related reports give the construction organization the following benefits:

- Enables early identification of productivity problems.
- Provides control of jobsite and company assets.
- Enables consistent practices and procedures that enhance accountability and productivity.
- Enables company office personnel (including the company owner) "to see and monitor the job from the office."
- Enables the preparation of financial statements that serve the needs of the company and external parties.
- Enables the collection of past project data that can be used to improve estimates and productivity for future projects.
- Provides a paper trail of events, expected and unexpected, that can be used to prove and quantify change orders, or to prevent or quantify disputes or claims.

New technology is available to reduce paperwork and to enhance project communication and productivity.

These benefits of paperwork and record keeping are not without costs. Project supervisors expend considerable time and effort filling out timecards, daily reports, meeting minutes, change requests, equipment logs, etc. This is time and effort that could be spent performing productive construction work such as supervising a crew or planning work activities. The cost of inaccurate or untimely paperwork and record keeping is even more than the cost of good record keeping.

These costs stem from the inability to identify correctable productivity problems, lost or stolen assets owing to a lack of controls, increased potential to lose a construction dispute or claim, etc.

On the surface, there appears to be a dilemma. The construction industry needs more accurate and timely record keeping; but the time it takes to do the necessary paperwork takes away from the time to do construction work.

Fortunately the construction industry is in the early stages of a profound revolution in jobsite technology that will change the industry more in the next ten years than in any other time in history. Barcode technology, digital cameras, fully integrated estimating and control systems, equipment guided by lasers and global positioning satellites, and Internet-based technology give the construction industry new ways to collect and utilize jobsite information to improve productivity. Smart buildings, construction robotics and the paperless jobsite are not fantasies; they are the future of the construction industry.

In this session we will discuss some of the many applications of new technology to improve jobsite productivity.

Exercise

Using New Technology to Increase Productivity — Not Just Faster, But Better

New technology, including bar code technology, digital technology, Internet technology, imaging, global satellite technology and lasers, can be used by the construction supervisor to reduce project paperwork and improve timely communication. Reduced paperwork and improved communication can result in improved project productivity.

However, simply using new technology to speed up an inefficient process does not optimize the construction process. When the construction firm and industry are changing the way they collect project data and communicate, it may be best to assess even the type of data or information that is collected.

In earlier sessions we identified processes for productivity improvement that require the new information for the construction supervisor. For example, it was suggested that the construction supervisor obtain information about project defect labor time such as "waiting time," "redo work," etc.

In this exercise, your group is asked to think out of the box to identify new project data or information that should be obtained using new technology. Divorce yourself from the traditional jobsite record keeping that is part of the construction process. Instead be innovative in your approach to setting out new information that can be gathered with new technology; information that can be used to improve jobsite productivity.

New project information to be gathered	Reason for collecting the information	How the information is to be gathered

Implementing New Technology for Labor Hour Reporting

The construction industry's high dependence on onsite labor costs makes timecard reporting a time-consuming function. While timecards might be filled out by a project accountant or by the individual workers themselves, more often than not, foremen fill out timecards for their individual crew workers. In addition to reporting on the total number of hours a worker works in a given day, it is necessary to record time spent performing specific tasks; e.g., time erecting concrete wall forms, time placing concrete, time stripping forms, etc. An example, "paper" timecard is shown in Figure 10-2.

Manually filled out timecards are time-consuming and tedious. Often the timecards have errors, are hard to read and are filled out inconsistently.

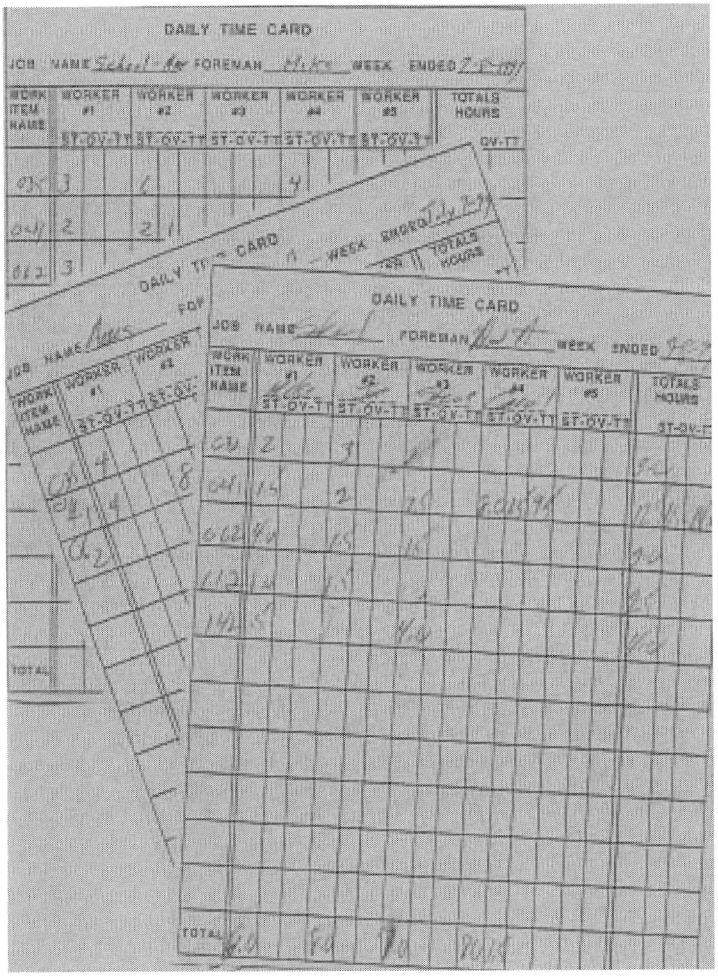

Fig.10-2

SESSION 10

IMPROVING PRODUCTIVITY WITH NEW TECHNOLOGY, REVIEW

The following difficulties are often characteristic of the construction timecard process.

- The time to fill them out is not structured, is excessive, and is not efficient

- Given the varied handwriting skills and the location at which they are filled out, timecards are often difficult to read.

- The degree of detail and time reporting varies from one individual to the next; for example, one foreman may break down a worker's time to the nearest ½ hour and another foreman may break it down to the nearest hour.

Shown in Figure 10-3 is new technology for doing paperless timecards. The system shown includes 1) a Bar Code Unit recording device, 2) a series of job and work item code cards and 3) a downloading device to transfer data via telephone lines to the main office computer.

Fig. 10-3

Bar code technology can be used to eliminate the paper timecard and improve the accuracy, consistency and timeliness of the labor reporting process.

The construction foreman carries the mobile Bar Code Recording Unit on his or her belt. The foreman also carries a Bar Code Card that has bar codes for cost codes preprinted on the card identification.

When a craftworker arrives in the morning, he or she hands the foreman the employee Bar Code Card and the foreman swipes the card into the Card Code Recording Unit. The foreman also swipes the Bar Code Recording Device over the Work Code on the Work Code card to indicate the work task the worker is assigned to perform. If the worker changes to another work task during the day, the worker merely returns to the foreman and the foreman swipes another cost code from the Work Code card. At the end of the workday, the foreman places the Bar Code Recording Device into a receptacle that attaches to the Downloading Device. All the timecard data is transferred via telephone lines to the firm's accounting payroll and job cost system at the main office.

Benefits of the bar coding time recording system relative to a paper timecard process include the following:

- Reduction in cost of doing timecard reporting
- Ability to monitor and reduce late starts and early quits
- Reduction of human error and the time it takes to record worker time
- Audit savings
- Improved accuracy, consistency and productivity

SESSION 10

IMPROVING PRODUCTIVITY WITH NEW TECHNOLOGY, REVIEW

Exercise

Cost Benefit Analysis for Automated Versus Manual Time Recording

In this exercise, you are asked to quantify the potential benefits of using an automated timecard process instead of having supervisors do them manually. Assume the following information:

Average number of onsite workers per day during the work year	100
Supervisor time savings per worker per week when filling out timecards with bar code process	6 minutes
Weekly salary of supervisor	$1,200 per week
Reduction in late starts and early quits of onsite worker with use of new technology for time reporting	12 minutes per day per worker
Average hourly wage rate of worker	$20 per hour
Work hours per year	2,000
Office accounting time to correct manual timecard entries	2 hours per week
Weekly salary of office accounting staff	$750 per week
Loss of productivity in field owing to miscoding of timecards (leading to incorrect job cost reports and failure to identify a correctable jobsite productivity problem)	1% of total onsite labor cost
General conditions costs (function of time)	7% times labor cost

Calculate the annual savings in dollars that can be saved using new technology for the labor time reporting.

10-10 Participant's Manual ■ STP ■ Unit 9

Controlling Materials, Tools and Supplies

New technology can also be used to improve inventory control, scheduling, and productivity of construction materials, tools and supplies. When visiting the construction jobsite, one often finds jobsite materials, tools and supplies in disarray, as shown in Figure 10-4.

Fig. 10-4

Little attention is given to providing storage areas and controls. The result is a lack of accountability for materials, tools and supplies, increased chance of theft, and a loss of productivity. Not being able to locate materials, tools or supplies leads to added waiting time for workers, unnecessary purchases of materials, tools and supplies, and wastage and theft. The cost of losing (or having an individual steal) a $100 tool at the jobsite is not limited to the $100 replacement cost. The real cost includes the idle work time of a crew when crewmembers scramble to locate the tool. Workers expend time looking for the tools and waiting for the tool to be replaced.

In effect the management of onsite materials, tools and supplies is a time-consuming function. To account for materials, tools and supplies via a paper reporting system is cumbersome and is dependent on timely and legible handwriting procedures. The result is that several construction firms have decided it is not worth the effort even to try to

Not being able to locate materials, tools or supplies leads to added waiting time for workers, unnecessary purchases of materials, tools and supplies, and wastage and theft.

control these items. Instead they view lost and stolen tools as a "cost of doing business." A case in point is that of managing and controlling tools. Many construction firms merely budget tools as 2% of the labor cost and view the tools as a job cost rather than an inventory asset. The result is that the 2% for tools becomes a cost of doing business.

Shown in Figure 10-5 is hardware to implement a bar code paperless tool and material control system.

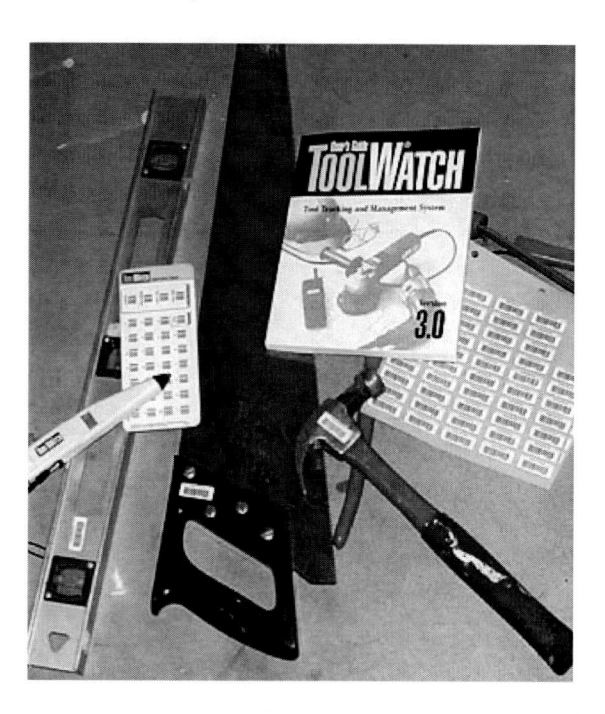

Fig. 10-5

Bar coding of materials, tools and supplies creates a perpetual inventory system rather than a periodic system. When a perpetual system is used, the materials, tools and supplies are accounted for (rather than merely counted) at the end of the project to determine what was used.

In this system each tool is coded with its own unique bar code. Accompanying software enables the firm to price tools to a project as they are checked out of an inventory control center. When tools are returned to the inventory control center (for example, a checkout room at the main office location), the costing of the jobs gets credited. In effect, the firm uses what can be described as a perpetual inventory system for tools and material. The location of each tool can be traced to an individual and a specific project. Bar coding of materials, tools or supplies can result in a perpetual inventory system rather than a periodic system. When a perpetual system is used, the materials, tools and supplies are accounted for (rather than merely counted) at the end of the project to determine what was used.

In addition to reducing paper and improving accountability, the bar coding system increases jobsite productivity. The software offers a report that tells supervisors when new tools are in short supply and need to be ordered. The system also lets a supervisor know instantly where a tool is and when it will be returned and available for another project. The entire system is compatible with the concept that accountability forces responsibility, which in turn enables productivity improvement. A similar process can be developed for the management and control of onsite materials and supplies.

Exercise

Tools and Material Management

Tools

The mismanagement of tools at the construction jobsite can lead to added worker waiting time at the jobsite, unnecessary purchasing of tools, theft and reduced worker morale.

Your group members are asked to share methods they have used to address this issue on jobsites. Discuss the benefits and disadvantages of alternative methods and difficulties that may have been encountered in implementing them.

Material

Assume a steel contractor maintains an inventory of various steel parts at the company's main office and delivers the part to specific jobs as needed.

In a perpetual inventory system for materials such as the steel items, each and every item is inventoried and a log is kept of the item when it is taken out of inventory. By viewing the inventory log at any point in time, the supervisor can determine the amount and type of inventory and make purchases ahead of time. This avoids the need to order materials or tools and wait, as often happens when the supervisor suddenly finds he needs something and it is not available or in stock.

In a periodic inventory system, the company merely counts how many items they have left at the end of a time period (say at the end of the month), and subtracts this amount from what was available at the beginning of the month (plus purchases during the month), to determine how much of the item was used. New purchases are made to restock the inventory.

Discuss the benefits and disadvantages of perpetual versus periodic methods and difficulties that may have been encountered in implementing the two methods.

New Technology and Equipment Productivity

Equipment, like labor, is key to a project and its productivity must be monitored and increased. This is especially true for such equipment-intense firms as roadway builders and excavators. All too often the construction firm has difficulty tracking productive and non-productive equipment time, identifying the location of equipment, and measuring and controlling operating and maintenance costs. As a result the firm often cannot evaluate the production and cost elements of equipment used at jobs. For example, my studies indicate that on most projects, equipment is standing idle for more than 60% of the workday. This is either because of poor scheduling or because the equipment has broken down. It is fair to say that non-productive equipment time is a larger problem than non-productive labor time.

It is time-consuming to keep adequate paper records on the location. Production and cost components of a piece of equipment such as an excavator, scraper or crane depend on the commitment of jobsite personnel to do the record keeping. In the end, the construction firm may not even attempt to do the record keeping. Instead equipment records usually are kept on a company basis rather than on a job basis. Instead of measuring daily or even monthly production or cost information for a piece of equipment on a job basis, the equipment is either charged to a job using published rental rates, or not dedicated to a job and not even charged to the job. Clearly, production and cost record keeping for equipment is a "black hole" in the industry.

The construction industry is starting to make use of global positioning satellite technology (GPS) to manage equipment. Shown in Figure 10-6 is hardware developed by Caterpillar to aid in the management of equipment.

As with labor, the productivity of equipment must be monitored and increased. All too often the construction firm has difficulty tracking productive and non-productive equipment time.

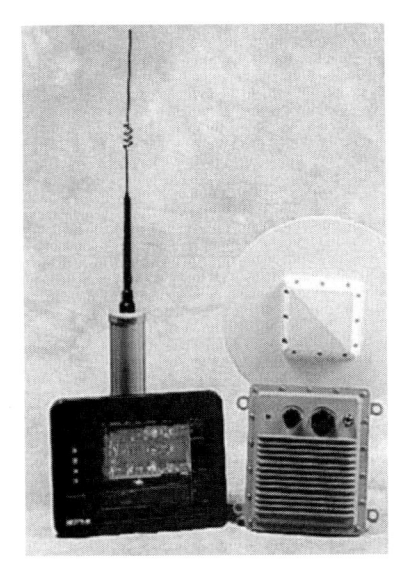

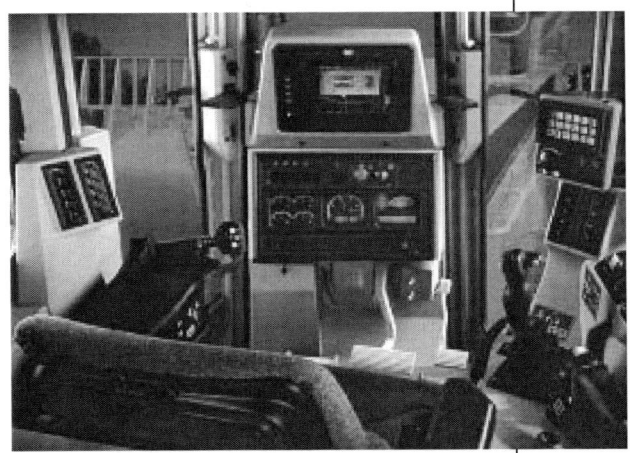

Fig. 10-6

The global satellite system (GPS) technology can be used to locate construction equipment and increase its productivity.

Using a dual portable radio, an antenna, a computer and color display and a GPS receiver, it becomes possible to locate equipment, reduce (if not eliminate) equipment theft, and improve productivity by reducing mistakes and making more optimal use of the equipment. For example, using the GPS system with accompanying software, the cut and fills excavation locations can be controlled so that the staking is eliminated and the equipment operator merely follows computer screen directions. For landfill type work, the GPS system and software can instruct the operator on the optimal number of passes based on compaction readings.

Along with GPS technology, new technology attached to equipment is enabling the contractor to keep records regarding maintenance and repair, downtime versus running time, and the exact location of the machine. Shown in Figure 10-7 is a report that gives the contractor this information instantaneously. This aids productivity by enabling the construction firm to implement preventive maintenance programs, monitor equipment performance, and evaluate operators and supervisors in their use of the equipment.

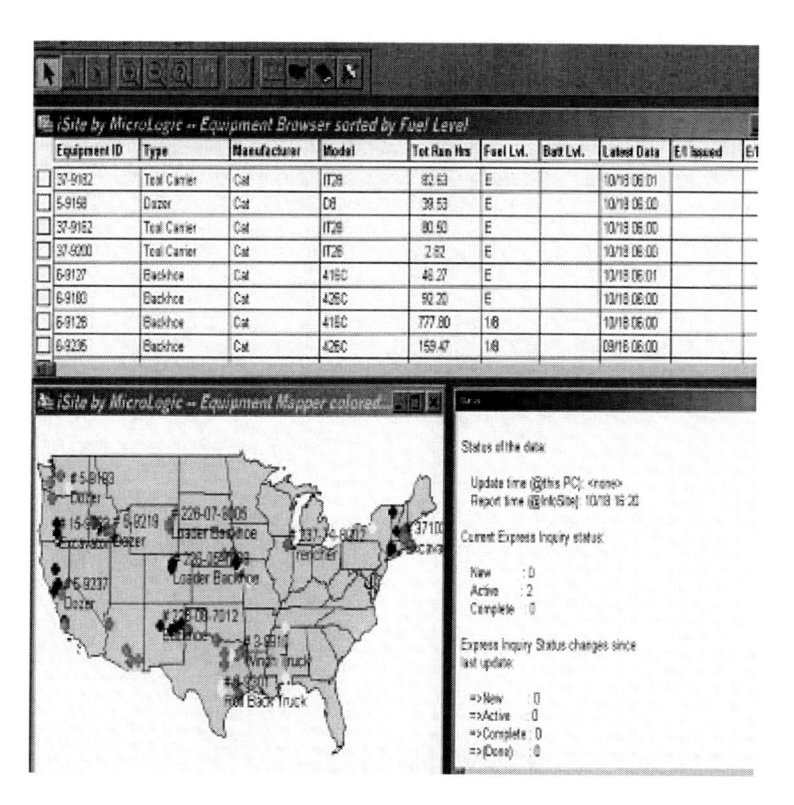

Fig. 10-7

GPS technology and electronic instruments that track equipment performance help the supervisor increase the productive use of equipment at the jobsite.

Daily Reports, Jobsite Record Keeping and Project Billings

In addition to jobsite record keeping, labor time reporting, and tracking materials, tools and equipment, the construction supervisor must report daily construction events that occur at the jobsite. Included in the required documentation are:

- Daily events such as quantities of work performed, weather conditions, instructions received, etc.
- Project changes like obstructions, instructions received, changed site conditions, etc.
- Progress billing information
- Change order information
- Requests for information regarding the project drawings and specification (RFIs)
- Meeting minutes

This is only an abbreviated list of the record keeping responsibilities of the construction supervisor. The record keeping function, while important, typically does not lead to increasing jobsite productivity. The time it takes to fill out manual forms takes time away from the supervisor to plan and monitor the work process. Given the choice between focusing on jobsite production tasks and doing paperwork, the supervisor often chooses the production tasks. The result can be sloppy or inaccurate paperwork (see Figure 10-8).

The time it takes to fill out manual forms takes time away from the supervisor to plan and monitor the work process.

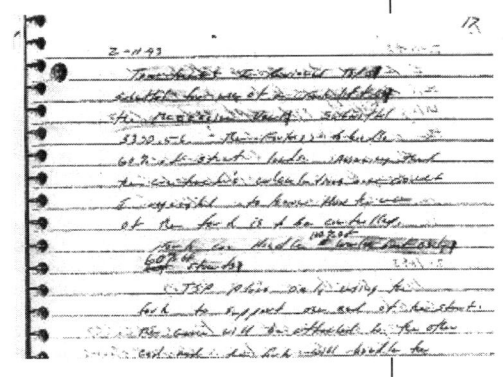

Fig. 10-8

Improving Productivity with New Technology, Review

An unstructured process of gathering jobsite information can lead to having supervisors record information that can hurt the firm.

In addition to being hard to read, manual record keeping is often inconsistent and in fact may prove troublesome to the construction firm. All too often a daily report such as that shown in Figure 10-8 may contain supervisor's remarks that may come back to hurt the construction firm. For example, the supervisor innocently writes "equipment not available, being worked on in shop" to indicate why he or she was not able to get access to a needed piece of equipment. However, read in a courtroom, this remark may indicate that an alleged owner delay comes down to the contractor. An unstructured process of gathering jobsite information can lead to this type of problem.

One of the major purposes of jobsite record keeping is to enable the construction firm to "play the project back like a movie" if needed. The need might relate to having documentation for a disputed work activity, or keeping track of important milestone dates. Jobsite record keeping should be limited to what information is needed. What is not needed should not be recorded. It should be done efficiently and in a structured format.

The use of computer laptops and PDAs enables the construction supervisor to reduce the time it takes to do jobsite record keeping.

New technology such as computer laptops and PDAs (shown in Figure 10-9) with accompanying software programs help construction supervisors save time record keeping. Equally important are computer software programs that catch errors. For example, the computer software program can be written to prevent a supervisor from entering labor time against a work code for which no quantities are in place.

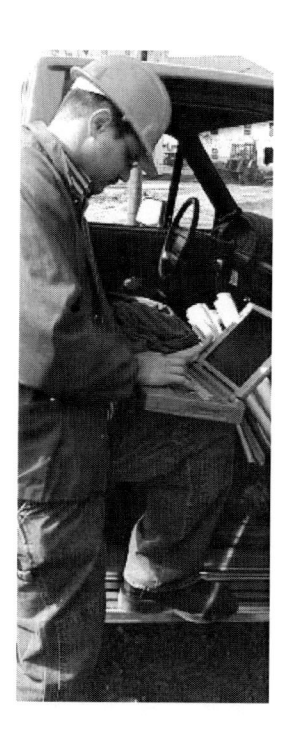

Fig. 10-9

Information gathered using computer laptops or PDAs can be downloaded to the construction company's main office via a telephone line. In addition, wireless technology makes it possible to transmit to the main office without a telephone.

One of the unique difficulties of the construction process is that projects are typically at locations far from the construction firm's main office. This results in delays in getting information to the jobsite from the main office and vice versa.

Productivity of the construction project is also negatively impacted by the fact that so many different firms or entities involved in a project need to communicate with one another. For example, the general contractor's ability to perform depends on timely and accurate information from the project owner, designer and various subcontractors. The many different entities of a construction project are illustrated in Figure 10-10.

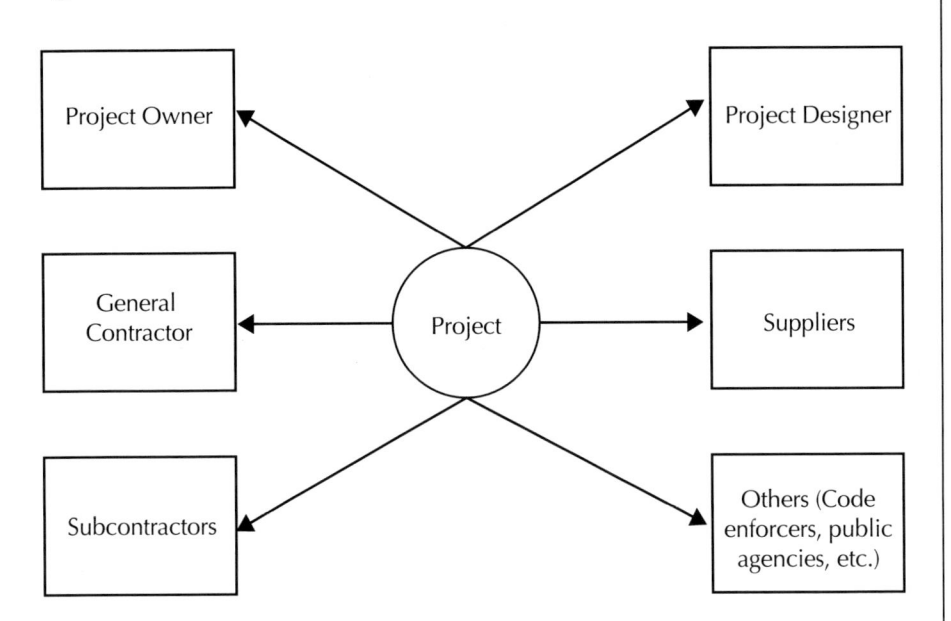

Fig. 10-10

All too often one of the parties is waiting for another to provide information — information necessary to production.

The lack of timely communication between any two of the project entities curtails productivity. Examples of lack of communication are:

- General contractor waiting for designer to respond to request for information (RFI).
- Subcontractor waiting for information from a supplier.

- Project owner, general contractor, subcontractors and designer waiting for decisions from public agencies.
- Subcontractors waiting for response from project owner and designer regarding approval of shop drawings.

These and other examples of untimely communication curtail productivity, create adverse relationships between project entities and lead to "blaming of the other guy" when production is delayed.

New computer technology and Internet capabilities enable improved communication between project entities. Project website "portals" such as that shown in Figure 10-11 provide all parties instant access to needed information.

— AIRPORT PROJECT (web site)

Contract Documents
Time Cards / Daily Reports
Progress Billings
Change Orders / Estimates
Schedules
Meeting Minutes

Fig. 10-11

The design of such websites allows information relevant to specific entities to be "shared." At the same time, privacy and security of information can be maintained through the use of security passwords.

Implementing New Technology

The construction industry and construction process will continue to go through a tremendous change owing to the current technology wave. New devices, new data and new methods of collecting information are evolving daily. At the same time, the construction industry is traditionally slow to change. Some construction employees are rather stubborn in defending their ways and are unwilling to change. This will continue to create difficulties in adapting all the new technology available; technology that can improve the productivity of the project and the firm.

In recognition of the potential difficulty of implementing new technology and to make the implementation cost effective, your group is asked to set out a list of do's and don'ts that should be considered by the construction firm and the supervisor in implementing the technologies described in this session.

Exercise

Session 10 Review

Look back over Session 10 and review these key points to be sure you understand them:

- Paper work and jobsite record keeping, while critical to a productive project, take away from the supervisor's planning and monitoring process.

- New technology available to the construction supervisor for jobsite record keeping and improving productivity:

    — Onsite labor time reporting

    — Materials, tools and supplies management

    — Equipment management

    — Daily reports, jobsite records and project billings

    — Project communication

- The construction firm and construction supervisor must take steps to plan and implement new technology in a cost-effective manner.

Using on the Job What You Learned Today

Jobsite Assignment

While on projects, consider measuring non-productive labor and supervisor or equipment time that relates to the use of a manual record keeping system. Use this information to consider the benefits of using new technology to perform record keeping functions.

Unit Review

Session 10 is the last session of this unit. Following this page is a list of *Supervisor Best Practices for Productivity Improvement.* The best practices have been prepared based on the information in each of the ten sessions in this unit.

You are asked to use the pages and "best practices list" as a reminder list when you supervise construction projects. You are encouraged to add additional "best practices" to the list as you develop them in your role as a supervisor.

Supervisor Best Practices for Productivity Improvement

SESSION 1: INTRODUCTION TO PRODUCTIVITY IMPROVEMENT

1. ❏ Explain the definition of productivity to all workers; productivity equals units of work placed per person-hour. Keep track of productivity increases relative to cost increases with the objective of trying to increase productivity faster than costs.

2. ❏ Take time to show workers the relationship between productivity and profits at a project. Show the workforce that only a small increase in productivity will have a significant impact on project profits and project schedule.

3. ❏ Always consider the four project variables of cost, time, quality and safety when making productivity decisions.

4. ❏ Emphasize safety as the most important project and work consideration; a productive job should be a safe job and vice versa.

5. ❏ Emphasize the importance of thinking out of the box when looking for productivity improvement.

6. ❏ View non-productive labor or equipment time as an opportunity to improve.

7. ❏ Try to get away from looking at things, and instead look at whether the thing (labor or equipment) is doing value-added work; i.e., is in a productive state.

8. ❏ Take random observations to benchmark representative percentages of productive, non-productive and support work states at projects. Try to determine why one project is better than another.

9. ❏ Emphasize that one should measure non-productive labor time not to blame individuals, but to study causation and means of improving.

10. ❏ Emphasize the positive to workers; indicate that they are doing many things right. Indicate that the goal of productivity improvement is to improve, not to blame.

SESSION 2: IMPROVING PRODUCTIVITY THROUGH PRE-PLANNING

11. ❏ Focus on all four phases of a construction project in the productivity improvement objective; 1) estimating, 2) pre-construction, 3) construction and 4) project closeout.

12. ❏ Develop a checklist of activities or tasks that should be done before construction starts.

13. ❏ Communicate estimating standards and assumptions to project personnel.

14. ❏ Identify "vital" work tasks — those tightly monitored — prior to construction. Consider schedule, cost, risk or variation and unfamiliarity with the work task in identifying vital tasks.

15. ❏ Identify potential areas of work difficulty and changes before starting construction.

16. ❏ Review supplemental conditions prior to construction to detect unique contract clauses that may affect productivity or add cost.

SESSION 2 (continued)

17. ❏ Break the labor estimate into daily production goals for work crews prior to the start of construction.
18. ❏ Develop a strategy of where to put things at a project prior to the start of construction.
19. ❏ Identify long lead items of material or work actions prior to the start of construction.
20. ❏ Involve subcontractors in pre-planning.

SESSION 3: "MORE" FOUR NEW SKILLS FOR THE EFFECTIVE SUPERVISOR

21. ❏ Focus on the accounting system as a means of "maintaining" productivity; view a more proactive approach as a means of improving productivity.
22. ❏ Budget time for measuring and challenging the work process.
23. ❏ Equip yourself and supervisors with a clipboard, wristwatch, calculator and pencil.
24. ❏ Take random measurements of productivity on a shortened cycle; for example, the number of crane picks from one hour to the next; number of panels placed in the morning versus afternoon, etc., as a means of drawing attention to improvement potential.
25. ❏ Measure material movement as a means of reducing non-productive material handling.
26. ❏ Budget time to challenge the work process at least once a month to determine an improved work method; write up the improved work method.
27. ❏ Require subordinates to identify an improved work method at least once a month.
28. ❏ Track productivity variation for a work method; expand the job cost report to measure productivity differences from one week to the next.
29. ❏ Prepare, carry with you and post what everything costs at your jobsite.
30. ❏ Focus your attention and that of your workers on managing and monitoring costly work tasks and costly materials, tools and equipment.

SESSION 4: PERSONNEL MANAGEMENT: MAKING A JOB LOOK LIKE A FIRM

31. ❏ Emphasize the importance of each worker to the project goals.
32. ❏ View labor as a friend, not a foe. Attaining improved labor productivity represents one of the few ways one can improve project cost, time, quality and safety.
33. ❏ Develop a philosophy of viewing people as equals, not as subordinates.
34. ❏ Focus on the four needs of every worker; measurement, communication, pride and financial compensation.
35. ❏ Give workers goals with which they can measure their performance.
36. ❏ Communicate production goals to workers as well as supervisors.
37. ❏ Attempt to listen, not just talk, as an effective communicator.

SESSION 4 (continued)

38. ❏ Attempt to promote a work environment in which every worker develops pride in what they do.

39. ❏ Manage workers with the premise that you must provide them an environment where they in effect manage themselves.

40. ❏ View each worker as different and try to keep track of what motivates each worker.

SESSION 5: EQUIPMENT MANAGEMENT FOR PRODUCTIVITY IMPROVEMENT

41. ❏ View equipment like labor in regard to its work state; it is either in a productive, non-productive or support state. Try to increase the percentage of time it is in a productive state.

42. ❏ View equipment as money rather than as a machine; know the hourly cost of all equipment at the jobsite.

43. ❏ Take time to locate equipment so that its placement leads to productive use and does not jeopardize safety.

44. ❏ Make a formal analysis of using equipment versus labor to do a task; consider all factors and the big picture in deciding to use one or the other.

45. ❏ Just as with labor, be attentive not to overwork equipment or extend its capacity.

46. ❏ Focus on looking ahead to keep equipment productivity; schedule work around equipment use as well as scheduling equipment around the work.

47. ❏ Focus on preventive maintenance of equipment to avoid breakdowns that lead to non-productive time.

48. ❏ Always focus on safety first when using equipment.

49. ❏ View equipment as having an ownership cost component (costs that incur as a function of time) and an operating cost component (costs that incur as a function of use). Emphasize that there is cost associated with idle equipment.

50. ❏ When two pieces of equipment work together, be attentive to balancing the productivity of the interdependent equipment.

SESSION 6: PRODUCTIVITY IMPROVEMENT AND PLANNING AND SCHEDULING

51. ❏ Emphasize the importance of planning as a means of 1) reducing the number of unanticipated problems that will occur and 2) developing a strategy to react to problems.

52. ❏ Emphasize that the more uncertain events that are likely to occur, the more important it is to have a written plan and update it.

53. ❏ Focus on preparing plans that set out milestone dates and how something will be accomplished rather than on when the entire task will be done; i.e., plan effort and performance.

SUPERVISOR BEST PRACTICES FOR PRODUCTIVITY IMPROVEMENT

SESSION 6 (continued)

54. ❑ Continually emphasize the relationship between planning and scheduling and productivity; focus on productivity improvement by attempting to match available resources to needed resources.

55. ❑ Emphasize that the master schedule or critical path method (CPM) diagram for a project is like a roadmap for getting from one point to another. Its use is necessary to getting to the end point in the least costly and most efficient manner.

56. ❑ Emphasize the importance of subcontractor's timely and accurate input to the overall project master schedule.

57. ❑ Update a project schedule frequently; the shorter the project, the more quickly it should be updated. Consider updating the schedule based on events rather than at a designated time interval.

58. ❑ Use a one- to four-week look-ahead detailed schedule to identify events that must occur today to ensure something will happen productively several weeks in the future.

59. ❑ Require foremen and supervisors to use a form to plan tomorrow's work today — lining up tools, material, equipment and labor.

60. ❑ Require supervisory personnel to carry a small notebook in their pocket and write memos to themselves as a reminder of actions they must take every day.

SESSION 7: MANAGING SUBCONTRACTORS

61. ❑ View a project as a system and remember that project time, cost, quality and safety objectives are jeopardized by the weakest link, including a non-performing subcontractor.

62. ❑ Develop a formalized process of performing a post-job analysis of subcontractors.

63. ❑ Get subcontractors to agree to specific management actions prior to the start of construction; monitor the performance of these actions and be authoritative in enforcing them.

64. ❑ Develop a philosophy of encouraging subcontractors to manage themselves; a win-win for everyone.

65. ❑ Require subcontractors to prepare and submit project plans and schedules that set out milestone dates and *how* they are going to get something done rather than merely *when* they are going to get it done.

66. ❑ Develop procedures that encourage subcontractor supervisors to plan tomorrow's work today.

67. ❑ Keep project records on subcontractor performance with the theme that accountability promotes productivity.

68. ❑ Plan and hold productive jobsite meetings. Plan the meeting agenda in advance and avoid meeting distractions or non-productive meeting time.

69. ❑ In working with subcontractors emphasize "we" rather than "they." Focus on problem solving rather than assigning blame.

70. ❑ Implement a "partnering" philosophy prior to and during construction.

SESSION 8: QUANTIFYING LOST PRODUCTIVITY

71. ❏ Focus on quickly identifying factors that negatively impact labor productivity: 1) increased work difficulty, 2) work sequencing, 3) environmental factors, 4) disruptions in work, 5) added support activities and 6) factors that affect the morale of workers.

72. ❏ Be attentive to the physical ability of a worker to do work; if the worker is overworked he or she will lose productivity and be more prone to have an accident.

73. ❏ Monitor the work process and sequencing of work relative to the planned work sequence. Document when work is done out of sequence relative to the plan.

74. ❏ Attempt to schedule work so that environmental factors such as temperature, precipitation, noise and lighting do not negatively impact productivity.

75. ❏ Document and try to minimize disruptions in the work process, including waiting for instructions or information.

76. ❏ Be attentive to planning work logistics and access to avoid material handling problems. Document when these situations are out of your control.

77. ❏ Be attentive to issues or events that cause a loss of worker morale or may result in a worker slowing up his or her production.

78. ❏ Attempt to measure or benchmark productivity decreases when unexpected factors such as out-of-sequence work occurs.

79. ❏ Before working overtime, consider its possible effects on productivity and safety.

80. ❏ Keep an expanding file of information about construction worker productivity and research studies that have quantified the loss of productivity.

SESSION 9: RECORD KEEPING, CONTROL, CHANGES AND DEFECT ANALYSIS

81. ❏ Focus on jobsite record keeping as a means of problem solving rather than as a means of policing workers.

82. ❏ When requiring individuals to fill out forms or collect data, 1) show them why the data or information is being requested, 2) show them that the data or information is in fact used and 3) give them feedback from the data or information.

83. ❏ Perform jobsite record keeping with the premise that the records provide a "movie" of the job.

84. ❏ Use a job control report that enables you to "see the status" of productivity from the report.

85. ❏ Immediately investigate a work task when the percentage of effort expended is greater than the percentage of work put in place.

86. ❏ Be attentive about separating change order work performed from base bid. Segment the labor hours and work put in place for the change order work.

87. ❏ Identify and focus on the productivity "defects" that result in non-productive labor or equipment time at the project.

SESSION 9 (continued)

88 ❑ Focus on measuring at least one type of defect during project performance and develop a continuous improvement program to reduce the defect.

89 ❑ When measuring a specific productivity defect such as redo work, focus on identifying the cause of the defect so that action can be taken to reduce the defect.

90 ❑ Involve workers in identifying defects and their cause. Invite suggestions for improvement.

SESSION 10: IMPROVING PRODUCTIVITY WITH NEW TECHNOLOGY

91 ❑ Focus on new technology as a means of quickly identifying problems so productivity can be increased.

92 ❑ Be attentive to developing consistent procedures at the project site, including timely and accurate record keeping. Promote an environment in which, when it comes to procedures such as the filling out of forms, everyone does the same thing.

93 ❑ Focus on improved time card accuracy and look into the use of bar code technology.

94 ❑ Develop a process for keeping track of tools, materials and supplies to reduce non-productive time spent searching for things.

95 ❑ Be attentive to new technology for operating equipment productively and more safely.

96 ❑ Be attentive to streamlining daily reports and quantity reports to enable more timely and accurate information. Evaluate new technology to perform these tasks more efficiently.

97 ❑ Attempt to centralize jobsite information and company information so that it is easily accessible to both.

98 ❑ Allot a time period every month to read about and investigate new technology for use at the jobsite.

99 ❑ Implement new technology with the theme of making things simpler, not more complex.

100 ❑ When new technology is implemented, take time to train individuals before requiring them to use the new technology.

Glossary

Addendum: a change in the construction contract documents prior to the letting of the project.

Arbitration: a process of resolving a construction dispute; an alternative to litigation.

Bar Code: electronic image on a card that is read by an electronic reader. Eliminates the need to write out data; used for time reporting and material and tool identification.

Bonus: something that is paid over and above what is due.

Brainstorming: generating a wide range of potential solutions to a problem; no analyzing.

Change Order: construction work outside the work defined in the initial construction contract documents, or work that was defined in the initial construction contract documents that is performed under conditions that were not expected.

Checklist: a reminder list that it is reviewed so that all appropriate actions are taken to enhance production.

CM (Construction Management): a construction project delivery process in which the project owner engages an entity to provide management and critique of the design and construction processes.

Computer: an electronic machine which, by means of stored instructions and information, performs rapid, often complex calculations or compiles, correlates, and selects data.

Continuous Improvement: a management process of measuring defects and variations in production, analyzing their causes, brainstorming and implementing improvement ideas, and measuring again. The cycle of measuring, analyzing, brainstorming and implementing continues until zero defects are attained.

Cost Code: a term used to describe a segment of the overall project work that is estimated, scheduled, and monitored.

Crew Balance Model: a modeling technique of plotting the work states of workers and equipment. Uses vertical bars to illustrate whether the various workers and equipment balance one another to achieve productivity.

Critical Path Method (CPM): a quantitative method of planning and scheduling a project as a function of the various work activities that make up the overall project.

Defect: an imperfection, such as the unnecessary double handling of material to perform a construction task.

Designer: an individual or firm that prepares the construction contract documents, and administers the construction process for the construction project owner.

Dilution of Supervision: a term used to describe a production process when added work or workers cause an undesirable ratio of supervisors to workers.

Discrete Method: a method of quantifying lost labor productivity for a change order, dispute, or claim whereby the cost or hours are measured and segmented as they are incurred.

Drawings: a construction contract document that two-dimensionally depicts the project quantities of work.

Earliest Start Time: when making scheduling calculations as part of the critical path method (CPM), this is the earliest time a work activity can start based on the technical, resource, and preference logic of prior work activities.

GLOSSARY OF TERMS

Earliest Finish Time: when making scheduling calculations as part of the critical path method (CPM), this is the earliest time a work activity can finish based on the technical, resource, and preference logic of prior work activities.

Education: the short-term process of developing the knowledge, skill, mind, and character to improve over a future period of time.

Environmental Factors: weather conditions such as temperature, humidity, noise, wind, and precipitation that affect construction productivity.

Estimating: an approximate calculation of the cost of performing work.

Fatigue: state of being weary from bodily or mental exertion.

Finance: the system or science of revenue and expenditures or of any money matters.

General Conditions: a construction contract document that specifies the roles of the various entities involved in the project.

General Contractor: an individual or firm engaged by the project owner to plan, schedule, coordinate, and monitor the construction process.

Group Behavior: a motivational base shared by individuals and conducive to recurrent interaction among them.

Humidity: the amount or degree of moisture in the air.

Impact: a term used in construction to define the result of unexpected events on construction productivity.

Internet: a vast globe-spanning network of networks that communicate with each other based on certain protocols.

Job Control Report: a timely written report that compares actual performance against planned performance, with the objective of identifying potential over- or underperformance.

Killer Clause: a term used to describe one or more clauses in the supplementary conditions of a contract document that are adverse to the interest of the contractor.

Kilocalories: the amount of heat needed to raise the temperature of one kilogram of water one degree centigrade.

Liquidated Damages: a monetary amount assessed against a contractor for not completing a project by the agreed-upon completion date.

Latest Finish Time: when making scheduling calculations as part of the critical path method (CPM), this is the latest time a work activity can finish without extending the planned completion date of the project.

Latest Start Time: when making scheduling calculations as part of the critical path method (CPM), this is the latest time a work activity can start without extending the planned completion date of the project.

Learning Curve: a mathematical model of repetitive operations showing proficiency versus practice.

Logistics: the placement and moving of materials and resources to accomplish a task.

Litigation: the process of resolving a dispute through law.

Maslow Theory: a personnel management theory proposed by Abraham Maslow that indicates that workers are motivated by various needs. As one need is filled, then another need must be offered to motivate the worker further.

GLOSSARY OF TERMS

Measured Mile Approach: a method of quantifying lost labor productivity for a change order, dispute, or claim. The productivity achieved in a non-impacted time period is contrasted with the productivity of the impacted time period.

Method Productivity Delay Model: a process for analyzing a construction work method that focuses on measuring work cycles and the identification of production delays.

Morale: the mental condition of zeal, confidence, enthusiasm, and willingness to accomplish a task.

MORE: an acronym for an approach to improving productivity that entails measurement, opportunity through challenging, risk analysis, and estimating and education of costs.

Motivational Maintenance Theory: a management theory that worker productivity can be increased by providing certain human needs such as responsibility and challenge, but can only be maintained by other factors such as worksite cleanliness and worker financial compensation.

No Damage for Delay Clause: a contract clause in the supplementary conditions that allows contractors to request a time extension, but does not entitle them to added costs when changes occur.

Non-impacted Day: a workday when production is normal and not affected by delays or external factors that negatively affect productivity.

Notification Clause: a contract clause in the supplementary conditions that places the burden on the contractor to inform the project owner or designer of a problem within a defined number of days after the event occurs (e.g., within 14 days).

One- to Four-Week Look Ahead Schedule: a form and process used to systemize the planning of work and required resources needed to accomplish the work. The plan set out using this form looks ahead one to four weeks.

Operating Cost: costs of operating a piece of equipment, such as maintenance and repair.

Ownership Cost: costs of owning a piece of equipment that incur whether the equipment is used or not. Ownership costs include the finance, insurance, and depreciation cost.

Pareto, Vilfredo: an Italian sociologist (1848-1923) who in his theories differentiated the vital few individuals or events from the useful many.

Performance Management: a management process of planning and monitoring effort or required resources rather than focusing only on results.

Partnering: a management process used in construction to develop trust and emphasize problem solving and improvement between the entities involved in the process.

Problem Solving: a process of collecting all the known facts regarding a problem, analyzing the objective and alternative solutions, and selecting a solution.

Productivity: units or dollars of output per person-hours of effort or input.

Queuing: to form in a line while waiting for something.

Rating Model: a management model by which observations are made of a worker or a machine to determine the percentage of time the worker or machine is in a productive, non-productive, or support work state.

Redo Work: work that has to be redone because it was done improperly the first time.

GLOSSARY OF TERMS

Request for Information (RFI): the formal process by which a contractor requests an explanation regarding the quantity or type of work to be performed that has not been well delineated in the contract documents.

Risk: a process that is not deterministic as to expected results; subject to variation.

Service Unit: when two production units are interdependent upon one another (e.g., a backhoe and trucks that carry soil for a construction site) the service, or stationary, unit is defined as the production unit doing the primary work.

Short Interval Production Schedule (SIPS): a form and process used to systemize the planning of work and required resources needed to accomplish it. Typically the plan is for the next day's work or for a few days' work.

Specifications: a construction contract document that specifies the quality of the work to be performed for a project.

Subcontractor: a contractor who/that does not have direct contract with the project owner.

Team Approach: the philosophy of several individuals who come together to solve a problem and put the overall objective ahead of individual objectives.

Technology: the science or study and application of the industrial arts.

Temperature: the degree of heat or cold, usually measured on a thermometer.

Theory X and Y: contrasting management theories as to what motivates a worker; theory X indicates that workers are motivated by financial gain, whereas theory Y indicates that workers are motivated by pride, responsibility, and challenges.

Time and Motion: the micro-measurement of the physical body movements of a worker as he or she performs a task.

Total Cost Method: a method of quantifying lost labor productivity for a change order, dispute, or claim whereby the cost or hours are determined by subtracting the estimate for the actual hours or dollars incurred.

Total Float: when using the critical path method (CPM) method of scheduling, this is the amount of free time, slack time, or delay time a work activity can withstand without affecting the planned project completion time.

Non-impacted Day: a workday in which production is normal and not affected by delays or external factors that negatively affect productivity.

Unions: an agreement or forming of leagues for mutual benefit.

Unit Cost: total cost divided by the number of units of production.

Updating: to bring up to date by measuring performance up to the date in question.

Useful Many: while abundant in number, these units or events do not greatly influence the result of a process or the overall objective or goal.

Variation Analysis: studying the variation in the results of a production process with the objective of determining the cause and implementing improvement processes.

Vital Few: a select number of units or events that dominate the results of a process or the overall objective or goal.

Waiting Line: a term used to describe a production process when two interdependent production units work together and they do not balance one another.

Work Sampling: a management model in which random observations are made of a worker or a machine to determine a mathematical depiction of the probabilities of being in one of two work states.

Index

A

Accounting ...1-13, 2-5, 3-2, 3-6, 7-5, 9-14, 10-3
Addendum 2-14
Arbitration 2-18
Arrival Unit ....5-23 to 5-32
Authority 7-10

B

Bar Code 6-8, 6-16, 10-8, 10-9, 10-12
Benchmarking 1-4, 3-7
Bidding 2-3
Bonus 1-15
Brainstorming 6-23, 9-16
Budgets ....2-20 to 2-24, 4-9 to 4-14
Building 1-11, 2-3

C

Challenging ....3-13 to 3-17
Change Orders 1-13, 2-13, 5-21,
                         9-12, 9-13, 10-17
Changes 8-1, 8-2, 9-1
Checklist 2-26, 2-27, 2-28, 2-29,
                   6-33, 6-34, 6-35
CM 7-3
Communication 4-5, 4-15, 4-16, 4-17,
                       7-1, 7-22, 10-1
Computer 10-18
Concrete 2-24
Concurrent Operations 8-4, 8-11
Continuous Improvement 9-16
Control 9-1, 9-5, 9-6, 9-7, 9-8
Cost Codes 1-18
Cost 3-4, 3-25, 3-26, 3-27
     Books 4-10
Depreciation 5-19
     Equipment 5-8
     Finance 5-19, 5-20
     Labor 3-4, 3-25, 3-26, 3-27
     Maintenance 5-19, 5-20
     Operating 5-19, 5-20
     Repair 5-19, 5-20
     Replacement 5-19, 5-20
Crew 1-7, 2-22, 3-17, 4-5, 4-12
Crew Balance Model 9-17
Crew Size 8-12
Critical Path Method ......1-20, 6-12 to 6-36

D

Defect 1-18, 2-2
Defect Analysis ....9-1, 9-14 to 9-21
Defining Work Items 6-13, 6-14, 7-13
Delay 3-16
Designer 1-12, 1-23, 2-13
Dilution of Supervision 8-13
Dispute Resolution 7-25
Discrete Method 8-33
Disruption 8-23, 8-24
Drawings 2-6, 2-13, 2-14, 8-5, 8-23
Duct Work 2-24

E

Earliest Finish Time 6-19
Earliest Start Time 6-19
Earned Value Method 8-35, 8-36, 8-37
Earthmoving 5-3, 5-4
Education 1-14, 2-2, 6-24
Electrical 2-24
Environmental Factors 8-16
Estimating 2-3, 2-5, 2-6, 2-7, 2-13,
                      2-20 to 2-24, 3-1, 3-25, 3-26
Equipment 1-2, 1-9, 1-13, 2-3, 3-18, 3-19,
               3-25, 5-1 to 5-32, 6-2, 7-2, 9-9, 10-15
     Breakdown 6-6
     Capacity 5-11, 5-12
     Logistics 5-5, 5-9
     Maintenance 5-5, 5-17
     Non-Productive 5-14, 5-15
     Operating Cost 5-19

INDEX OF TOPICS

Ownership Cost 5-19
Safety 5-18
Schedule 5-16
Support State 5-13
Expert Approach 8-37

F

Fatigue 8-6
Finance 2-5

G

General Conditions 2-14
General Contractor 7-3, 7-4
Global Satellite System 10-15, 10-16
Goal 6-3
Group 4-1
Group Behavior 4-25, 4-26, 4-27, 5-2

H

Highway 3-18
Human Element .8-31
Humidity 8-17

I

Impact 8-3, 8-4
Impacted Day 8-25
Incentives 4-18, 4-19, 4-20
Industrial Engineering 8-35
Interdependent Production 5-22
Internet 10-1

J

Job Control Report .9-3, 9-4, 9-5, 9-6, 9-7, 9-8, 9-10, 9-11
Job Cost Report 1-19, 3-23, 3-24, 6-26

K

Killer Clause 2-1, 2-14, 2-16, 2-29
Kilocalories 8-6, 8-7

L

Liquidated Damages . . .1-15, 2-15, 2-16, 2-18
Labor 1-2, 1-13, 2-3, 4-1, 5-6, 5-10, 7-2
Latest Finish Time 6-19
Latest Start Time 6-19
Learning 8-1
Learning Curve 8-4, 8-5, 8-12, 8-15
Lay Down Area 8-5
Lighting 8-4, 8-20, 8-21
Logistics 8-4, 8-28, 8-30
Litigation 2-3
Lost Labor Productivity . . . . .8-1 to 8-38
Lowest Cost 5-31

M

Management 1-15, 1-16
Process 1-15, 1-16
Results 1-15
Manufacturing 1-2, 1-3, 1-4, 1-7
Maslow Theory 4-21, 4-22
Masonry 2-24
Master Schedule 6-11
Materials . . .1-2, 1-13, 6-6, 9-19, 10-11, 10-14
Material Handling 3-9, 3-10, 6-29
Measured Mile Approach 8-34
Measurement . . . . . . .3-1, 3-7, 3-8, 3-9, 3-28, 4-2, 4-5, 4-9 to 4-14
Meetings 4-6, 7-1, 7-21, 7-23
Method Productivity Delay Model 9-17
Milestone Date 7-1, 7-14, 7-15
Money 4-18, 5-3
Monetary Benefits 4-18
Monitoring 3-17, 3-20
Morale 8-4, 8-5
MORE . . . . .3-1 to 3-28, 4-2
Motivate 4-1, 4-4, 4-8, 5-3
Motivational Maintenance Theory . .4-22, 4-23

N

No Damage for Delay Clause 2-16, 2-18
Noise 8-4, 8-19
Non-Productive Time 6-7, 6-8, 6-10
Notification Clause 2-15, 2-18

O

One- to Four-Week
Look Ahead Schedule . . .6-1, 6-29, 6-20, 6-26
Operating Cost 5-5, 5-19, 5-20
Opportunity 3-1, 3-4, 3-13
Overtime 8-1, 8-5, 8-8, 8-9, 8-10
Ownership Cost 5-5, 5-19, 5-20

P

Paperwork 10-17
Pareto, Vilfredo 1-20
PDA 10-18
Performance Management 7-13
Partnering 7-25
Personnel Management 4-1, 4-28
Planning . . . . .1-20, 6-1 to 6-36
Precipitation 8-18
Pride 1-22, 4-5, 4-6, 4-7, 4-18, 5-3
Preliminary Plan 6-4
Pre-Planning . . . . .2-1 to 2-28, 6-5
Proactive .1-17, 1-22
Problem Solving 7-23
Procedures Manual 1-15
Process 2-2
Production . . . . .2-1, 2-20 to 2-24, 2-1
Productivity . . . . .1-1 to 10-22
    Data 3-3
    Defined 1-3, 2-2, 5-6
    Fade 3-11
    Improvement 1-1
Project 1-11
    Building .1-11
    Close Out .2-3

Cost 1-3
Owner 2-13
Public Works 1-11
Quality 1-3
Safety 1-3
Profitability 1-9, 1-10, 1-11
Public Works 1-11
Punch List 1-13, 1-18, 6-7

Q

Quality 1-21, 2-3, 7-7, 7-21
Queuing . . . . .5-22 to 5-32, 6-2

R

Rating Model .9-17
Record Keeping . . . . . . .7-1, 7-20, 9-1 to 9-23,
                                  10-1 to 10-22
Redo Work . . .1-13, 1-18, 6-7, 6-9, 6-20, 6-21
Reminder List 6-4, 6-36
Request for Information 10-17, 10-20
Research and Development 1-15
Risk 1-19, 2-9, 3-1, 3-4, 3-19,
              3-20, 3-22, 3-23, 3-24, 3-28, 4-2
R. S. Means 4-10, 5-24

S

Safety 1-3, 1-22, 2-3, 5-18, 7-7, 7-21
Schedule .7-12, 7-18
Scheduling . . . . .2-6, 2-8, 6-1 to 6-36
Self-Perform 4-3
Service Unit . . . . .5-23 to 5-30
Short Interval Schedule 6-1, 6-4,
                     6-31, 6-32, 6-36, 7-17
Specifications 2-13, 8-5, 8-23
Stacking of Trades 6-4, 8-13, 8-14
Structural Steel 2-24
Subcontractor 1-2, 1-15, 1-23,
                2-10, 6-15, 7-1 to 7-28, 8-1
Supervision 1-1, 1-3, 3-1, 3-3

Index of Topics

Supervisor 1-15, 1-19, 1-22, 2-4,
2-5, 2-6, 2-8, 2-10, 2-14,
2-15, 2-16, 2-20, 2-21, 3-15,
4-3, 4-5, 4-7, 4-9, 4-11, 6-9

T

Team Approach 7-25
Team Building 7-1, 7-27, 8-2
Technology ....10-1 to 10-22
Temperature 8-4, 8-5, 8-17, 8-18, 8-21
Theft 1-13, 1-18, 6-7
Theory X and Y 4-21
Time and Motion 3-5
Timecard 9-18, 10-7, 10-10
Tools 1-18, 9-9, 10-11, 10-14
Total Cost Method 8-34
Total Float 6-18, 6-19, 6-20, 6-21, 6-22

U

Unimpacted Day 8-25
Unions 1-12
Unit Cost 9-8
Updating ....6-4, 6-25 to 6-28
U.S. Economy 1-22
Useful Many 1-20, 2-6, 2-8, 2-11, 2-12

V

Variation Analysis 1-19
Vital Few 1-20, 2-1, 2-6, 2-8, 2-10, 2-12

W

Waiting 8-4
Waiting Line ....5-22 to 5-32, 6-2
Wastage 6-7
Weather 1-3, 1-23, 5-10, 6-6, 8-3
Website 10-20
Work Activity ....6-13 to 6-15
   Contingency 6-15
   Defining 6-13, 6-15
   Sequencing 6-14
Work Method .....1-17, 3-13, 3-14 to 3-17,
3-21, 3-22
Work Rules 4-20
Work Sampling 9-17
Work States ....1-7 to 1-24
   Productive 1-7, 1-24
   Non-Productive 1-7, 1-8, 1-13, 1-14, 1-24
   Support 1-7, 1-8, 1-24

Participant's Profile

Your name _____

How long have you worked in the construction industry? _____ years

Your company's name _____

What kind of work does your company do? Check any that apply.

❏ building ❏ heavy ❏ highway ❏ M/U ❏ industrial ❏ _____

How long have you been with this company? _____ years

What is your job title or function? _____

How many people do you directly supervise? ___ people

Where do you work? ❏ jobsite ❏ home office ❏ other

What project are you working on now? Project name, location, type of project.

_____

Check the STP courses you have previously taken:

❏ *Construction Supervisor*

❏ *Heavy/Highway Construction Supervisor*

❏ Unit 1: *Leadership and Motivation*

❏ Unit 2: *Oral and Written Communication*

❏ Unit 3: *Problem Solving and Decision Making*

❏ Unit 4: *Contract Documents and Construction Law*

❏ Unit 5: *Planning and Scheduling*

❏ Unit 6: *Understanding and Managing Project Costs*

❏ Unit 7: *Accident Prevention and Loss Control*

❏ Unit 8: *Project Management: The Supervisor's Role*

❏ Unit 9: *Productivity Improvement*

❏ Unit 10: *General and Specialty Contractor Dynamics*

Who pays your course fee? ❏ company ❏ I do ❏ other_____

Why did you enroll in this course? Check any that apply.

❏ I've taken other STP courses and I wanted to take this one also

❏ I was asked or told to take this course by _____

❏ The Supervisory Training Program (or this course) was recommended by _____

_____

❏ I want to take all 10 courses so I can get a certificate from AGC

❏ I read or heard about STP (or this course) and it seemed worthwhile

❏ Other _____

REFERENCE WORKSHEETS | SESSION 1

PRODUCTIVITY IMPROVEMENT
PARTICIPANT'S PROFILE — CONT.

What is the thing you like best about your work?

_____
_____
_____

What is the most difficult part of your work?

_____
_____
_____

What are your expectations or goals for the time you spend in this course?

_____
_____
_____

If there is a specific question, topic, situation or problem you want to be sure we talk about sometime during this course, please list or describe it below:

_____
_____
_____

What are your personal activities and interests?

_____
_____
_____

If there is any other information that has a bearing on your participation in this course, please list or describe it below — your career goals, other construction training courses you've taken, special assignments you've had or might have in the future, something else you have on your mind.

_____
_____
_____
_____
_____

RWS 1-1

Pre-Knowledge Survey

____ ____ ____ ____
last four digits

This survey is designed to check your knowledge about productivity improvement on the construction site. This is not graded, and the information in it is for your use only. Answer each question to the best of your ability. Circle the letter next to your choice, or respond as directed in the question.

1. Productivity is determined solely by how hard a person works.
   a. True
   b. False

2. Productivity has increased faster in the construction industry than it has in he automobile industry.
   a. True
   b. False

3. The amount of non-productive labor time at a construction project varies from project to project but averages around 16%
   a. True
   b. False

4. There is typically more variation or risk with the concrete forming task than there is with the concrete placing task.
   a. True
   b. False

5. The construction supervisor has typically used a monitoring or accounting approach to construction productivity as opposed to a critiquing or analysis approach.
   a. True
   b. False

6. The construction firm has typically benchmarked its best productivity for a work task as a means of setting out estimating and production goals.
   a. True
   b. False

7. A worker typically has a higher hourly cost than a construction crane.
   a. True
   b. False

8. The majority of construction workers view themselves as working for a firm, not a job.
   a. True
   b. False

9. The typical construction supervisor expends more time and energy coming down on problems as opposed to investigating opportunities.
   a. True
   b. False

10. In the typical construction firm, the project estimate is broken down into daily production goals for the workers.
    a. True
    b. False

11. Money is the single most important motivator to all workers.
    a. True
    b. False

12. Job site working conditions are viewed as a motivating factor as opposed to a maintenance factor.
    a. True
    b. False

13. On the majority of construction sites, equipment is in a non-productive state more often than is labor.
    a. True
    b. False

14. Planning entails determining when something has to be done and scheduling entails determining what has to be done.
    a. True
    b. False

15. The work activities that are defined for a project plan and schedule should not be the same as the take-off items in the project estimate.
    a. True
    b. False

16. The project activities that are the most difficult to update when updating a project schedule are the work activities that have not started as of the date of the update.
    a. True
    b. False

17. The construction supervisor should be more attentive to a work activity or task on the critical path as opposed to a work activity that has considerable schedule float.
    a. True
    b. False

18. Requiring a subcontractor to fill out a daily production planning and schedule form is an example for requiring the subcontractor to management itself.
    a. True
    b. False

19. When a construction worker works ten six-hour days doing hard physical work, the worker only loses productivity in the hours he or she is working past the normal 40-hour work week.
    a. True
    b. False

20. The ratio of supervisory hours to worker hours is a factor in determining worker productivity.
    a. True
    b. False

21. Work space is a factor in determining the amount of construction productivity that is achieved.

22. The construction industry has historically used a job cost report that is produced daily as a means of monitoring productivity.
    a. True
    b. False

23. There are three elements to an effective control system:
    1) plan
    2) compare
    3) reprimand

    a. True
    b. False

24. Continuous improvement entails the measurement of a defect and an analysis of the cause of the defect.
    a. True
    b. False

RWS 10-1

Post-Knowledge Survey

This survey is designed to check your knowledge about productivity improvement on the construction site. This is not graded, and the information in it is for your use only. Answer each question to the best of your ability. Circle the letter next to your choice, or respond as directed in the question.

1. Productivity is determined solely by how hard a person works.
   a. True
   b. False

2. Productivity has increased faster in the construction industry than it has in he automobile industry.
   a. True
   b. False

3. The amount of non-productive labor time at a construction project varies from project to project but averages around 16%
   a. True
   b. False

4. There is typically more variation or risk with the concrete forming task than there is with the concrete placing task.
   a. True
   b. False

5. The construction supervisor has typically used a monitoring or accounting approach to construction productivity as opposed to a critiquing or analysis approach.
   a. True
   b. False

6. The construction firm has typically benchmarked its best productivity for a work task as a means of setting out estimating and production goals.
   a. True
   b. False

7. A worker typically has a higher hourly cost than a construction crane.
   a. True
   b. False

8. The majority of construction workers view themselves as working for a firm, not a job.
   a. True
   b. False

9. The typical construction supervisor expends more time and energy coming down on problems as opposed to investigating opportunities.
   a. True
   b. False

REFERENCE WORKSHEETS | SESSION 1

PRODUCTIVITY IMPROVEMENT
POST-KNOWLEDGE SURVEY — CONT.

10. In the typical construction firm, the project estimate is broken down into daily production goals for the workers.
    a. True
    b. False

11. Money is the single most important motivator to all workers.
    a. True
    b. False

12. Job site working conditions are viewed as a motivating factor as opposed to a maintenance factor.
    a. True
    b. False

13. On the majority of construction sites, equipment is in a non-productive state more often than is labor.
    a. True
    b. False

14. Planning entails determining when something has to be done and scheduling entails determining what has to be done.
    a. True
    b. False

15. The work activities that are defined for a project plan and schedule should not be the same as the take-off items in the project estimate.
    a. True
    b. False

16. The project activities that are the most difficult to update when updating a project schedule are the work activities that have not started as of the date of the update.
    a. True
    b. False

17. The construction supervisor should be more attentive to a work activity or task on the critical path as opposed to a work activity that has considerable schedule float.
    a. True
    b. False

18. Requiring a subcontractor to fill out a daily production planning and schedule form is an example for requiring the subcontractor to management itself.
    a. True
    b. False

19. When a construction worker works ten six-hour days doing hard physical work, the worker only loses productivity in the hours he or she is working past the normal 40-hour work week.
    a. True
    b. False

20. The ratio of supervisory hours to worker hours is a factor in determining worker productivity.
    a. True
    b. False

21. Work space is a factor in determining the amount of construction productivity that is achieved.

22. The construction industry has historically used a job cost report that is produced daily as a means of monitoring productivity.
    a. True
    b. False

23. There are three elements to an effective control system:
    1) plan
    2) compare
    3) reprimand

    a. True
    b. False

24. Continuous improvement entails the measurement of a defect and an analysis of the cause of the defect.
    a. True
    b. False

Productivity Improvement

RWS 10-2

Responses to Post-Knowledge Survey

1. Productivity is determined solely by how hard a person works.
    b. False. Productivity is affected by many factors, including work effort, management, weather, planning, etc.

2. Productivity has increased faster in the construction industry than it has in the automobile industry.
    b. False. Productivity has increased more slowly in the construction industry for a variety of reasons, one being too much focus only upon results rather than upon managing the process.

3. The amount of non-productive labor time at a construction project varies from project to project, but averages around 16%.
    b. False. Most studies indicate that more than *40%* of the labor time is non-productive.

4. There is typically more variation or risk involved in the concrete forming task than there is with the concrete placing task.
    a. True. Risk is defined as variation from the expected average. The nature of forming is such that productivity varies widely from one day to the next. The supervisor needs to pay considerable attention to risky tasks.

5. The construction supervisor has typically used a monitoring or accounting approach to construction productivity, as opposed to a critiquing or analysis approach.
    a. True. The supervisor typically compares performance to prior jobs or the estimate. Supervisors would benefit from looking for better ways to do things on a specific job.

6. Construction firms typically have benchmarked their best productivity for a work task as a means of setting estimating and production goals.
    b. False. The industry and the supervisor typically have focused on the average productivity achieved or expected. This focus detracts from the potential to improve.

7. A worker typically has a higher hourly cost than a construction crane.
    b. False. In many cases equipment costs more per hour; therefore it is important to keep equipment as productive as labor.

8. Most construction workers view themselves as working for a firm, not a job.
    b. False. This is one of the most difficult challenges for the construction supervisor. Many of his or her workers are only with them for a job. This makes it harder to know and motivate each and every worker.

9. The typical construction supervisor expends more time and energy coming down on problems than he/she expends investigating opportunities.
    a. True. Unfortunately, the supervisor often finds himself or herself "putting out fires." It would be advantageous for the supervisor to spend some time focusing on opportunities.

10. In the typical construction firm, the project estimate is broken down into daily production goals for the workers.
    b. False. The supervisor and the crew typically are not given production goals, even though they should receive them.

11. Money is the single most important motivator to all workers.
    b. False. Many studies have found that workers are equally or more motivated by responsibility, measurement, feedback, and pride.

12. Job site working conditions are viewed as a motivating factor as opposed to a maintenance factor.
    b. False. Workers expect job conditions to be good; it is a maintenance factor. Typically if the job conditions are worse than expected, productivity decreases.

13. On most construction sites, equipment is non-productive more often than is labor.
    a. True. Equipment is often idle at the job and does not get the attention of the supervisory management. It should.

14. Planning entails determining when something has to be done and scheduling entails determining what has to be done.
    b. False. Just the opposite.

15. The work activities that are defined for a project plan and schedule should not be the same as the take-off items in the project estimate.
    a. True. Ideally they should be, however--that is how the schedule and estimate become one and the same system.

16. The project activities that are the most difficult to update when updating a project schedule are the work activities that have not started as of the date of the update.
    b. False. The activities that are the most difficult to update are the activities that have started but are not yet complete at the time of the update.

17. The construction supervisor should be more attentive to a work activity or task on the critical path as opposed to a work activity that has considerable schedule float.
    a. True. For the most part this is true in that the critical activities determine the overall project duration.

18. Requiring a subcontractor to fill out a daily production planning and schedule form is an example for requiring the subcontractor to management itself.
    a. True. What is good for the general contractor typically is good for the subcontractor. One way to manage a subcontractor is to require self-monitoring; i.e., practice good management.

19. When a construction worker works ten six-hour days doing hard physical work, the worker only loses productivity in the hours he or she is working past the normal 40-hour work week.
    b. False. When a worker gets fatigued doing overtime, each and every hour is negatively impacted.

20. The ratio of supervisory hours to worker hours is a factor in determining worker productivity.
    a. True; if there is too much supervision, it is not cost effective. However, under-supervision typically leads to workers being less productive.

21. Work space is a factor in determining the amount of construction productivity that is achieved.
    a. True; most studies indicate that there is a "best" work area space to perform work tasks. If less area is available, worker productivity will decrease.

22. The construction industry has historically used a job cost report that is produced daily as a means of monitoring productivity.
    a. True; the supervisor compares actual to budget. Even though this is the most common means, the problem is that the budget in itself represents averages and not what can be achieved.

23. There are three elements to an effective control system:
    1) plan
    2) compare
    3) reprimand

    b. False; a control system entails
       1) comparison of actual
       2) to plan
       3) to detect a potential problem, and
       4) the attempt to correct the problem.

24. Continuous improvement entails the measurement of a defect and an analysis of the cause of the defect.
    a. True; by focusing on defects, identifying the cause, and taking appropriate actions, improvement can be achieved.

Unit 9

PLEASE FILL OUT THIS FORM AND SEND IT IN!

Productivity Improvement
Participant's Registration and Course Evaluation

Please complete both the **Registration** and **Evaluation** sections of this form. Your instructor must sign the **Registration** section. This form must be returned to the Associated General Contractors of America for your name to be entered in the database of people who have completed this course. Your instructor can send in this form with your class as a group, or you can send it in yourself by folding on the dotted line and taping it so the post-paid address shows.

Participant's Registration:

Participant Information:

Name (as shown on your Driver's License)

Home Address

City   State   ZIP

Date of Birth: _____
                Month/Day/Year

Last 4 numbers of your Social Security Number:

___ ___ ___ ___

> Help us avoid mix-ups between persons with similar names by using your name **exactly** as it appears on your Driver's License. We use your name, birthdate and the last four digits of your Social Security Number to accurately record your course completion.

Participant's Company/Organization:

Company/Organization Name

Company/Organization Address

City   State   ZIP

About the course:

Name of organization that sponsored the course

Instructor's Name

Course start date   Finish date

How many separate sessions did the course meet:

❏ 10   ❏ 5   ❏ 3   ❏ _____

How many total hours? _____

This participant has successfully completed the *Productivity Improvement* course.

Instructor's Signature

Instructor's Company/Organization

( )

Instructor's Work Address   City   State   ZIP   Work Phone

Please turn the page and complete the EVALUATION section

UNIT 9

REGISTRATION AND EVALUATION FORM

Participant's Course Evaluation:

❶ Did *Productivity Improvement* meet your expectations?

☐ it exceeded my expectations ☐ it definitely met them ☐ it was just OK
☐ it didn't quite measure up ☐ it fell way short

❷ Would you recommend this course to others in your company or organization?

☐ yes ☐ no   Why?

_____
_____
_____

❸ What ideas or skills you learned in this course will be most useful to you on the job?

_____
_____
_____

❹ What would you add to this course to make it better (topics, ideas, skills, situations, solutions)?

_____
_____
_____

❺ Check any **Supervisory Training Program** courses you plan to take in the future.

☐ *Leadership and Motivation* ☐ *Understanding and Managing Project Costs*
☐ *Oral and Written Communication* ☐ *Accident Prevention and Loss Control*
☐ *Problem Solving and Decision Making* ☐ *Managing the Project: The Supervisor's Role*
☐ *Contract Documents and Construction Law* ☐ *Productivity Improvement*
☐ *Planning and Scheduling* ☐ *Contractor and Specialty Contractor Dynamics*

☐ *Construction Supervisor* or *Heavy/Highway Construction Supervisor*

❻ In a few words, tell us what you think of the *Productivity Improvement* course.

_____
_____

Do we have your permission to quote you? ☐ yes ☐ no

UNIT 9

REGISTRATION AND EVALUATION FORM - OPTIONAL QUESTIONS

We don't want to pester you with so many questions that you toss out this whole evaluation form, so **this page is optional**. However, we hope you will provide as much feedback as you can because we base revisions and improvements to *Productivity Improvement* on responses from participants and instructors.

Instructions: *For each session*, check any boxes that describe how you feel about *that session*. For example, if you feel that the topics covered in Session 3 on developing the project plan have *some* relevance to your work, you would check the box as shown below. (If *some* is not your answer, just ■ the *some* box and ✓ one of the others.)

	1. Introduction to Productivity Improvement	2. Pre-Planning	3. "MORE" 4 Skills for Effective Supervisors	4. Personnel Management	5. Equipment Management	6. Productive Planning and Scheduling	7. Managing Subcontractors	8. Quantifying Lost Labor Productivity	9. Record Keeping, Changes, Defect Analysis	10. New Technology/Review
Concepts and skills presented were:										
too complex or difficult										
just about right										
too general or easy										
The amount of time spent on these topics was:										
too much										
about right										
not enough										
The relevance of these topics to my work was:										
much										
some						✓				
little										
none										
The activities in this session were:										
useful										
boring										
confusing										
interesting										
fun										
well designed										
busy work										
The reading material in the Participant's Manual was:										
clearly written										
hard to understand										
about the right amount of information										
too much to read										
needed more explanation										

Please use the back of this page for any additional comments or observations that you feel might be helpful to the developers of the Supervisory Training Program. Thank you.

UNIT 9

PRODUCTIVITY IMPROVEMENT

Name _____

Address _____

City _____ State ____ ZIP _____

Phone (_____) _____

BUSINESS REPLY MAIL
FIRST CLASS MAIL   PERMIT NO 1017   ARLINGTON, VA

POSTAGE WILL BE PAID BY ADDRESSEE

Associated General Contractors of America
2300 Wilson Blvd., Suite 400
Arlington, VA 22201

Attn: Director, Supervisory Training Programs

NO POSTAGE
NECESSARY
IF MAILED
IN THE
UNITED STATES

PLEASE COMPLETE AND SUBMIT THIS APPLICATION ACCORDING TO THE DETAILED INSTRUCTIONS ON THE BACK OF THIS SHEET.

Application for a Supervisory Training Program (STP) Completion Certificate

❶ This application is for the following STP participant who has completed all ten courses

Name	SS # (last 4 numbers)	
Address	Phone	Birthdate
City	State	Zip

❷ This application is submitted by the following STP class sponsor, organization or person

Name	Organization Name	
Address	Phone	Fax
City	State	Zip

❸ Send the certificate to the following person at this address

Name	Organization Name	
Address	Phone	Fax
City	State	Zip

❹

Course Title	Date Completed	Name of Sponsor	Location
Unit 1: Leadership and Motivation			
Unit 2: Oral and Written Communication			
Unit 3: Problem Solving and Decision Making			
Unit 4: Contract Documents and Construction Law			
Unit 5: Planning and Scheduling			
Unit 6: Understanding and Managing Project Costs			
Unit 7: Accident Prevention and Loss Control			
Unit 8: Managing the Project			
Unit 9: Productivity Improvement			
Unit 10: General and Specialty Contractor Dynamics			

For AGC use only
App received by: ☐ Director, STP _____
App received by: ☐ Database recordkeeper _____
Participant Database Record # _____
Certificate sent _____

TO ALLOW ADEQUATE LEADTIME FOR PROCESSING, SUBMIT THIS APPLICATION AT LEAST **30 DAYS** BEFORE YOU WANT THE CERTIFICATE IN YOUR HANDS.

Instructions for Filling Out and Submitting the Application for a Supervisory Training Program (STP) Completion Certificate

Who Can Obtain This Special Recognition from AGC?

AGC provides a special certificate of recognition to persons who complete **all ten courses** of the Supervisory Training Program.

The two overview courses for construction supervisors, *Construction Supervisor* and *Heavy/Highway Construction Supervisor* **are not counted** among the ten courses needed to qualify for this recognition certificate. Each overview course has its own certificate.

Who Can Fill Out and Submit This Application?

Normally, this application will be filled out and submitted by the organization that sponsored the STP courses taken by the participant who wishes to be recognized. If this is not possible, this application may be filled out and submitted by the participant.

Where Should The Completed Application Be Sent?

Mail or fax the completed application to: Director, Supervisory Training Programs
AGC of America
2300 Wilson Blvd., Suite 400
Arlington, VA 22201
Fax: (703) 837-5405

What Is the Deadline for Submitting This Application?

To allow adequate leadtime for processing, submit this application at *least 30 days before you want the certificate(s) in your hands*. Applications are processed in the order in which they are received.

What Are The Special Instructions for Filling Out the Application Form?

Section ❶: Fill in each blank, including the Social Security number and birthdate blanks. These two items have been used in the STP database to make sure that course completion data submitted at various times (or by various sponsors) have been credited to the correct participant.

Sections ❷ and ❸: Fill in each blank as appropriate. If you are submitting this application as an individual participant, list your name, address, etc. in Sections 2 and 3.

Section ❹: Fill in as much of this information as possible. It will enable your application to be processed more efficiently and quickly. This information is used to verify your course completions against the STP database.